# COMPARATIVE PUBLIC MANAGEMENT

# COMPARATIVE PUBLIC MANAGEMENT

## WHY NATIONAL, ENVIRONMENTAL, AND ORGANIZATIONAL CONTEXT MATTERS

KENNETH J. MEIER,
AMANDA RUTHERFORD, AND
CLAUDIA N. AVELLANEDA, EDITORS

Georgetown University Press / Washington, DC

Library of Congress Cataloging-in-Publication Data
Names: Meier, Kenneth J., 1950– editor. | Rutherford, Amanda, editor. | Avellaneda, Claudia N.
Title: Comparative public management : why national, environmental, and organizational context matters / Kenneth J. Meier, Amanda N. Rutherford, and Claudia N. Avellaneda, editors.
Description: Washington, DC : Georgetown University Press, 2017. | Includes bibliographical references and index.
Identifiers: LCCN 2016024117 (print) | LCCN 2016040084 (ebook) |
ISBN 9781626164000 (hc : alk. paper) | ISBN 9781626164017 (pb : alk. paper) | ISBN 9781626164024 (eb)
Subjects: LCSH: Public administration.
Classification: LCC JF1351 .C5878 017 (print) | LCC JF1351 (ebook) | DDC 351—dc23
LC record available at https://lccn.loc.gov/2016024117

♾ This book is printed on acid-free paper meeting the requirements of the American National Standard for Permanence in Paper for Printed Library Materials.

18 17 9 8 7 6 5 4 3 2 First printing
Printed in the United States of America

Cover design by Jeremy John Parker.

# Contents

# Illustrations

## Figures



## Tables

# Preface

The field of public management has seen exponential growth in studies that link some aspect of management to organizational performance. As an empirically driven field, we now have a wealth of findings, many of which appear to be inconsistent with each other. Why, for example, is managerial networking important in the United States, moderately effective in the United Kingdom, but of little consequence in the Netherlands?

A recent theoretical article by Laurence O'Toole Jr. and Kenneth Meier, an earlier version of this book's introduction, argues that public management studies need to consider the political, environmental, and organizational contexts. They propose a contingency framework for public management in which context influences the types of managerial actions that can be used effectively in public organizations. This framework offers the potential to integrate the numerous existing studies of public management and provides a starting point for a new generation of public management scholars.

This book is the next step in the context agenda and demonstrates how individual studies of public management can be set within the framework to produce greater generalizability. After an expanded presentation of the theory of context, seven empirical studies of how management affects performance in different contexts are presented. The contexts vary from schools in the Netherlands to local governments in Brazil to health care in Africa to higher education in the United States. The first group of studies treats context as a variable and presents interactive relationships, and the second group provides examples in which the authors use context as a framing variable and explain how the specific context fits within the general framework proposed by O'Toole and Meier. Collectively, these empirical chapters provide a comprehensive comparative assessment of the impact of management on organizational performance.

Our view of "context" is broad and includes all the constraints on the organization, its potential resources, as well as how the variables relate to each other such as the functional form of relationships (see Johns 2006; Bamberger 2008). Context can include the national political context, sectoral elements (public versus private versus not for profit), industry characteristics (e.g., health care, education, national defense) or economy-wide factors such as the degree of economic development or the nature of the production system. Context can also include normative elements and orientation of political regimes.

Although context has been widely integrated into studies on private sector leadership, it has not played a prominent role in the public sector literature with some exceptions (see Pollitt 2008, 2012).

Our long-term objective is to build a more general theory of public management that specifies how context influences the management–performance relationship. This text is only the first attempt at testing this framework; as the concluding chapter of this book suggests, much more research remains to be done to determine when and how context creates variance in the findings linking management to organizational outputs and outcomes. Further, the components of context at the core of this book—the separation of powers, federalism, process, performance appraisal systems, complexity, turbulence, munificence, social capital, clarity of goals, centralization, and professionalism—may still be an incomplete picture of the internal and external environments in which organizations are situated. The theoretical chapter generates a large number of hypotheses concerning how context affects the impact of public management on performance. In understanding how the contexts of individual chapters compare, scholars are better able to understand the scenarios in which management is best understood (in this book, complex organizations tasked with multiple and conflicting goals within a larger unitary system) or where management is most in need of additional study (where organizations are simpler and more placid, and lack social capital and professionalism). The seven empirical chapters demonstrate how testing can be done with current data sets, but these tests barely scratch the surface of possibilities. The final chapter provides a synopsis of the progress that has been made but also points out areas where potentially important questions can be addressed using the theory and approach of this book in future research. We see the final chapter both as a road map for a comprehensive agenda on comparative public management and as a challenge to the field to not only push our studies into new contexts and areas but also integrate existing and future findings. This objective cannot be achieved by a single individual or a single team of individuals. We invite other scholars to take up the quest for comparative public management. Tell us where the framework works; more important, tell us where it fails and how it needs to be changed. The framework and the studies presented in this book are only the first step in an ongoing process.

We would like to thank a variety of people who contributed to making this book possible. First, financial support for the management conference in 2014 was provided by the Texas A&M European Union Center and its Project for Equity, Representation, and Governance. Guy Whitten, the director of the Center, provided encouragement and support; and Ann Klaus, the Center's associate director, assisted with the logistics involved in bringing scholars to the United States. Second, the conference took place at the conclusion of the

PhD Seminar in Advanced Public Management in the spring of 2014. The students in that course were subjected to endless studies of Texas school districts, and they probably felt relieved that none of the conference papers forced them to relive their nightmares. Third, working with Don Jacobs and the team at Georgetown University Press was a pleasure. They provided support and encouragement to the project.

# Introduction

## *Comparative Public Management: A Framework for Analysis*

LAURENCE J. O'TOOLE JR.
AND KENNETH J. MEIER

Research effort to model and estimate the effect of public management on public-organizational and public-program performance is a growth area in public administration. Building on earlier, primarily case study efforts, more recent investigations have emphasized relatively clear specifications and, where possible, large-*N* quantitative research (examples from a much larger set include Lynn, Heinrich, and Hill 2001; Boyne and Walker 2004; Boyne et al. 2006; Walker, Boyne, and Brewer 2010; Akkerman and Torenvlied 2011; and O'Toole and Meier 1999). Much progress has been made. Several aspects of management, along with resources and task difficulty, help to explain the range of performance-related results. The functional form by which management relates to performance, however, still needs systematic analysis, and management is often a multilevel phenomenon, particularly in networked settings, so plenty of additional research questions remain. This introductory chapter continues to develop the research agenda for public management and performance by noting an additional gap and by beginning to address it: the relationship of what we might call context to the management–performance relationship. Our objective is to begin to build a parsimonious framework at a relatively abstract level by focusing on several general dimensions of organizational context.

By "context," here we mean a concept more inclusive than "environment," or "organizational environment," as the terms are sometimes used in the fields of organization theory and management. Our notion is consistent with that of Johns (2006, 386), who defined context as those "situational opportunities and constraints that affect the occurrence and meaning of organizational behavior *as well as functional relationships between variables*" (emphasis added). As Bamberger (2008, 840) explains, "For those seeking to explain the behavior of organizations, such situational factors may include such industry-, sector-, or economy-wide characteristics, as well as other normative and institutional structures and regimes." A few years ago, the editors of the *Academy of Management Journal* pointed out that during a one-year period that was monitored (2006–7), one-quarter of the articles published in the *AMJ* focused on context (Bamberger 2008). We seek to bring the systematic study of context into public management research, and especially those theories that attempt to explain the relationship between management and performance across nations. This topic has not been widely treated in the scholarship on public management, although important contributions can be identified (for thoughtful treatments of time, place, and technology as parts of context, see especially Pollitt 2008, 2012). Our long-term objective is to develop a more general theory of public management that specifies how context influences the management–performance relationship.

As is common in public management research, and often in social science more generally, theoretical and empirical scholarship has aimed toward general knowledge of causal relationships, but the actual efforts at validation typically avoid or ignore many aspects of contextual variation. Among the results of this limitation is that some researchers eschew the very goal of general theory in favor of qualitative and sometimes interpretive work that is not likely to cumulate—for example, Denhardt and White (1982, 168) argue that an "interpretive purpose would be served by explicating the meaning social actors bring to organizational situations." A second result among those who maintain the objective of general theory is to fall back on subjective managerial assessments of their organizations' performance, so as to enable comparisons to be made, even though different programmatic and organizational settings may be situated in quite different contexts. A systematic assessment indicates that this option is not a productive one, and it is likely to lead to misleading and invalid results (Meier and O'Toole 2013a, 2013b).

A third result is that validation efforts are often restricted to contextually similar settings, thus effectively physically controlling for the set of variables encapsulated by context. Much can be learned through this approach, we believe, and thus examinations of management and performance across—for instance—English local governments, or Danish or Dutch primary education, or New York City public schools, or US nursing homes are welcome. Each set of studies within each type of management system, however, necessarily screens out possible contextual variation on a whole set of dimensions. The result is clusters of interesting findings within each set of empirically similar settings. From this result, two issues arise. First, generalizing from, for instance, Danish public education to the world of public management raises real concerns regarding external validity. And second, comparing the sets of empirical findings across very different contexts can show that precise findings differ in contextually different analyses, and can even disclose inconsistencies and puzzles if one tries to aggregate the results.

To develop a somewhat more systematic assessment of how much contextual variation is present in research on public management and performance, we reviewed the first twenty-three volumes of the *Journal of Public Administration Research and Theory* from the founding of the *Journal* through April 2013.[1] *JPART*, of course, is only one outlet, but it is the most widely cited journal in the field and should be broadly representative of the best scholarship. We examined all articles exploring the relationship between management and performance, regardless of methods used, and coded them for various simple aspects of context. Of the sixty-six articles focused empirically on management and performance, there has been considerable variation regarding policy field or sector, and also by level of government. However, and perhaps not surprisingly, there has been much less variety in national setting. All but fifteen of the articles were based on data from the United States; of the analyses reaching beyond the United States, seven of these rely on data from the United Kingdom. No other country was represented more than once, and only three studies examine data outside North America or Europe.[2] A reasonable conclusion is that before we can feel any confidence in working toward a general theory of public management and performance, we need to know much more about the influence of context than we are now able to glean from the available studies.

For all these reasons, the field could use a framework for context regarding management and performance—a logical explanation for how and why various aspects of context might predictably and systematically modify the relationship between management and performance. If this argument is correct, the development of such a framework would permit the accumulation of systematic findings across national, environmental, and other contextually varying settings and, therefore, get us closer to a general theory of public management and performance.

We do not mean to radically simplify. Various aspects of management seem to be important, and context may mediate their relationships to performance in differing ways. Similarly, "performance" is typically a complex notion, and virtually all public organizations are tasked with multiple goals. How context might affect the management–performance relationship might vary with different aspects of performance, and also in distributional consequences across various stakeholders. Additional performance criteria are also worth investigating (Boyne 2003).[3]

One recent study in this direction (Meier and O'Toole 2011) developed a set of theoretical ideas on how the authors' own general model of management and performance might vary between the public and private sectors (see also Petrovsky, James, and Boyne 2015). Certainly, developing this line of theory is well within the developed traditions of the field of public management, because—unlike with generic management scholars—most of those within public management would agree with Wallace Sayre's well-known aphorism that the public and private sectors are alike "in all unimportant respects" (Sayre 1958). That recent study hypothesized how the managerial influences on performance might vary predictably by sector. That analysis began by making a set of assumptions supported by the literature and then sketched several hypotheses.

In this chapter we identify several variables other than sector that we think are worth including in a broader framework of context. For each one, we sketch several hypotheses and, for certain ones, note findings or theoretical arguments that might tentatively support such ideas. Developing and validating a theory of context is likely to be a long-term enterprise, and one to which many researchers and many studies can contribute. The empirical chapters in this book are a step in this direction.

Our approach is as follows. First, we outline our general, abstract notion of how one might think about context affecting the relationship between management and performance. We then proceed to identify several dimensions or aspects of context and consider briefly how each aspect might shape the management–performance relationship. Finally, we suggest a checklist of contextual factors that could be used to characterize studies in the interest of an improved theory of context.

## THE LOGIC OF CONTEXT

The logic of considering context relative to the impact of management on public organizational performance is that context conditions the relationship between management and performance. To begin with a simplified model linking management to organizational outcomes, we have:

$$O_t = \beta_1 M + \beta_2 C + \beta_3 X + \varepsilon \quad (1)$$

where $O$ is a measure of organizational performance (outputs and/or outcomes) at time $t$; $M$ is a vector of managerial actions;[4] $C$ is a vector representing organizational context; $X$ is a set of control variables; $\beta_1$, $\beta_2$, and $\beta_3$ are estimable parameters; and $\varepsilon$ is an error term.

The logic of context, however, is not that it is merely a linear additive term in management, but rather that it interacts with management and makes certain variables more important in some contexts and less important in others. In short, the logic of context requires estimating an interactive model, as follows:

$$O_t = \beta_1 M + \beta_2 C + \beta_3 X + \beta_4 MC + \varepsilon. \tag{2}$$

The logic of context, however, is not just that the fourth term in this model is statistically significant ($\beta_4 \neq 0$), but also that a given context fundamentally changes the relationship between management and performance. If one rearranges the terms in the model and then isolates on the terms indicating the impact of management, we get:

$$O_t = M(\beta_1 + \beta_4 C) + \beta_2 C + \beta_3 X + \varepsilon. \tag{3}$$

The slope estimate for management in this equation, thus, is ($\beta_1 + \beta_4 C$), which indicates that the impact of management on performance will vary depending on the value of the context vector. As an illustration, in an organization that is a traditional hierarchy, one might suspect that networking by managers would be less valuable than the same type of networking might be within a structure that was organized as a fluid network (O'Toole 1997). The impact of the second term in the slope, $\beta_4 C$, for example, could increase the impact of management, could decrease it to zero, or could even reverse the sign so that management strategies that are effective in one context might be completely dysfunctional in other contexts.

The model given in equation 2 can be implemented only if the organizations being examined vary in context, because it assumes that context is a variable. Most public organization data sets have contextual variation only on some dimensions simply because the need for valid, comparable data on outputs or outcomes requires that organizations perform similar functions. These data limitations, in turn, mean that only some of the contextual factors can be investigated in an interactive model. So though English local governments or Texas schools vary somewhat on contextual variables, their variation pales when one compares them with Korean quasi-governments or Colombian local governments. In such cases, the solution is to treat context as a qualitative variable, or to do what some scholars might term justifying the case study being examined (Konisky and Reenock 2013). What characteristics of English local governments related to structure, political environments, and other contextual factors might be relevant? By clearly specifying the context of studies along dimensions specified in this chapter, we think substantial progress—and the first step in developing a theory of how context affects the relationship between management and public organizational performance—can be made.

The second step in creating an empirical literature on context and public management is to apply existing models of public management in as many different contexts as possible. A modest level of education, for example, can be translated into competitive advantages in performance in a developing country such as Colombia (see Avellenada 2009b), but does not appear to matter in Danish schools (Andersen and Winter 2011). The accumulation of these studies in widely varying contexts and with specific delineation of the context will provide the building blocks that scholars can then use to explain how context conditions the impact of management on performance. No one study can be definitive, but each study can add information that is relevant to the relationship of management and context. As empirical studies accumulate, additional theorizing will be necessary to refine the framework so that it will retain its ability to generalize.

## TOWARD A THEORY OF CONTEXT

In this main section of the chapter, we outline several dimensions of context and sketch a set of expectations in two areas—characteristics external to the organization (both political and general, environmental ones), and factors internal to the organization. The external discussion seeks to bring together the literature on the political environment from political science and the literature from organizational theory regarding environments in general. In both cases, more complex environments create opportunities and constraints for managers. The political context focuses on the concentration of political power and considers the separation of powers, federalism, corporatist versus adversarial processes, networks, and performance appraisal. The discussion of the organizational environment adds social capital to the traditional trio of complexity, turbulence, and munificence. The internal dimension includes goals, hierarchy, and professionalization.

Although the chapter sketches numerous hypotheses, much of the theoretical logic that covers the great bulk of these is straightforward: In more complicated external settings, we expect public managers to need to expend more effort to assist in generating or protecting performance than they would need to do in simple, ordered, and placid settings. Doing so should mean that any given or marginal unit of managerial effort may be less productive overall than when the settings are quiet and orderly—because of the heavy lifting required in the former. At the same time, management is likely to explain more of the overall variance in performance across the organizational units when the setting is complicated. The hypotheses, therefore, will generally focus on the marginal effect of a given level of management and also focus on the total variation explained by management factors. This logic covers most of the nineteen hypotheses developed regarding the political and external environmental contexts. The remaining five hypotheses deal with the internal features of the organization.

## EXTERNAL CONTEXT I: POLITICS AND THE CONCENTRATION OF POWER

The starting point for a framework of context and public management is the political context, simply because public organizations are expected to be responsive to the demands of political sovereigns. The variation in political contexts around the world is extensive, and no delineation of this aspect of context, let alone how this context might affect public management, can be complete. Instead, the political context must be treated in broad-brush strokes to focus on a few key variables that are logically linked to public organizations. We think the most promising aspect of political context on which to focus is power, and whether political power in a country or area is concentrated or dispersed (Lijphart 1999, 3–5). This view is greatly influenced by the seminal work of Norton Long (1949, 1952), who declared that "power is the lifeblood of administration." It also links into the contemporary political science concern in comparative politics with veto points (Tsebelis 2002); in simplified terms, a veto point is "an individual or collective actor whose agreement is necessary for a change of the status quo" (Tsebelis 1999, 593), and this concept is generally applied to political institutions with formal authority. Some political systems concentrate political power, while others disperse it, with multiple veto players along with the resulting checks and balances.

Political power can be fragmented either in formal structures or via rule-governed processes. Formal structures of fragmentation include the separation of powers, federalism, and networks. A separation-of-powers system disperses power among political institutions, thereby allowing each to act as a veto point in some or all circumstances (e.g., the United States), whereas a unitary political system concentrates power in a single political institution (e.g., the United Kingdom[5]). Power can be further dispersed via a federal system, whereby autonomous or semiautonomous regional or local governments have independent authority. In many cases collaborative networks of actors, none with the authority to compel the participants, disperse power even further (O'Toole 1997; Skelcher 2010). Separation of powers and federalism are formal structures, and political power can also be concentrated or dispersed by rules that establish governing processes. A clear distinction can be made between corporatist political systems (Esping-Andersen 1990) and more adversarial political systems (often termed "liberal political systems"). The former rely on a consensus and establish processes that focus on the inclusion of all relevant interests and a consensual decision-making process that binds all participants; the latter do not consciously seek to be inclusive and create a variety of political forums, with no decision considered final or binding on all participants.

This brief discussion does not do justice to the bewildering array of political systems (Lijphart 1999), but rather it serves in general to note that some political systems are consensual and concentrate political power, whereas others are adversarial or fragment political power. In the former political systems, public managers face a political consensus about the bureaucracy and its programs, whereas in the latter ones, public managers need to become political actors and seek to forge a coalition that supports agency actions (Hood and Lodge 2006; Long 1949).

Variations in the political context or in the concentration of political power can have two influences on the impact of management on organizational performance. First, they can change the mix of managerial activities that are likely to pay off—that is, they can enhance some management skills and devalue others. Second, they can increase or decrease how much management itself matters in affecting performance.

Fragmented and adversarial political systems, as Long so eloquently noted, require that public managers take on the political task of building a consensus for the agency's programs and policies. In a system with concentrated political support, decisions by the political sovereigns resolve issues of policy direction and the allocation of resources, and thus allow public managers to focus on managing the internal operations of the bureaucracy. This means that public managers in the dispersed context must devote more attention to managing in the environment than managers in consensual systems. This set of considerations leads to the first hypothesis:

> H1. Managing outward (in the environment) will (H1a) be more in evidence and (H1b) have more impact on performance in political contexts that disperse power.[6]

Relatively little evidence on these points is available as of yet. Managerial networking outward is frequently related to substantively important performance improvements in dispersed political contexts, such as public education (Meier and O'Toole 2003) and law enforcement (Nicholson-Crotty and O'Toole 2004) in the United States, whereas networking seems less important in English local authorities, with a unitary system but a moderate amount of political dispersion (Andrews et al. 2010), and it seems to be relatively unimportant in more concentrated and corporatist political contexts like Denmark (O'Toole and Pedersen 2011; Meier et al. 2015).

The requirement that managers focus more on the environment and actually perform what is a political function of building support (or, bluntly, making policy) means not only that managers in politically dispersed contexts face a more daunting task but also that their role in program performance is likely to be greater.[7] By this we do not mean that managers in politically dispersed contexts are more likely to succeed and have successful programs, but only that their activities will account for more variance in program success or failure. Given the nature of the tasks, in fact, we should expect managers in politically dispersed contexts to overall supervise less successful programs:

> H2. Management overall will have a greater impact on program performance in political contexts that disperse power.

> H3. The dispersal of political power will reduce the likelihood of program success, and the marginal impact of any managerial action is likely to be lower.[8]

Political power can also be concentrated via formal enhancements that affect the relationship between political sovereigns and public bureaucracies. New Public Management created a system of performance accountability whereby political sovereigns set goals for bureaucracy and permit bureaucratic discretion in attaining these goals with a process for the evaluation of results (Pollitt and Bouckaert 2000; Moynihan 2008). Some countries operate with elaborate systems of macro performance appraisal, such as the US Government Performance and Results Act and the subsequent Program Assessment Rating Tool. In theory, these assessment systems strengthen the ability of political sovereigns to oversee the bureaucracy and concentrate power so that bureaucrats can improve performance; thus:

> H4. Performance management systems that contribute to the concentration of political power should positively affect the marginal contribution of management to performance and increase its impact.

This hypothesis needs to be qualified, however. It assumes that political sovereigns are interested in improving the performance of government programs, that they will provide clear goals for bureaucrats to implement, and that they will actually pay attention to and use performance information (Pollitt 2006; Nielsen 2014). The US experience suggests that politicians are often more interested in downsizing government than in improving overall performance. Pollitt's (2006) cross-national review shows little actual use of performance information by political sovereigns. The hypothesis is also contingent on political sovereigns acting as principals in a principal–agent relationship,[9] and not engaging in cheating by refusing to provide clear, unambiguous goals or not honoring the implied contract to reward better performance.[10]

## EXTERNAL CONTEXT II: COMPLEXITY, TURBULENCE, AND MUNIFICENCE

If one leaves aside the explicitly political context of public organizations, it remains important to recognize that such organizations are path-dependent open systems. The path-dependent nature of public organizations derives from their efforts to routinize actions and deal with problems in a predictable, sequential nature. The path-dependent nature of organizations means that what they do today is very similar to what they did yesterday. In open system contexts, environmental forces can influence the performance of such agencies; and managers, as part of their responsibilities, need to monitor this environment and sometimes seek to tap aspects of it for organizational purposes or buffer organizational production processes from it. Monitoring takes time and attention, whereas tapping or buffering takes managerial effort.

How might the organization's task environment condition the relationship between management and performance? The "task environment of a given organization consists of all those organizations with which it must interact to grow and survive" (Osborn and Hunt 1974, 33). Whether the environment consists of a few or a multitude of such other relevant organizations, we expect its characteristics to condition the effect of management on performance.

Such organizational environments can be characterized along numerous dimensions (e.g., Rainey 2009, 95–101). Here we consider three frequently mentioned aspects of organizational environments: their complexity, turbulence, and munificence (Dess and Beard 1984; also see Aldrich 1979 for a further differentiation of aspects of organizational environments).

By *complexity* we refer to the environment's degree of homogeneity or heterogeneity and concentration or dispersion. The more different kinds of organizations occupy a public agency's environment, the more complex it is; and the more dispersed, rather than concentrated, these other organizations are—the more separate organizations that are clearly relevant to the core organization's task—the more complex is the core organization's environment. Evidence indicates, not surprisingly, that greater environmental complexity is associated with lower organizational performance (Andrews 2009), but this research does not address the question about how complexity might affect the relationship between management and performance. What might be expected? The more complex an organization's environment, the more managerial effort we would expect to be devoted to managing outward, much as was hypothesized in the treatment of politically dispersed contexts in the preceding section. The logic about political dispersion also applies to dispersion more generally in the task environment. In a sense, environmental complexity is also related to the subject, previously covered, of consensual-versus-fragmented and adversarial political systems. This is so because in corporatist arrangements, interests typically aggregate into peak associations that deal in bargaining processes with public organizations and, indeed, governments. So the earlier deduced logic can be applied to environmental complexity, with modifications. Specifically:

> H5. Managing outward (H5a) will be more in evidence in settings that are more dispersed and less homogeneous (i.e., more complex), so managing outward (H5b) will have more performance-related impact in environmentally complex settings.

Similarly,

> H6. Operating in a more heterogeneous and dispersed task environment will reduce the likelihood of program success, and the marginal impact of any externally directed managerial action is likely to be lower.

> H7. Operating in a more complex environment will reduce the path dependence of a public organization's operations, so the autoregressive parameter of performance will decline as externally directed managerial efforts increase.

Hypothesis H7, on the relationship with the external management and the autoregressive parameter (and, more fundamentally, between environmental complexity and the autoregressive parameter), can be expected to hold if the organization does not rely heavily on structural and other buffering devices, which might also substitute for the buffering portion of external managerial effort.

Complex environments pose challenges for public managers and of necessity draw their attention. Although they can be expected to lower chances for program success and reduce performance, management capacity might mitigate the lower marginal impact of external management. With substantial capacity—for instance, a larger, more expert management cadre, perhaps with significant policy-analytic expertise—more complex environments may be more manageable. (For a detailed discussion of management capacity and analyses of its performance effects in two sets of empirical settings, see Meier and O'Toole 2010, and Andrews and Boyne 2010). In other words, management capacity can enable public organizations to mitigate the decline in the managerial effects on performance that might otherwise be expected in complex contests:

> H8. Management capacity mitigates the lower marginal impact of externally directed managerial action that would otherwise be expected in a more heterogeneous and dispersed task environment.

*Turbulence* refers to "externally induced changes . . . that are obscure to administrators and difficult to plan for" (Aldrich 1979, 69). Dess and Beard (1984) consider turbulence to be an aspect of dynamism. Uncertainties in the environment, rapid changes, and unpredictability are all likely to reduce organizational performance (Andrews 2009).[11] Similarly, more turbulence is likely to draw more managerial effort outward. As with the discussion above, we can expect turbulence to attenuate the marginal effect of such management on supporting or improving program performance:

> H9. Managing outward will be more in evidence in settings that are turbulent, and managing outward will have more performance-related impact in environmentally turbulent settings.
>
> H10. More turbulent organizational environments will reduce the likelihood of program success, and the marginal impact of any managerial action is likely to be lower.
>
> H11. Operating in a more turbulent environment will reduce the path dependence of a public organization's operations, so the autoregressive parameter of performance will decline as externally directed managerial efforts increase.

Once again, management capacity offers the prospect of retaining the relationship between external management and performance in turbulent environments—by the same logic as that sketched above for environmental complexity:

H12. Management capacity mitigates the lower marginal impact of externally directed managerial action that would otherwise be expected in a more turbulent task environment.

*Munificence* references the availability of needed resources (Rainey 2009, 95). The needed resources may be of several kinds, although often the focus is on financial resources. How might one expect varying levels of munificence to affect the relationship between management and performance? Here we find it useful to distinguish two aspects of externally directed management: exploiting environmental opportunities and buffering the organization's production processes from environmental challenges.

When a public organization's environment is high in munificence, more opportunities—in the form of valued resources—are available. Indeed, earlier research indicates that greater munificence is associated with better performance (Andrews 2009). Managers may recognize that external efforts can pay big dividends. Tapping munificent environments may also mean more prospecting managerial strategies; managers will be more likely to try to enhance performance on additional metrics and/or expand performance to heretofore-ignored or underemphasized service populations. Conversely, when task environments are low in munificence, managers are likely to try to protect or buffer the core organization from the resource-poor surroundings, which may include other organizations interested in tapping the core organization's resources or jurisdiction. This circumstance can also generate more managerial efforts outward—although ones of a different sort. If this logic holds, therefore, we are likely to see the least external managerial efforts in moderately munificent environments:

H13. More munificent organizational environments will offer opportunities for enhancing organizational interests and performance, so managers will increase their efforts to tap environmental opportunities over such efforts when external resources are moderate (neither plentiful nor overly constrained).

H14. In more munificent organizational environments, managers will direct relatively more of their effort to tap environmental resources to enhance performance. A stronger relationship between such external management and performance is expected. Higher performance may take the form of more outputs/outcomes on the most salient metric, more outputs/outcomes in additional performance metrics, and/or more outputs/outcomes for a larger service population.

H15. In more munificent organizational environments, the marginal return from external management will be greater.

When organizational environments are low in munificence, there may be more reason to buffer or protect organizational production from the limitations and constraints stemming from the environment. In other words, one can expect two different aspects of external management to be more prominent—to be more often employed—at high and low levels of environmental munificence than when munificence is at moderate levels. Under circumstances of high munificence, we expect more external management to try to tap resources for the organization; under low munificence, we expect more external management to try to buffer organizational production processes from the environment. Furthermore, we expect the marginal value of these two aspects of external management to be higher, respectively, at high and low levels of munificence than at moderate levels. Accordingly:

H16. Less munificent organizational environments will offer reasons to protect organizational interests and performance, so managers will increase their efforts to protect against less promising environments when compared with situations in which external resources are moderate (neither plentiful nor overly constrained).

H17. In less munificent organizational environments, managers will direct more of their effort toward protective external efforts to insulate internal operations from environmental constraints and thus stabilize performance. "Higher" performance may take the form of more stabilized outputs/outcomes on the most salient metric, or strategic redirection of organizational effort toward core performance metrics and/or core service populations.

H18. In low-munificence organizational environments, the marginal return from external management will be greater than in moderately munificent environments.

## Munificence and Social Capital

One element of munificence that merits separate discussion is the social capital of the community. Social capital has multiple definitions, but for our purposes can be defined as the interpersonal networks and organizational memberships that citizens possess; such ties enhance a sense of efficacy, facilitate collective action, and generate interpersonal trust. Managers who operate in environments with ample social capital generally will have less difficulty in implementing effective programs because social capital allows greater coproduction of services, eases the communication of information, and generates more acceptance of programs that provide public goods (Andrews 2010):

> H19. The level of social capital in a community interacts with management to enhance the impact of management on performance.

Hypothesis 19, however, should be qualified to note that this expectation holds for situations in which program goals are consistent with the norms and values of the individuals generating the social capital. It is quite possible for social capital to be a source of resistance to government programs, particularly those that benefit another group (Hero 2007). An implication is that trust in government and regime support would be expected to be important, related contextual factors.[12]

## THE INTERNAL ORGANIZATIONAL CONTEXT

The internal context of an organization is likely to affect management's relationship to performance in two ways. First, the context provides the starting point that includes the goals of the organization and the constraints and resources that the manager faces. Managerial decision making can be considered, simply put, as the effort to maximize outcomes (i.e., goals) relative to resources, subject to the constraints of the organization. Second, the context should also affect what managerial actions are needed and what actions are likely to be effective. In the logic of context that was noted above, internal organizational context interacts with management. Three particularly salient elements of context are discussed here and linked to specific hypotheses—goals, hierarchy (and its related concept, centralization), and professionalization.

### Goals

Organizations are goal-oriented collectivities; they exist to achieve some expressed purpose. In the real world, however, organizations often have ambiguous goals (Rainey 2009). Goal ambiguity can arise from two sources: goal conflict, and the inherent ambiguity of some goals. Public organizations have multiple masters, and these masters—particularly when political power is not concentrated—can have conflicting goals for the organization. Although, in theory, an effective political process can resolve goal conflicts and provide clear and consistent goals for public organizations, in practice public organizations are often tasked with conflicting goals or goals that are ambiguous (Chun and Rainey 2005). Goal conflict, in turn, is manifested as goal ambiguity because managers face program demands that are not compatible with each other. Goal ambiguity can also arise because some goals are inherently ambiguous. The goal of educating children does not deal with the specifics of whether the education is to be for vocational purposes or for future education. Nor does it clarify how much emphasis should be placed on standardized tests versus creative thinking, or numerous other ends of education.

Scholars know little about what managers do when faced with goal conflict—that is, do they seek to clarify goals, thus either risking goal displacement or institutionalizing conflict when the clarification demonstrates that goals do conflict?[13] A logical strategy for an organization is to deal with conflicting goals sequentially (Cyert and March 1963), or to assign them to different parts of the organization in hopes that they can be buffered from each other or reconciled at some future point. However a manager deals with goal conflict and goal ambiguity, the presence of either or both makes the task of management more difficult and is likely to affect performance:

> H20. The presence of goal conflict and goal ambiguity increases the impact of both internal and external management and means that management will account for a greater proportion of the variance in program outcomes.
>
> H21. As goal ambiguity (and conflict) increase(s), the marginal contribution of a given level of management declines.

## Hierarchy and Centralization

Public organizations come in a wide variety of forms; many of these are quite different from the traditional Weberian bureaucracy with a strong hierarchy, clear lines of authority, and written rules to cover most if not all situations. At the risk of gross oversimplification, we can arrange these organizational forms along a dimension that is strongly hierarchical and centralized at one pole of the continuum and collegial and decentralized at the other pole. Although one can have a hierarchical organization that is decentralized (e.g., the individual units of an army in wartime), in general, hierarchy and centralization covary. The degrees of hierarchy and centralization affect both the level in the organization where management will matter and also the form that management will take. Management will clearly matter most at the point where the organization vests discretion. The literature on representative bureaucracy demonstrates that representation matters at the street level in organizations that vest discretion in frontline bureaucrats (e.g., schools and police forces; Meier and Morton 2015), but matters at the middle-management level in those organizations where key decisions are made at the supervisor level (e.g., child support; see Wilkins and Keiser 2004).

In regard to the form that management will take, as discretion is vested in lower levels, the activities of top management shift somewhat toward human resources functions, especially the selection of individuals who will carry out the goals of the organization. Top management also will focus on goals and strategy but leave operations and tactics to those closer to the point of implementation. The hypotheses generated as a result focus on which sets of managers to study rather than the relative impact of the managers in general:

> H22. The strongest relationships between management and organizational performance will be at the organizational levels where the organization vests the most discretion.
>
> H23. As organizations become decentralized and vest discretion in lower levels, the top management of the organization shifts from hierarchical direction to goal setting and the selection of organizational personnel.

As an aside, the impact of any managerial action—say, external networking—should not necessarily change with decentralization, but which managers are performing the function is likely to change. This means that measuring networking at the correct level of the organization is important, simply because at some levels it is unlikely to be prominent and unlikely to have any impact.

## Professionalism

Public service both is professionalized and has itself become a profession (Mosher 1982). The recruitment of professionals into public organizations—doctors, scientists, engineers, and the like—has been a consequence of the technical demands of public policy. This influx of professions is important, because professions bring their own values about policy, and how to accomplish policy objectives, to the organization. Professionals also tend to make decisions based on expertise, rather than relying on hierarchy. The influence of professionalization on the relationship between management and performance can thus be linked to the discussion of decentralization, as sketched above. Public service has also become a profession in its own right, with its own process for certifying who is a public servant, codes of ethics, career patterns, and so forth. The esteem of the public service as a profession varies greatly even among developed countries; one needs only to compare the level of bureaucrat bashing in the United States with that in Western Europe. Similarly, individual professions can vary greatly in esteem, as witnessed by the high regard for teachers in Finland versus the United States (Mintrom and Walley 2013).

The level of professionalization and the esteem accorded to these professions alter how managers are likely to manage and, therefore, perhaps affect the level of skills needed to have an impact on performance. The consensus of the literature is that professionalization requires collegial management styles and the decentralization of decision making to the lowest level possible. At the same time, professionalization should not affect the need for and the impact of external networking, although it is likely to change the composition of networks significantly to more closely reflect the norms of the profession. These are not necessarily unique hypotheses and could be treated simply as a special case of the decentralization/hierarchy hypotheses above.

The clear impact that professionalization should have, however, is to escalate the level of management skills that are necessary. Managers will be expected to have skill and education levels on a par with the professions that they manage; in many cases, the managers will be drawn from the ranks of the dominant professions in the organization. This might well be the reason that a college education is a reasonable indicator of management quality in a developing context but matters little in a developed one. This point—diminishing marginal returns to management capital—plus the idea that direct hierarchical control is unlikely to work and therefore managers in professionalized public organizations need a higher-level set of management skills—generates the following hypothesis:

> H24. As public organizations become more professionalized, the impact of management on performance will increase (i.e., explain more variation), but the marginal influence of a "unit" change in management will decline.

## A Proposal for Future Research

This chapter has argued that scholars of public management need to consider the context that surrounds public organizations and their management. The chapter has proposed the idea that context affects management by interacting with management and thus changes the relationship between management and performance. The theory also suggested that the political context of an organization has parallels to the general environmental context of that organization and these contexts can be expected to produce similar results. These simple ideas expressed in a simple equation, however, will not be easy to implement in a research program, or even in several of them. Ideally, what would be needed are samples of organizations that have widely varying contexts, for which there are accepted performance metrics, and for which one has information about management or could collect such information. We would, therefore, encourage researchers to undertake explicitly cross-national studies of management and performance in particular policy sectors, while also specifying analytically how the contexts differ. These can contribute to a broader understanding of the influence of certain contextual features on this relationship.

Within countries as well, systematic comparisons are welcome. Unfortunately, the demand for a comparable performance metric essentially means the examination of organizations that are performing the same or similar functions. This approach converts many context variables into constants, or near-constants, across the units and means that we can say little or nothing about the (near-)invariant aspects of context and their impact on how management matters for performance. Devising such a data set would be a Herculean task that would absorb far more resources than the field of public management currently has available.

Accordingly, a more modest strategy can be proposed. This chapter has identified what we believe to be a set of key context variables; and though there probably is no universal agreement on what context fully entails, there would seem to be a consensus on the elements discussed here. A significant step forward could be made if scholars were to add to their studies a table—such as table I.1 below—that provides information regarding the specific context of their empirical investigation(s). As an illustration, using a common example of research on the management of Texas schools in 2012, the analyst might note that the political structure is unitary (i.e., there is no separation of powers) and has a single level (although with federal influences), with adversarial political processes, a developed performance appraisal system, and moderate levels of social capital. The environment would be characterized as complex (demands to educate different races, income levels, etc.), turbulent (owing to immigration and other factors), and modest to poor on the munificence scale (owing to several budget reductions). The internal context of the organization could be characterized as having ambiguous goals (and multiple goals), as having a decentralized and nonhierarchical structure, and as professionalized.

Public management scholars are producing a respectable volume of studies linking management in its various aspects to organizational performance. It is now past the time to ask, simply, whether management matters. Rather, there are two important questions: When does management matter? And what factors affect how much it matters? Answering these questions requires careful attention to the context in which management operates. This chapter suggests that much needs to be done to link context to management and performance, and it has specified twenty-four hypotheses. Clearly, no single study can address twenty-four hypotheses. The short-term strategy of using

**Table I.1** The Public Management Context Matrix

| *Political Context—Concentration of Power* | | |
|---|---|---|
| Separation of powers | Unitary | Shared |
| Federalism | One level of government | Multiple levels |
| Process | Corporatist | Adversarial |
| Performance appraisal | Established | No formal system |
| *Environmental Context* | | |
| Complexity | Complex | Simple |
| Turbulence | Turbulent | Placid |
| Munificence | Rich | Poor |
| Social capital | Present | Absent |
| *Internal Context* | | |
| Goals | Clear and consistent | Multiple and conflicting |
| Centralization | Centralized, hierarchical | Decentralized |
| Professionalism | Professional | Not Professional |

*Note:* For the sake of simplicity, we have dichotomized the variables in this table; but we recognize that they are each interval variables. The table is less complex than it appears, because many of the variables are likely to be collinear (i.e., the concentration-of-powers variables are likely to be positively correlated).

the context matrix in table I.1 to clearly designate the context of any given study, however, can provide building blocks that scholars might use to create a strong theory of context. The context matrix can also be used to find contextual situations that differ dramatically from those available in the existing sets of studies (English local governments, Texas schools, Dutch education, etc.). Only by subjecting our theories to testing across disparate contexts can we validate general managerial relationships and also understand the importance of contextual conditions in shaping the management–performance relationship. The context matrix itself is theory neutral, in the sense that it can be used in conjunction with numerous management theories. It offers a route toward understanding both the general and the contingent aspects of public management.

## OVERVIEW OF THE BOOK

In the following chapters, this volume attempts to take the next step in the context agenda by demonstrating how individual studies of public management can be set within the proposed theory to provide greater generalizability.

The contexts in the empirical chapters vary from schools in the Netherlands to local governments in Brazil and from health care in Africa to higher education in the United States. The approach also varies, with some studies treating context as a variable and presenting interactive relationships and others using context as a framing variable and explaining how the specific context fits within the general theory.

Chapter 1—by Cameron Wimpy, Marlette Jackson, and Kenneth J. Meier—provides the first examination of context as a part of the management equation (whereby context is expected to interact with management and condition the results of public management on performance). The authors examine the role of administrative capacity (i.e., the quality of administration) on health outcomes in thirty-six African nations over an eleven-year period using the path dependence of being a British colony as the contextual variable. The impact of administrative capacity on government program performance is quite likely to be affected by context. Bureaucratic capacity can easily be undercut by a lack of resources, by a corrupt political system, or by a variety of other factors. This study uses one of these contextual factors—path dependence—and illustrates how it conditions the impact of government capacity. Government bureaucracies deal with problems by breaking them into small parts and addressing one part at a time. When such policies rely on the cooperation of citizens, the bureaucracies need to repeat the process as a new clientele arrives until the resulting behaviors or conditions change. Health care is particularly affected by this long time frame and path dependence. Immunization programs, prenatal care, clean water, sanitary systems, and similar preventive efforts require continued operation to do the intake process for new clients, to maintain water systems, to distribute nutritional information and supplies to expectant mothers, and the like. Health is a coproduced good, and so it also requires high levels of trust among the population, which also take time to develop. Findings show that administrative capacity is associated with significant reductions in child mortality and that these reductions are significantly greater in former British colonies. Additional analysis examines the same relationships for the incidence of cholera, HIV infections, malaria, and tuberculosis and also suggests that the effects are nonlinear.

In chapter 2 Rhys Andrews explores the separate and combined effects of environmental complexity and organizational strategy on the performance of English local governments using multivariate statistical techniques. Empirical results show that environmental complexity is negatively related to performance, but that an innovative strategic stance moderates the negative effect of complexity on performance. Both a defensive and a reactive strategic stance, however, worsen the complexity–performance relationship. Following the hypotheses posed here in the introduction related to complexity as an important component of an organization's external context, the analysis in chapter 2 therefore provides support for the idea that strategic choices matter when public organizations confront a complex environment.

Chapter 3, by Claire Stieg and Amanda Rutherford, revisits classic debates centered on comparing and contrasting public and private organizations. Rather than attempting to continue the discussion on specifying the characteristics of private and public organizations, the objective of this chapter is to examine the performance outcomes of public and private managers. By testing the effectiveness of management on outputs and outcomes, we are able to step away from defining the differences between public and private organizations and move toward better explaining the effect that variance in structure and organization may have on performance. Analyses are conducted on an original data set about presidents of institutions of higher education in the United States universities rated during a twenty-one-year period by the Carnegie classification system as doctoral/research universities, as research universities–high research activity, or as research universities–very high research activity. Performance variables span areas of student performance (graduation rates and degree completion), student access (share of low-income students and average institutional award), and institutional research (federal grants and contracts and gifts and endowment). Findings suggest that presidents with reputations as scholars often raise the performance of their organization, whether public or private, perhaps because of a certain outlook compared with other, non-research-minded presidents. Conversely, presidents who most recently were employed as the president of another institution consistently perform better in public institutions, though the effect of any socialization gained through prior position is much more mixed in private institutions.

Transitioning to the context of primary and secondary schools, in chapter 4 René Torenvlied and Agnes Akkerman test whether managerial networking is consistently linked to educational outcomes. Studies of Texas school districts, performed over the last fifteen years, reveal that both internally and externally oriented management activities make an important difference for organizational performance. The external validity of these findings, however, is mainly restricted to a specific domain in a specific US state. This chapter uses data on Dutch primary education to replicate and extend the Texas school district studies. Despite an initial lack of empirical support, analyses ultimately find strong evidence for the fundamental mechanisms linking management with performance postulated by the model of public management outlined here in the introduction. The key to success is a careful specification of institutional context of both denominational and nondenominational schools within the

Dutch research setting. For nondenominational schools, principals' contact with local government turns out to be crucial; this stems from their public orientation and their obligation to accept all registered pupils in the municipality. Principals of denominational schools can focus more on youth care professionals, and these contacts contribute most to the performance of these schools. Findings in this chapter provide strong support for the general model of public management in both the US and European contexts.

In chapter 5, Mads Leth Jakobsen, Anne Mette Kjeldsen, and Thomas Pallesen illustrate the importance of context in traditional assumptions related to public service motivation (i.e., that employees motivated to engage in public service are considered a positive asset by any organization). But are these motivated employees always a benefit when they are required to increase performance? Using survey data from Danish public service providers at a recently merged public hospital, this chapter examines whether hospital staff members who are motivated to engage in public service should be characterized as loyalists or saboteurs in relation to two types of performance-increasing organizational changes: an austerity type of reform that aims to increase output and contain costs, and a strategic reform that aims to improve hospital service. Analyses show that employees motivated to engage in public service are more supportive when performance requirements are service-oriented changes rather than an austerity reform that may conflict with public service values. Moreover, political leaders and their top public managers confront more potentially strong saboteurs, who are motivated and powerful, in relation to the austerity reform policies than in relation to the strategic service-oriented change policies.

Chapter 6, by Claudia Avellaneda, shifts to the context of South American local governments. The chapter examines whether the decision context (issue salience, actors' interrelations, credible commitment, and political environment) affect local public managers' decisions to delegate municipal spending and explores the direct and moderating effects of local managers' qualifications on their delegation decisions. Analysis is conducted through an original survey experiment using Honduran incumbent mayors who are both the political and administrative leaders in their municipalities. Each mayor was asked to respond about how he or she would hypothetically allocate a large sum of money that was donated by an international donor agency to his or her municipality. Results indicate that, in general, mayors prefer not to delegate spending; but when they do delegate, mayors opt for a local instead of a national association of municipalities. Although issue salience has no effect on mayors' decisions to delegate, the local political context (competitiveness and ideological conflict) does affect mayoral delegation.

In chapter 7 Ricardo Gomes and Claudia Avellaneda focus on the influence of political and managerial characteristics on municipal revenue performance in Brazil. After they control for a range of municipal indicators, their results suggest that those municipalities led by reelected mayors tend to obtain fewer state and federal grants. Municipalities led by younger mayors seem to be more successful in securing federal grants, whereas those led by leftist mayors also do well in securing state grants. More generally, their findings provide empirical tests of the hypotheses related to external contextual variables related to politics and the concentration of power described above in the introduction. If expanding revenues translates into greater social investment, this study contributes to local development by determining whether politics, managerial competency, or contextual factors influence subnational growth in the Latin American context.

The book's conclusion—by Amanda Rutherford, Laurence J. O'Toole Jr., and Kenneth J. Meier—reviews findings in the empirical chapters for additional insights on the role of context in public management. Two additional hypotheses are added to those offered in the introduction, and recommendations are provided for scholars of public administration on how to expand this line of research. It will be critical to consider context as the study of public management continues to become more comparative in nature so that findings in the setting of a specific industry or a specific country can be compared with those in another setting.

## NOTES

This chapter is a revised version of "Public Management, Context, and Performance: In Quest of a More General Theory," by Laurence J. O'Toole Jr. and Kenneth J. Meier (2015); it was adapted for this book with the permission of Oxford University Press.

1. We acknowledge with thanks the considerable assistance of Snizhana Radzetska in conducting this review.
2. The three countries are Colombia, Nepal, and South Korea. The remainder of volume 23, plus materials in subsequent volumes and online, indicate that a wave of non–United States studies is breaking over the field.
3. Indeed, context might also affect other relationships, including the role of organization structure, incentives, culture, and other variables, and how they relate to each other as well as to performance. To avoid incorporating mind-numbing and likely unproductive complexity regarding this last set of relationships, nonetheless, we focus in this analysis only on how several aspects of context can be expected to influence directly the management–performance link.
4. Virtually the entire literature on management, both public and private, indicates that many managerial actions can be consequential. To keep the present logic to

its core argument, we omit for the moment any specifics about what constitutes the vector of relevant managerial actions. Later in the chapter, we offer some possibilities.

5. Even the United Kingdom fragments political power, with devolution to Scotland and, in a lesser case, to Wales. One might also consider the difference between majoritarian and coalitional political systems in terms of concentrating power.
6. Here we introduce a distinct aspect of the thus-far-undifferentiated notion of management: management outward. Though scholars do not fully agree on the various aspects of management that carry performance-related implications, one frequently distinguished aspect is this externally oriented portion of management. For instance, Moore (1995) distinguishes among managing upward, downward, and outward. Lynn, Heinrich, and Hill (2001) do not explicitly identify a management effort outward, but instead treat management as a production- and interior-focused influence; however, they do incorporate a set of political and environmental variables into their reduced form model of governance. They therefore may be seen to imply that management sometimes deals with such influences. O'Toole and Meier (1999) distinguish externally oriented ($M_2$) from internally focused ($M_1$) managerial efforts. They further distinguish external managerial efforts to exploit or tap external forces ($M_3$) from external managerial efforts to protect or buffer the organization from external forces or perturbations ($M_4$). We believe it is useful to distinguish in some fashion the external from the internal management functions, but using this distinction does not necessarily bind one to any particular formulation.
7. It might also be the case that where power is dispersed, the plural political authorities can exhibit variation in program decisions and resourcing. So the variation in outputs and outcomes could also be a function of this feature. In this chapter we focus on the actions and influence of managers as the central theme.
8. We distinguish the importance of management and the marginal impact of a given unit of management. The importance of management means that it accounts for more of the variance in outcomes. The marginal impact is how much an individual unit can contribute (e.g., whether a manager has earned a professional degree). Context can affect both the importance of management and its marginal impact.
9. A more precise statement would also include the point that in separation of powers systems, the multiple principals may sometimes blame each other for reported suboptimal performance results, as documented by the system. In unified systems, political executives are likely to have stronger incentives to set clear frameworks for performance. In short, we expect the evidence for H4 to be weaker in separation of powers systems
10. Similarly, not only principals but also agents can game such systems; see Bevan and Hood 2006.
11. Andrews examines the relationships between these environmental characteristics—in both subjective and objective (or archival) senses—and performance. In the current study, we omit consideration of how managerially perceived environments might modify the relationship between management and performance.

12. Other external dimensions that might be considered in a complete theory are the level of development and the incorporation of culture factors, including citizen trust, the status of bureaucrats, and other factors.
13. Goal displacement is possible because, in the effort to clarify goals, the manager might include only a portion of the mission of the agency. Performance appraisal systems that focus on measurable outcomes are often criticized for oversimplification and, in the process, contributing to goal displacement.

# 1

# Administrative Capacity and Health Care in Africa

## *Path Dependence as a Contextual Variable*

CAMERON WIMPY, MARLETTE JACKSON,
AND KENNETH J. MEIER

Management clearly matters in a wide variety of both national and substantive contexts—ranging from public schools in the United States, the Netherlands, and Denmark to local governments in England and Colombia to national governments. The impact of management on different aspects of performance, however, varies across these different contexts. In the introduction to this book, O'Toole and Meier present a theory of context whereby context is expected to interact with management and condition the results of public management on performance. Ideally, they argue that one would study management across contexts so that context might be a variable that could be used as an interaction effect within a single equation (see equation 2 in the introduction). Their second-best proposal is for scholars to document the context of their studies along such dimensions as the political context (the degree to which political power is concentrated), the environmental context (complexity, turbulence, munificence, and social capital), and the internal organizational context (goals, centralization, and professionalism). We follow the first strategy in this chapter by examining the role of administrative capacity in health outcomes in thirty-six African countries, using the path dependence of being a British colony as the contextual variable.

The analysis proceeds in five parts. First, we introduce the concept of administrative capacity—a variable that is often assumed in studies of public management but rarely measured and included as an explanatory variable. Second, we present a theoretical argument that bureaucracy or administrative capacity is subject to path dependence. The creation of administrative capacity takes time to develop, and the effectiveness of administrative capacity should be enhanced to the degree that bureaucracy has a longer history of effective performance. We use experience as a former British colony as our indicator of effective historical performance, based on a reading of the qualitative historical and political literature. Third, we introduce the substantive area of concern, health outcomes in Africa, with a focus on a health care indicator, child mortality, that should be highly sensitive to administrative capacity and the ability to deliver basic services. Fourth, we present a panel analysis of thirty-six African countries over an eleven-year period that shows administrative capacity is associated with significant reductions in child mortality and that these reductions are significantly greater in former British colonies. Additional analysis examines the same relationships for the incidence of cholera, HIV infections, malaria, and tuberculosis (TB) and also suggests that the effects are nonlinear. Fifth and finally, we assess the meaning of the present analysis for the study of how context conditions the impact of management on performance.

## ADMINISTRATIVE CAPACITY

Administrative capacity or, alternatively, the quality of administration is a central feature of governance. Policies are rarely self-implementing, which dictates the establishment of an administrative organization to oversee programs and deliver actual services. In most cases, policy actions are expressed as goals—the improvement of health outcomes, the reduction in poverty, the increase in human capital, creating democratic citizens—and the specific programs are left for administrative agencies to design and implement (Rourke 1984). This aspirations form of policy in turn requires a level of administrative expertise to understand the causal linkages in the policy under question, or in some cases to discover such linkages and design solutions. Administrative capacity is needed for this, and government bureaucracies are the political institution that is most designed to develop policy expertise. All bureaucracies engage in specialization and breaking down complex problems into smaller parts where the solutions might not be as daunting. The logic of near-decomposable systems (Simon 1965) holds that these small solutions can then be reaggregated in such a manner as to generate an effective overall policy. Bureaucratic specialization is facilitated by the hiring of professionals and technicians with specific skills that are applicable to the problem being addressed. Administrative capacity in this manner should be directly associated with administrative quality because it permits the organization to make better decisions.

Administrative capacity is also linked so closely to two other concepts that they may be descriptions of the same phenomena. Administrative stability as a concept taps into a bureaucracy's permanence and its ability to address problems by breaking them down over time or by using prior experience to solve problems. Although one might use turnover or some other indicator of administrative stability, it is often measured as the size of the administrative component (see chapter 4 in this volume, by Torenvlied and Akkerman). Similarly, there is a literature examining the concept administrative intensity, an organization's relative ratio of administrative effort to production, as a dependent variable (Boyne and Meier 2013). This literature is driven by two predominant hypotheses—the public choice hypothesis, that administrative intensity is a function of bureaucratic waste and aggrandizement; and the functional hypothesis, that administrative intensity is an effort to address organizational problems. In the later interpretation, administrative intensity can be considered the equivalent of administrative capacity, with its links to improved organizational outcomes.

Despite this universal understanding of administrative capacity and its linkage to administrative quality and role in effective programs, the public management literature has generally ignored capacity. Many studies examine a set of organizations that are well established, and among which the range of administrative capacity is relatively small and thus becomes treated as a constant in the process. Even within such studies, variation in capacity is often difficult to measure and is often indicated by very indirect indicators, such as the size of administrative staff (Bowman and Woods 2007; Huber and McCarty 2004; Johnson and Randall 2013; Meier, O'Toole, and Hicklin 2010).

Indirect measures such as size have one inherent limitation. Bureaucracies can be large because they are specializing and developing expertise, or they can be large because they are inefficient but have still convinced the political branches to fund them. Better measures of capacity actually try to assess quality—the ability of the bureaucracy to effectively implement policy. In most cases such measures are based on elite opinion, using a set of raters that have experience with the governments in question. Within the United States, perhaps the foremost example of elite measures of administrative capacity is the Government Performance Project (Ingraham, Joyce, and Donahue 2003; Ingraham 2007; for an application, see Krueger and Walker 2010). A parallel measure for many developing countries, including those in this study, has been created by the World Bank (see below).

The objective of this chapter is to relate administrative capacity to health outcomes in Africa (see table 1.1 and the discussion in the conclusion for a more detailed description of how this setting fits into the context matrix). The impact of administrative capacity or public administration quality on health care outcomes is relatively straightforward. The greatest relative gains in health outcomes tend to be preventive measures that protect individuals from diseases that could lead to premature death. Health care in these situations is not the high-technology type of care associated with major medical centers but rather primary care, immunizations, sanitation, and other relatively simple actions. In the countries under study, this involves dealing with malaria, TB, cholera, and HIV infection, as well as providing prenatal care and primary care health workers. The ability of government bureaucracies to carry out such programs, particularly to implement them outside the capital city, becomes essential. Administrative capacity should be a good measure of the ability to effectively implement these large but low-technology health care programs. The impact of such programs should be felt most on overall indicators of public health, such as child and infant mortality rates (Gupta and Verhoeven 2001). The influence of administrative capacity in Africa generally takes place in a political context characterized by unitary nonfederal system governments with adversarial processes and no formal performance appraisal. Environments are complex and turbulent but poor and lacking in social capital. The internal context is centralized but also nonprofessional and associated

**Table 1.1** The Public Management Context Matrix: African Countries and Primary Health Care

| *Political Context—Concentration of Power* | | |
|---|---|---|
| Separation of powers | **Unitary** | Shared |
| Federalism | **One level** | Multiple levels |
| Process | Corporatist | **Adversarial** |
| Performance appraisal | Established | **No formal system** |
| *Environmental Context* | | |
| Complexity | Complex | **Simple** |
| Turbulence | **Turbulent** | Placid |
| Munificence | Rich | **Poor** |
| Social capital | Present | **Absent** |
| *Internal Context* | | |
| Goals | **Clear and consistent** | Multiple and conflicting |
| Centralization | **Centralized, hierarchical** | Decentralized |
| Professionalization | Professional | **Not professional** |

with multiple and conflicting goals. These generally problematic contexts for policy places a high premium on administrative capacity.

## PATH DEPENDENCE

The impact of administrative capacity on government program performance is quite likely to be affected by context. Bureaucratic capacity can easily be undercut by a lack of resources, by a corrupt political system, or by a variety of other factors. This study will take one of these contextual factors—path dependence—and illustrate how it conditions the impact of government capacity. Government bureaucracies deal with problems by breaking them into small parts and fixing one part at a time. When such policies rely on the cooperation of citizens, the bureaucracies need to repeat the process as new clientele arrive until the resulting behaviors or conditions change. Health care is particularly affected by this long time frame and path dependence. Immunization programs, prenatal care, clean water, sanitary systems, and similar preventive efforts require continued operation to do intake for new clientele, to maintain water systems, to distribute nutritional information and supplies to expectant mothers, and the like. Health is a coproduced good, so it requires high levels of trust among the population, which can take time to develop.

Our measure of path dependence is a simple one that codes whether a country is a former British colony. Although all colonial governments in Africa were exploitive and focused on generating returns for the home country rather than developing effective future governing structures, scholars generally perceive the British experience as least abusive (Agbor 2011; Barro 1999; Clague, Gleason, and Knack 2001; Lipset, Seong, and Torres 1993). The expressed philosophy of British governance was indirect rule, whereby indigenous rulers were co-opted by the British to assist in governing (Herbst 2000, 81).[1] This symbiotic relationship meant that British colonies had a vested interest in developing local bureaucratic capacity by investing in education for local administrators and training in administration and management to a greater degree than in other African colonies (see Kingsley 1967, 307). This investment meant that at the time of independence, the British colonies in Africa had, on average, greater indigenous administrative capacity than did the French, Portuguese, or Belgian colonies. This legacy also meant that former British colonies had a head start in distinguishing between the administrative state and personal gain, so that increases in administrative capacity were built on a stronger base than in other colonies. The generalist nature of the British administrative service meant that after independence, the former colonies could enter into contracts with foreign officials for their technical and scientific expertise and at the same time retain key management positions in the bureaucracy (Kingsley 1967, 309).

The experience of the former British colonies differs markedly from other forms of colonial heritage. For example, when the Portuguese left Mozambique in 1975, there were no trained Mozambican doctors (Walt and Cliff 1986).[2] By contrast, Grier (1999) concludes that many of the existing differences in postcolonial development between the British and French colonies can be explained by education levels at the time of independence. In the case of the French colonies, the existing power structures were often reorganized and major responsibilities of governance were most often carried out by French officials. Conversely, the British colonies experienced far less meddling in existing local power structures when compared with the French (Crowder 1964). In a study of the Hausa peoples, who inhabit the overlapping Hausaland region of Nigeria and Niger, Miles (1994) concluded that there were marked differences in development in Nigeria (a former British colony) when compared with Niger (a former French colony). These findings were further echoed in a more recent case study of Cameroon (Lee and Schultz 2011), which was split into two colonial administrations (British and French).[3] The authors concluded that the British-administered area of West Cameroon had higher levels of public goods provisions and better-performing local governance institutions when compared with the French-administered East.

## THE STATUS OF HEALTH IN AFRICA

Public health outcomes in Africa lag significantly behind those in much of the rest of the world. Among the best indicators to measure overall health outcomes in a country are child and infant mortality rates, because life expectancy at birth is greatly determined by the survival chances of infants and children (Klasen 2008; Hill and Amouzou 2006). According to the United Nations (2013), in 2012 the child mortality rate (deaths under the age of five years) in Sub-Saharan Africa was 98 children per 1,000 live births, the highest regional rate in the world. The rate for North Africa was better, at 24 per 1,000 live births, but that was still substantially above the rate for developed countries of 6 per 1,000 live births. Particularly high were the child mortality rates of Sierra Leone (234 per 1,000 live births), Rwanda (182), South Sudan (181), Sudan (171), and Zambia (169). These numbers might also underestimate the problem, because in poor countries with marginal health care, many births are not recorded and as a result some childhood deaths are also not counted.

Child mortality provides a good overall indicator of a nation's health and also a good test for the role of administrative capacity because perhaps as many as two-thirds of childhood deaths can be prevented by relatively rudimentary public health measures (Rao, Lopez, and Hemed 2006). In tropical Africa, the main causes of infant and child deaths are infections, protein-calorie malnutrition, and birth trauma (Page and Coale 1972; Newland 1982). Infections such as HIV/AIDS also play a role (Mboup et al. 2006). Walker, Schwartlander, and Bryce (2002) found that controlling for competing causes of mortality, HIV infections caused 8 percent of under-five deaths in 1999. Children in the developing world, especially in Sub-Saharan Africa, often suffer from more than one disease at a time. This generates a "synergism of infection," whereby children tend to suffer from several diseases at the same time while also being affected by malnutrition. The combination of factors leads to dramatically higher levels of childhood mortality.

As Reidpath and Allotey (2003) conclude, using the child mortality rate as an overall indicator of a nation's health reflects the intuition that structural factors affecting the health of entire populations have a disproportionate impact on the child mortality rate. Because a large percentage of childhood deaths can be prevented by access to adequate nutrition, clean water, and rudimentary health care, they are a highly sensitive indicator to use in assessing the impact of administrative capacity on the government's health policy performance. This sensitivity means that even rough measures of overall public administration quality should have fine enough distinctions to translate into differences in public health.

## OTHER HEALTH OUTCOME DETERMINANTS

Public health outcomes are affected by a wide variety of factors other than administrative capacity, including the level of health care infrastructure, economic development, the level of democracy, and the degree of conflict. Each of these factors either influences access to health care or creates situations that increase the risk to health. Controls for each set of variables, therefore, need to be included.

### The Health Care Infrastructure

Any effort to assess the role of bureaucracy vis-à-vis health outcomes needs to control for the existing health care infrastructure. Access to health care is rationed in all societies, either by market mechanisms or by queuing. As the supply of health care providers increases, individuals are more likely to gain access to primary care. In particular, the number of frontline health care professionals is likely to be important. In Santerre, Grubaugh, and Stollar's (1991) examination of Africa, they found that a 10 percent increase in the number of physicians per capita led to a 5.4 percent decrease in the infant mortality rate. These findings were echoed by Benson and Shekar (2006), who found that the number of per capita physicians tracked consistently with health care quality.

Access to health care also involves transaction costs, such as travel in areas that are underserved. A large number of studies find that access to health care in developing countries is much more difficult in rural areas than in urban ones. This has resulted in consistent findings that urban areas tend to have lower mortality and morbidity rates than rural areas (Monsted and Walji 1978; Page and Coale 1972; Gaisie 1979), although the size of the rural/urban differential is also affected by other factors, such as education, marital status, and family size (Mott 1982; Monsted and Walji 1978).

### Economic Development

One of the strongest determinants of health outcomes at the aggregate level is economic development (Mosley and Chen 1984; Boyle et al. 2006; Murray and Lopez 1997). Economic development contributes to better health outcomes in a variety of ways. First, economic development is associated with greater access to clean water and clean air, thus reducing the ability of waterborne and airborne diseases to reach epidemic stage. Immunization rates also are higher in more developed countries. Second, economic development is associated with greater investments in health care, both as the result of the increased supply of health professionals and as the result of increased demand by the population. Third, as an individual's economic status improves, he or she is more likely to have the funds to invest in health care and to seek out solutions to health problems.

### Democracy

Public health scholars have linked democracy to positive health outcomes. The democratic process creates incentives for elected officials and policymakers to meet the needs of the general population, and in much of Africa access to clean water, adequate nutrition, and basic medical services are significant needs. Zweifel and Navia (2000) and Kudamatsu (2012) both find a positive correlation between democracy and positive health outcomes in Africa.

### Conflict

Health outcomes in a developing country are heavily dependent on adequate food supplies, clean water, and access to primary medical care. None of these factors are equitably distributed among the population, and these distributions are likely to be affected by both ethnic fractionalization and armed conflict. Ethnic fractionalization creates both political and social divisions in a polity. Such divisions reduce social interactions and can result in basic services being distributed on the basis of ethnic ties rather than strictly on the basis of need. More homogeneous societies should find it easier to deliver the programs that improve health outcomes. Both La Porta and colleagues (1999) and Alesina and colleagues (2003), for example, find that ethnic fragmentation is positively correlated with infant mortality.

Armed conflict, a frequent occurrence in many African countries, disrupts the delivery of basic health services, has a detrimental impact on food production and distribution, and frequently dislocates individuals from their homes to refugee camps (Iqbal 2006; Koch 2012). Ghobarah, Huth, and Russett (2004) find that civil wars destroy property, disrupt economic activity, and divert resources from health care. Davis and Kuritsky (2002) report that severe military conflict in Sub-Saharan Africa raised infant mortality by 12 deaths per 1,000 live births.

## DATA AND METHODS

The data for our analyses come from several sources. The Mo Ibrahim Foundation compiles indicators from various sources on a wide variety of variables. The Ibrahim Foundation is our source for the measure of administrative capacity based on the foundation's effort to rank African countries on their quality of governance across the broad categories of safety and the rule of law, participation and human rights, sustainable economic opportunity, and human development, using data from existing sources. In addition to the Ibrahim Foundation, we collected data from the US Central Intelligence Agency's (CIA) *World Factbook*, the *Economist* Intelligence Unit, the World Health Organization, and Polity. Our final data set covers thirty-six African countries for the period 2000–2010, thus yielding 396 country-years as our units of analysis.

### The Variables

Our primary explanatory variable is a measure of public administration quality developed by the World Bank (see table 1.2 for a list of variables used in this study; when a term in the text is capitalized, it refers to the variable name as listed in the table; generally, however, the text uses descriptive language for the variables). This variable "assesses the extent to which civilian central government staff is structured to design and implement government policy and deliver services effectively."[4] For those countries with subnational governments that play a significant role in policy implementation, the assessments also cover these subnational governments. The documentation, however, notes that the primary focus is on the central government and that the basic scores of the central government are adjusted upward or downward based on the performance of the subnational governments.

The measure is essentially an elite opinion measure based on assessments of individuals with experience with the specific governments. The assessments are based on three components—the managing of the government's operations, ensuring quality in policy implementation, and coordinating human resources management outside the core government administration. This third dimension addresses the ability to work with and coordinate with nonprofits and other nongovernmental organizations to deliver services. The variable is a component of the broader Country Policy and Institutional Assessment (CPIA), which is compiled by the World Bank as a yearly appraisal of a given country's policies and institutions. This assessment is only done for countries that are eligible to borrow from the International Development Association branch of the World Bank, which gives highly concessional loans. The CPIA scores range theoretically from a low of 1 to a high of 6, but no country in Africa received a score above 4 during the period under study. A score of 1 means that a country has little management capacity, that major personnel actions do not reflect merit criteria, that institutional responsibility for implementation is weak or unclear, and that the government sector has little ability to coordinate the policy actions of nonprofits or other organizations. A measure of 4 essentially signifies that the capacities and abilities of the country are moderate with the application of merit principles, that some ability to coordinate policy actions is present, that institutional responsibility for action exists, and that a moderate level of public management is evident. The CPIA is used not just by the World Bank but also by the African Development Bank in their decision processes, and has been subject to continued review and adjustment since the late 1970s. Although the CPIA has not been used in public management research to date, its use by major international organizations gives it some face validity as a measure of administrative capacity. We employ this variable as a proxy measure of administrative capacity as we defined it in the previous sections.[5]

Assessing the impact of administrative capacity on organizational performance requires controlling for a variety of other variables that could also affect performance. We argue theoretically that administrative capacity should be affected by path dependence; administrative capacity takes time to develop, and this development is not likely to simply be linear. In terms

**Table 1.2** Coding, Expected Relationships, and Sources for All Variables

| *Variable* | *Expected Relationship* | *Coding (Source)* |
|---|---|---|
| Child Mortality | Dependent variable | Rate per 1,000 births (Ibrahim Index / IGME) |
| Public Administration Quality | – Increase in quality leads to decrease in child mortality | 1–6 scale (World Bank) |
| Former British Colony | – Former British colonies experience less child mortality | 1 = Former British Colony<br>0 = Not British Colony |
| Access to Improved Water | – More clean water decreases child mortality | Proportion of population with access to potable water (Ibrahim Index / World Health Organization, WHO) |
| Cholera | Dependent variable | Number of reported deaths per capita (WHO) |
| Domestic Armed Conflict | + Conflict leads to higher child mortality | 0–100 scale of intensity (Ibrahim Index / Economist Intelligence Unit, EIU) |
| Doctors per Capita | – More doctors decreases child mortality | (Ibrahim Index / WHO) |
| Ethnic Fractionalization | + Fractionalization leads to higher child mortality | 0–1 Herfindahl Index (Alesina at al. 2003) |
| HIV | + Disease leads to higher mortality | Prevalence among adults (WHO) |
| Internet Subscribers | – More internet access decreases child mortality | Percent of population subscribing to internet (Ibrahim Index / ITU) |
| ln(GDP per Capita) | – More development leads to less child mortality | Natural log of GDP per capita (World Bank) |
| Malaria | Dependent variable | Cases per capita (Ibrahim Index / WHO) |
| Percent Muslim | +/– Control variable | CIA *World Factbook* |
| Percent Rural | + Less access to health care leads to higher child mortality | Percent of population living in rural area (CIA *World Factbook*) |
| Polity IV | – More democratic leads to lower child mortality | –10 to 10 (Polity Project) |
| Tuberculosis | Dependent variable | Cases per capita (Ibrahim Index / WHO) |

of path dependence in administrative capacity, African countries experienced radically different colonial legacies. Some consciously sought to build administrative capacity, while others simply treated the African colonies as resources to be exploited as rapidly as possible. Scholars of democratic and economic development have often pointed to these colonial legacies as important moderating factors for most distinguishing factors that are used to explain development (Agbor 2011; Barro 1999; Clague, Gleason, and Knack 2001; Lipset, Seong, and Torres 1993). Specifically, the heritage of being a former British colony has been highlighted as an important consideration for distinctions in development when compared with other former colonial powers. As noted above, the British colonial legacy is particularly important in creating administrative capacity, such that former British colonials not only inherited extensive administrative capacity but also had human resources systems that continued to support a trained civil service. The measure is a dichotomous variable coded 1 for former British colonies.[6]

## Additional Control Variables

Numerous factors contribute to a nation's health outcomes, and getting an estimate of the impact of administrative capacity on these outcomes requires that the factors be included in the study. The public health infrastructure should be positively related to health outcomes. The Ibrahim Index includes two variables that are obvious choices: the number of doctors per capita, and the percentage of the population with access to improved (potable) water—both of which have been found to be important in the literature (Jain 1985; Robinson and Wharrad 2000; Benson and Shekar 2006). Both these variables are linked to access to health services. Access to health care also varies within a country for populations living in urban versus rural areas. As such, we include a measure of the percentage of the population living in rural areas from the Ibrahim Index.

Health outcomes are also affected by the level of economic development. We use a measure of economic development, operationalized as the natural log of gross domestic product (GDP) per capita, from the World Bank. As an additional measure of development, we include the percentage of internet connectivity, which is included in the Ibrahim Index via the International Telecommunications Union. This variable assesses a different dimension of development than GDP in that it captures technological development.[7] As such, it should facilitate the government's communication and coordination in combating health problems.

An additional contextual measure is the level of democracy; we use the combined autocracy/democracy score from the Polity IV index (Marshall, Jaggers, and Gurr 2012). The countries in our data set range from among the world's most autocratic (Swaziland, Libya, Eritrea, and Sudan) to its most democratic (Cape Verde and Mauritius). Democracy and economic development have been strongly linked in the literature, thus making this a natural contextual control for the examination of development in the public administration and health sectors.

Finally, ethnic and religious heterogeneity and the level of conflict should both be related to health outcomes and administrative capacity. We use the ethnic heterogeneity measure calculated by Alesina and colleagues (2003), which is a Herfindahl index.[8] Higher indexed scores indicate higher levels of heterogeneity. The role of ethnic heterogeneity as an explanatory factor for political outcomes has been debated at length in various literatures, with mixed findings (Fearon and Laitin 2003; Posner 2004a, 2004b, 2005). Given this debate, we further test this contextual role as it applies to health outcomes. We also include a measure of religion from the CIA *World Factbook*: the percentage of the population that adheres to Islam. We do not necessarily expect one religion to influence health outcomes (either positively or negatively) over another. We use this as a contextual control for different cultural influences across the continent, including the significant difference of being in North Africa versus Sub-Saharan Africa.

The level of intragroup conflict within a country could affect access to health care and upset other related avenues of administration. To the extent that the government is not in control of the entire country, the delivery of health services is bound to lack universal application. As such, we include a measure from the Ibrahim Index that calculates the intensity of domestic armed conflict for each country-year.

## Dependent Variables

As a first test of the effectiveness of bureaucratic capacity for health outcomes, we consider the level of child mortality for each country-year as our initial dependent variable. We take this measure from the Ibrahim Index, which originally sourced it from the United Nations' Inter-Agency Group for Child Mortality Estimation. The variable measures the rate of under-five child mortality per 1,000 births.

As an additional test, we include a series of models with alternative dependent variables. For these models, we employ measures of cholera, HIV, malaria, and TB. The cholera variable is the per capita rate of reported cholera deaths in a given country-year. HIV is measured as the percentage of its prevalence among the adult population. Malaria and TB are each measured as per capita rates for every 1,000 people. These data are all derived from the World Health Organization. In table 1.2 above, we display all the variables, coding,

**Table 1.3** In-Sample Summary Statistics for the Variables Used in Analyses

| *Variable* | *N* | *Mean* | *Std. Dev.* | *Minimum* | *Maximum* |
|---|---|---|---|---|---|
| Child Mortality | 396 | 136.98 | 43.82 | 27.5 | 250.3 |
| Public Administration Quality | 396 | 2.88 | .519 | 1 | 4 |
| Former British Colony | 396 | .333 | .472 | 0 | 1 |
| Access to Improved Water | 396 | 63.11 | 14.27 | 28 | 95 |
| Cholera | 396 | .926 | 2.89 | 0 | 28.07 |
| Domestic Armed Conflict | 396 | 58.84 | 33.11 | 0 | 100 |
| Doctors per Capita | 396 | 1.25 | 1.11 | 0.450 | 6 |
| Ethnic Fractionalization | 396 | .690 | .206 | 0 | 0.930 |
| HIV | 374 | 4.63 | 5.57 | 0.100 | 27.30 |
| ln(GDP per Capita) | 396 | 6.15 | .723 | 4.466 | 8.45 |
| Malaria | 385 | 116.23 | 86.31 | 0.1 | 354 |
| Percent Muslim | 396 | 32.50 | 32.24 | 0 | 99.70 |
| Percent Rural | 396 | 64.99 | 16.10 | 12.70 | 91.70 |
| Polity IV | 396 | 1.85 | 4.70 | –7 | 10 |
| TB | 396 | 48.17 | 28.33 | 3 | 153 |

and sources used in the analyses, along with our expected relationships for each one with the health outcomes. In table 1.3, we present summary statistics for all variables.

## Methods

We treat the various health outcomes as continuous variables, and, as such, we employ ordinary least squares estimation. Because our data vary across time and space, we take a number of additional steps, including panel-corrected standard errors, to account for any contemporaneous spatial relationships (Beck and Katz 1995). We also employ time fixed effects (year dummy variables) to account for any common shocks to all the cases in a given year.[9]

We estimate a series of models, starting with a simple bivariate model with child mortality regressed on public administration quality. We then move to a fully specified model, using the same outcome and our additional contextual and control variables. Because we are interested in how bureaucratic capacity varies in its effects on health outcomes across contexts, we include an interactive specification, which allows former colonial status (British or not) to moderate the effect that public administration quality has on child mortality.

Finally, we present the series of fully specified models with the interactions for each of the disease outcomes.

## Results

The bivariate estimation (table 1.4) of the variable Child Mortality regressed on the variable Public Administration Quality indicates that we can expect a reduction of 23 child deaths per 1,000 live births for every one-unit increase in the quality of public administration. Of course, this estimate is biased because we are not yet controlling for other variables, but it does highlight an interesting relationship, which we continue to test in our additional models.

In table 1.5 we present our fully specified model, with Child Mortality as the health outcome of interest. In this case, we can see that a one-unit increase in Public Administration Quality is associated with about a 26-child reduction in the incidence of child mortality per 1,000 live births. This is a huge effect size, an approximate reduction of 25 percent in child mortality compared with the average country.[10] The other significant variables all adhere to our expected relationships. In looking at the contextual variables, Former British Colony is associated with a 6-child reduction in child mortality, whereas a one-unit increase in Ethnic Fractionalization is associated with about a 46-child increase in child deaths per capita.[11] The only variables to not achieve statistical significance were GDP and conflict intensity. However, we are most interested in how context affects bureaucratic capacity vis-à-vis health outcomes, so we focus largely on the findings of our interactive models.

The second column of table 1.5 presents our interaction between being a former British colony and public administration quality. The significant interaction shows that public administration quality has a larger impact on child mortality in former British colonies than their alternative colonial heritage

**Table 1.4** Bivariate Estimation of Public Administration Quality on Child Mortality

| *Variable* | *Estimates* |
|---|---|
| Public Administration Quality | –23.7*** |
| | (1.12) |
| Constant | 205*** |
| | (1.83) |
| Observations | 429 |
| $R^2$ | .07 |

*Note:* Standard errors are in parentheses (two-tailed tests, despite directional hypotheses). Panel corrected standard errors are reported underneath ordinary-least-squares parameter estimates, $^{***}p < 0.01$.

**Table 1.5** The Effects of Public Administration Quality on Child Mortality

| *Variable* | *Base Model* | *Contextual Model* |
|---|---|---|
| Public Administration Quality (PAQ) | –25.9*** | –20.9*** |
| | (1.6) | (2.17) |
| Former British Colony | –6.57** | 38.8** |
| | (2.23) | (15.5) |
| PAQ × Former British Colony | | –15.7*** |
| | | (4.73) |
| Access to Improved Water | –.498*** | –.434*** |
| | (.0538) | (.0412) |
| Domestic Armed Conflict | .0288 | .0208 |
| | (.0199) | (.0192) |
| Doctors per Capita | –10.2*** | –12.1*** |
| | (.952) | (1.46) |
| Ethnic Fractionalization | 45.5*** | 48.9*** |
| | (4.72) | (4.52) |
| Internet Subscribers | –14.8*** | –15.2*** |
| | (4.1) | (4.24) |
| ln(GDP per Capita) | .998 | 3.04 |
| | (2.49) | (2.51) |
| Percent Muslim | .154*** | .153*** |
| | (.0101) | (.0108) |
| Percent Rural | .414*** | .455*** |
| | (.0831) | (.082) |
| Polity IV | 1.54*** | 1.71*** |
| | (.176) | (.202) |
| Constant | 201*** | 169*** |
| | (21.5) | (19.7) |
| Observations | 396 | 396 |
| $R^2$ | .44 | .45 |

*Note:* Time dummies are not shown. Standard errors are in parentheses (two-tailed tests, despite directional hypotheses). Panel corrected standard errors are reported underneath ordinary-least-squares parameter estimates, * $p < 0.1$, ** $p < 0.05$, *** $p < 0.01$.

counterparts. A one-unit increase in administrative quality is associated with a reduction of 20.9 child deaths per 1,000 live births in non-British former colonies and a reduction of 31.6 child deaths per 1,000 live births in former British colonies. Consider the 2000 example of Sierra Leone, which had the highest rate of infant mortality among the countries in our data set, with about 1 in 4 children not surviving.[12] This is not surprising, given that they were experiencing a civil war at that time. Nevertheless, based on the results of our model, Sierra Leone (a former British colony) would have experienced about a 15 percent reduction in child mortality if its score on public administration quality had moved from 3 to 4.[13] Otherwise, the results for the other variables in this model do not change in any meaningful way from those discussed above.

To better present our interaction effects, in figure 1.1 we plot the effects of Public Administration Quality when Former British Colony status is present and when it is not. This indicates that the presence of being a former British colony changes the effect for public administration quality from expecting a reduction of 20 child deaths per 1,000 live births in countries with a non-British colonial heritage to a reduction of 36 deaths when the country was a former British colony. We then plot the fitted values of expected child mortality for each colonial status (British or not) across the values of public administration quality. We can see there is a significant difference in the slopes of these

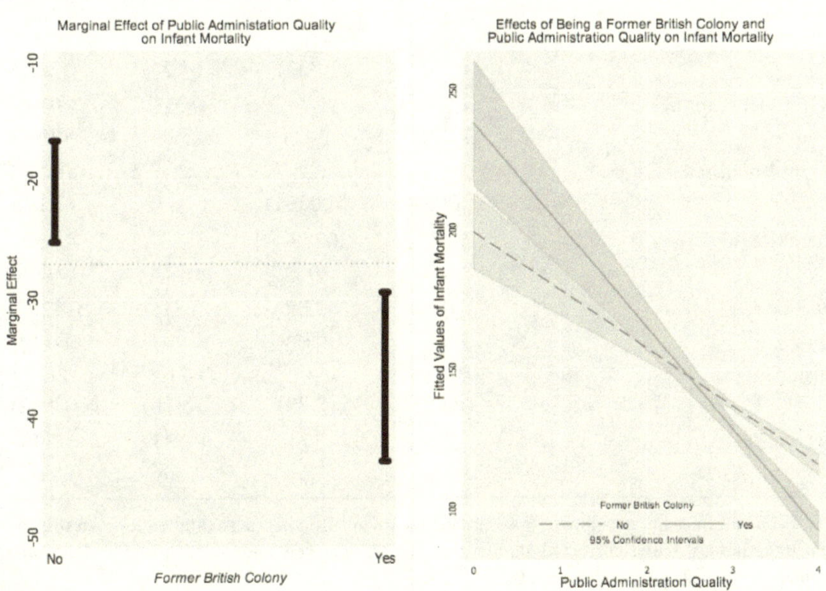


**Figure 1.1** The Effects of Public Administration Quality and Former British Colony on Infant Mortality

*Note:* The graph on the left presents marginal effects of Public Administration Quality on infant mortality conditioned by whether or not the country was a Former British Colony. The graph on the right presents the fitted values of infant mortality across the range of Public Administration Quality conditioned by being a Former British Colony or not.

**Table 1.6** The Effects of Public Administration Quality on the Rate of Disease

| *Variable* | *Cholera* | *HIV* | *Malaria* | *TB* |
|---|---|---|---|---|
| Public Administration Quality (PAQ) | –1.32*** (.29) | –1.92*** (.333) | –28.1*** (3.3) | 1.56 (1.75) |
| Former British Colony | 6.85* (3.83) | 16.3*** (2.4) | 109*** (28.5) | –2.05 (6.98) |
| PAQ × Former British Colony | –2.25* (1.26) | –3.85*** (.779) | –43.4*** (8.92) | –1.38 (2.39) |
| Access to Improved Water | .01 (.0103) | .0231** (.00718) | .429*** (.082) | –.505*** (.0434) |
| Domestic Armed Conflict | .01** (.001) | .0484*** (.00705) | .0917 (.0566) | –.195*** (.0327) |
| Doctors Per Capita | –.18 (.152) | –1.72*** (.238) | –19.1*** (3.22) | –1.32* (.781) |
| Ethnic Fractionalization | .42 (.926) | –5.05*** (.423) | 224*** (5.53) | –6.8** (2.96) |
| Internet Subscribers | .70* (.39) | –1.34 (.833) | –8.07* (4.24) | 5.01** (2.27) |
| ln(GDP Per Capita) | .23 (.29) | 2.96*** (.41) | 6.35* (3.84) | –19.8*** (.908) |
| Percent Muslim | .01*** (.003) | –.051*** (.00361) | .427*** (.0472) | .0675*** (.0146) |
| Percent Rural | 2.77* (1.27) | .0778*** (.0125) | 1.25*** (.128) | –.955*** (.0502) |
| Polity IV | .02 (.03) | .0226 (.0469) | 5.81*** (.663) | .826*** (.113) |
| Constant | 1.33 (2.49) | –10.1*** (2.89) | –71.5* (30.6) | 263*** (7.82) |
| Observations | 396 | 374 | 385 | 396 |
| $R^2$ | .16 | .60 | .39 | .33 |

*Note:* Time dummies are not shown. Standard errors are in parentheses (two-tailed tests, despite directional hypotheses). Panel corrected standard errors are reported underneath ordinary-least-squares parameter estimates, * $p < 0.10$, ** $p < 0.05$, *** $p < 0.01$.

predictions, indicating that former colonial status has an important moderating effect on public administration quality insofar as it explains child mortality.

Last, we turn to a discussion of our interactive models for the alternative health outcomes of cholera, HIV, malaria, and TB. Across the models shown in table 1.6, we can see that the effects for the variable Public Administration Quality are significant in all models, with the exception of TB. One possible reason for this is that TB is an airborne disease that is typically treated via isolation and particularized drugs (Floyd, Wilkinson, and Gilks 1997), which relate to other sectors beyond public administration (e.g., health facility infrastructure). The other diseases are all often treated on a more preventive basis through the mass distribution of mosquito nets for malaria (Vallely et al. 2007), education and condoms for HIV (Alary et al. 2002), and water treatment for cholera (Tappero and Tauxe 2011; see also Kwofie 1976).[14] The variable Former British Colony also behaves the same way across these models, which is a further indication of the extent, and limits, of contextual distinctions for predicting health outcomes.

When examining the cholera model, for example, we can say that a one-unit increase in public administration quality is associated with about a 1.32 per capita incidence reduction in the number of cases when the country was not a British colony. However, when the country was formerly a colony of Britain, we expect to see a case reduction of nearly 4 per capita in the incidence of cholera for every one-unit change in public administration quality. The results for HIV and malaria are also quite substantial when examined in their own metrics. These findings further substantiate our theoretical expectations about the role of bureaucratic capacity in improving various health outcomes.

## IMPLICATIONS

This chapter has examined the impact of administrative capacity in Africa and its impact on the health outcomes of childhood mortality. Because a large proportion of childhood mortality is preventable with basic public health activities in disease prevention and food distribution that limit malnutrition, the measure is highly sensitive to the quality of administration. This is an area where the barriers to performance are not high-technology limits but rather simple processes of distributing malaria nets, providing clean water, conducting health education, and administering immunizations. Similarly, the problems related to malnutrition are frequently malfunctions in the distribution of food rather than a total absence of calories.

Two aspects of context are relevant to the impact of administrative capacity on health outcomes in Africa. First, in terms of the contextual model presented in this book's introduction, public administration in Africa, even with the Herculean task of generalizing to more than fifty countries, is clearly distinct from most of the cases examined in the public management literature. In terms of the political context, the African countries are weak states that are highly centralized. Their legislatures, judiciaries, and governing institutions other than their executive branches tend to be weak, so they resemble unitary systems in practice if not in format. Their processes are decidedly not corporatist, and there are few if any formal processes of performance appraisal. For the most part, their governments do not operate as federal systems. The result is a concentration of power, but one that is often not focused on policy. The administrative environment can be generally characterized as complex (with multiple pressing problems), highly turbulent, poor in resources, and containing little social capital. The internal context can be classified as having multiple and conflicting goals (policy vs. personal gain), centralized and hierarchical, and lacking in professionalism.

Second, because the context of African countries (even overgeneralized, as in the paragraph above) differs greatly from the type of organizations usually studied, we opted to focus on a contextual variable that actually varied across the region. We used the fact of whether the country was a former British colony as a measure of path dependence—the inheritance of an administrative system and procedures that stressed some aspects of self-government and the creation of Western-style bureaucratic organizations.

The findings demonstrate not only that administrative capacity has a large impact on the incidence of child mortality but also that context matters. In the former British colonies, the impact of administrative capacity was significantly greater (by about 75 percent) than in countries with other colonial heritages. Much of the impact on administrative capacity vis-à-vis childhood mortality appears to be through the process of disease prevention. In the cases of malaria, cholera, and HIV infections, administrative capacity was also negatively related to disease rates (only TB appeared to be unaffected by capacity). Similar to the findings for childhood mortality, the impact of administrative capacity on malaria, cholera, and HIV infections was at least twice as great in former British colonies as in the rest of Africa.

Although the findings of this chapter are striking, we should note the limitations of this study. First, examining management and administrative performance at the national level masks a great deal of variation and deviates greatly from the more common assessment of organizational variation within a country. Within each of the countries included, there is likely variation in impact and capacity among individual organizations. Second, the context variable Former British Colony is a blunt category that masks significant variation among the various former colonies. Third, major aspects of public management—such as networking, managerial strategy, the development of human resources, and even public service motivation—were not included in this study; in fact, they may be difficult if not impossible to study at this level of aggregation. Fourth, much health policy in Africa is implemented by the presence of international nongovernmental organizations, which greatly augment the capacity of the existing national governments. The role of these not-for-profit organizations merits explicit study.

Even with the limitations of this study, there is still potential for significant future research using cross-national cases such as the present one. First, unlike a great deal of the literature, the models used in this chapter are linear and additive. Given the frequency of nonlinear relationships in the literature and the undeveloped state of administration in Africa, we might expect administrative capacity to benefit from increasing returns to scale. Second, being a former British colony is only one small part of the contextual variation in Africa. The continent's countries vary in religion, ethnic fractionalization, economic development, and health infrastructure—all of which might affect the relationship between administrative capacity and performance. Third, this chapter has examined only a single policy area—health care—and only a small set of outcome indicators. We might expect to find similar influences of administrative capacity in other areas, such as transportation, education, economic development, and even democratization. This study thus has illustrated the potential payoff from cross-national studies of public management in Africa, but it has not come close to exhausting their potential.

## NOTES

1. This is a generalization across numerous colonies and the degree of indirect rule varied greatly across British colonies and was not consistently applied; see the discussion by Herbst (2000). The British indirect rule policy, and the distinction it produced from other colonial powers, was already well established by the mid-1930s (Whittlesey 1937).
2. According to a report from the United Nations Development Program, in 1999 Mozambique's literacy rate was less than half those of most of its neighbors.
3. It is worth noting that Cameroon was a German colony before World War 1.
4. The Ibrahim Foundation rescores this variable and merges it with several others. To make sure we were measuring administrative quality and capacity only, we opted to use the original data gathered by the World Bank.
5. The lack of 5 and 6 ratings is telling. African bureaucracies in general are characterized by patrimonialism, corruption, and overcentralization; see Chabal and Daloz (1999). The concept of patrimonialism is used to denote the inability of bureaucrats to distinguish between their public roles as bureaucrats and their own private gains. Patrimonialism quite clearly leads to corruption and the inefficient and inequitable distribution of services. African bureaucracies generally also have much less capacity to deliver services in rural areas; see Jreisat (2002). This lower level of capacity compared with developed nations is another reason for using a primary indicator of public health like child mortality rather than measures that focus on the mortality or morbidity of adults.

6. The mean level of public administration quality was 2.92 for former British colonies and 2.85 for the other countries in this study. The interaction effect examined below, as a result, is not the result of higher levels of administrative quality alone.
7. The ln(GDP) per Capita and Internet Subscribers variables are correlated at $r = .59$.
8. The formula for this index is 1 minus the sum of the squared percentages of the share of the population for a given ethnic group (Alesina et al. 2003).
9. There are other methods of dealing with time in pooled time series data. As robustness checks, we also estimated models with lagged dependent variables in addition to Prais-Winsten analysis. In each case our results had little substantive variation with respect to our variables of interest.
10. Given the low level of administrative capacity (no nation rated above 4), there appear to be substantial additional gains that could be made on this dimension.
11. This effect size is magnified by the nature of the limited range of the fractionalization measure. A more appropriate effect size is that a reduction of 1 standard deviation in fractionalization is associated with a drop of 9.5 child deaths per 1,000 live births.
12. The exact count was 250.3 per 1,000 children born. This high number is not surprising given that Sierra Leone was engulfed in civil war at this time. The lowest child mortality rate in our sample was Cape Verde in 2009 and 2010, with only 27.5 under-five child deaths per 1,000 births.
13. This reduction would have only been by about 8 percent if Sierra Leone had not been a British colony.
14. Conversely, patients with AIDS are at particular risk for TB and are therefore often considered a priority for preventive treatment when available and feasible (Creese et al. 2002).

# 2

# Environmental Complexity and Public Service Performance in England

## *Does Organizational Strategy Matter?*

RHYS ANDREWS

Interest in the performance of public organizations has grown rapidly during the past ten years or so. As governments around the world have become concerned about the efficiency and effectiveness of public services (Pollitt and Bouckaert 2000), researchers have also paid increasing attention to the organizational, managerial, and environmental factors that influence public service performance (Ashworth, Boyne, and Entwistle 2010). One important feature of this research effort has been the emphasis on the external circumstances that facilitate or constrain the work of public organizations (Andrews et al. 2005; Meier and Bohte 2003). As a result, the external context in which public services operate is now widely recognized to be an important determinant of outcomes (O'Toole and Meier 2015). According to the organizational studies literature, low levels of munificence (resource availability) and high levels of environmental complexity (heterogeneous clients and suppliers) and dynamism (unpredictable changes in munificence and complexity) are the main challenges present within the organizational task environment (Dess and Beard 1984). Nevertheless, comparatively little attention has been given to the ways in which public organizations respond to their environments and their success or failure. Existing studies have tended to concentrate on the managerial strategies that are likely to mitigate the negative performance effects of low munificence (see Meier and O'Toole 2002) and dynamism (or turbulence) (Boyne and Meier 2009). A small number of studies also consider the impact of environmental shocks or jolts on public service performance (e.g., Meier and O'Toole 2009; Andrews et al. 2013). In this chapter the managerial strategies likely to overcome or exacerbate the effects of environmental complexity on performance are analyzed, drawing on data from English local governments—a setting that in recent times has been characterized by high levels of complexity.

The relationship between management, the external environment, and organizational outcomes is a concept at the heart of many influential organizational theories, such as institutional theory (DiMaggio and Powell 1983), population ecology (Hannan and Freeman 1989), and resource dependency (Pfeffer and Salancik 1978). Contingency theory, especially, suggests that certain organizational strategies are more likely to be successful when organization environments are more or less complex and dynamic (Donaldson 2001; Miles et al. 1978). Despite widespread acknowledgment of the salience of the idea that organizations can respond positively to the circumstances that they confront (Boyd and Gove 2006), the environment–performance link posited by contingency theory has rarely been tested in the public sector. In particular, there has been no comprehensive exploration of the impact of alternative organizational strategies on the connection between environmental complexity and public service performance.

The relative degree of complexity in the organizational environment is a product of the sheer number and diversity of the human and material factors with which organizations must contend (Duncan 1972). As such, it is generally hypothesized to be a burden on managers, who must devote more attention to understanding and managing the multiplicity of clients, stakeholders, competitors, and sources of revenue outside the organization's boundaries. This, in turn, implies that complexity is likely to be bad for performance, but also that certain managerial and organizational practices and routines may be more or less likely to facilitate an effective response to a heterogeneous environment. In particular, contingency theories suggest that organizations must be more proactive in how they manage environmental complexity if they seek to achieve superior performance. Hence, a focus on innovating and finding new ways to meet the needs of clients and stakeholders is assumed to be a more appropriate strategy than a focus on incremental improvements to the status quo in a complex environment (Miles et al. 1978). Is environmental complexity associated with worse public service performance? Does organizational strategy make a difference to the complexity–performance relationship? More specifically, does a prospecting, outward-facing strategy enable organizations to better manage a complex environment than a defensive, inward-looking one? To answer these questions, this study undertakes a multivariate statistical analysis of the relationships between ethnic diversity, organizational strategy, and the performance of English local governments, drawing on primary and secondary sources of data.

The structure of the chapter is as follows. In the next section, I explore the concept of environmental complexity and its relationship with public service performance. Following that, the potential moderating effects of a prospecting, defending, and reacting strategy on the complexity–performance relationship are examined, and hypotheses about these effects are developed. Next, the chapter outlines the organizational context of the study and how it fits within the comparative public management framework presented in the introduction to this book, before the data and measures are discussed. Thereafter, the results of statistical tests of the hypotheses are described and interpreted. Finally, the theoretical and practical implications of the findings are explored.

## ENVIRONMENTAL COMPLEXITY AND PUBLIC SERVICE PERFORMANCE

The concept of environmental complexity has a venerable history within the literature on organization studies. Beginning with Emery and Trist's (1965) analysis of the causal texture of organizational environments, numerous attempts have been made to precisely define what is meant by complexity and how it shapes organizational behavior (Cannon and St. John 2007). Duncan (1972) argues that complexity is composed of two main elements: (1) the number of different factors within the environment, and (2) the degree of heterogeneity between the different environmental factors. According to Duncan (1972), these two elements of complexity may be present to varying degrees within organizations' external environments (e.g., customers, suppliers, and competitors) and internal environments (e.g., occupational groupings and functional units). Crucially, complexity is seen to pose problems for organizational decision makers, especially within the external environment, because this is much less malleable and susceptible to managerial intervention than the internal context. A wide range of dissimilar external factors, as Tung (1979, 675) puts it, place ever-greater demands on "the CEO's cognitive abilities to grasp and comprehend the relationships that exist among them." All of this highlights the reality that in a complex environment, additional managerial attention must be devoted to understanding the external context in which an organization is operating.

Later conceptions of environmental complexity have drawn on Dess and Beard's (1984) analysis of the different dimensions of the organizational task environment. According to Dess and Beard, environmental complexity comprises both the heterogeneity and the dispersion of an organization's domain. In particular, in a heterogeneous environment, an organization is grappling with a wide range of markets and services, and the multitude of customers and suppliers that this implies. In these circumstances, managers require more information-processing systems as well as skills, which leads to greater strain on an organization's resource capacity (Dutton, Fahey, and Narayanan 1983). Public-sector organizations typically operate in a complex environment when they are required to serve a heterogeneous population. Complexity in the public sector is therefore likely to reflect the relative homogeneity or heterogeneity of service users, especially the different social and cultural groups from which they are drawn, given that user needs are rarely addressed on an individual basis but are instead targeted to certain populations.

Because the environmental complexity that public organizations face is likely to reflect the demographic characteristics of their clients, the performance effects of complexity are a product of the diverse needs and demands of the different social groups within the client population. In particular, if the public is relatively homogeneous (e.g., mostly white middle class), it may be comparatively straightforward to elicit their preferences and provide a "standardized" service that addresses their needs. By contrast, for a heterogeneous population (e.g., one consisting of many different ethnic groups), greater effort may be required to identify their preferences, and it may be necessary to provide a wider range of services to meet their requirements (Boaden and Alford 1969). Environmental complexity may therefore lead to a vast expansion in the multiple and potentially conflicting organizational goals that managers are expected to meet (Pandey and Rainey 2006). In public organizations, the "goal ambiguity" associated with perceptions of high levels of goal complexity has been shown to result in poor performance (Chun and Rainey 2005). All of this suggests that environmental complexity will be negatively related to public service performance.

## ENVIRONMENTAL COMPLEXITY, ORGANIZATIONAL STRATEGY, AND PERFORMANCE

To address the potential challenges posed by environmental complexity, public organizations are likely to need to innovate and develop policies that will enable them to meet the multiple demands that arise from client heterogeneity. Specially designed initiatives can be designed to tackle the dilemmas associated with diversity in the target population, especially programs to support the array of different community groups that may be served by an organization (Lowndes and Thorp 2011). At the same time, the broad strategic approach adopted by organizational leaders is likely to influence an organization's prospects of being able to develop effective initiatives for dealing with the diversity of service needs that it confronts. This indicates that the interactive effects of complexity and strategy on performance may be of considerable importance. However, alternative strategic choices are known to have divergent implications for performance (Meier et al. 2010), so it may well be the case that some strategies represent a better bet than others when seeking to respond to environmental complexity. In fact, this very point is at the heart of contingency theories, which suggest that organizations must seek to align their strategies with the environmental circumstances that they face (Donaldson 2001).

With respect to the links between complexity, strategy, and public service performance, it seems prima facie likely that an outward-looking and innovative organization will be more attuned to meeting a diverse array of social demands and needs. By contrast, an inward-looking strategy may make organizations less alert to the opportunities for developing initiatives that go beyond a one-size-fits-all approach. In recent times, a number of alternative approaches to conceptualizing the nature of strategic endeavor in the public sector have emerged that can provide useful insights into how the interaction between complexity and strategy might play out. The strategy typology developed by Miles and Snow, in particular, has become one of the most important and influential (Bryson, Berry, and Yang 2010).

According to Miles and colleagues (1978), organizational strategies can be categorized into four ideal types. *Prospectors* are organizations whose strategic outlook is firmly focused on innovation and the exploration of new markets and services. They are often pioneers and "first movers" in their industry. Within the public sector, prospecting is likely to involve an independent quest to explore and try out new approaches to meeting service users' needs. *Defenders* are organizations that adopt a conservative view of new product development. They typically stick to their core business niche, with a focus on improving efficiency, rather than attempting to identify new opportunities. Public organizations adopting a defending strategy will likely focus on the incremental refinement of tried-and-tested approaches to service delivery. *Analyzers* share elements of both the prospector and defender strategy. *Reactors* are organizations that develop no consistent response to change and uncertainty in their organizational environments. Typically, a reactor waits for direction from powerful stakeholders and regards all developments within their operating environment as threats that may affect their survival. In the public sector, reacting will generally entail doing whatever supervisory agencies recommend is the best way forward for providing services.

Conant, Mokwa, and Varadarajan (1990) and DeSarbo and colleagues (2005) argue that organizations adopt different strategies for different purposes—for example, by robustly defending the organization's core niche to protect its existing markets, while actively prospecting for new products or services in an effort to create new markets. As a result, strategy variables should be seen as continuous rather than categorical, implying that Miles and Snow's "analyzer" category is redundant because all organizations are likely to prospect and defend to some extent.

Organizational strategies are likely to have an important independent effect on public service performance, although those effects may vary for different strategies and in different organizational and national settings (Meier et al. 2007, 2010). Within the context of English local government, prior research suggests that prospecting may work best, whereas defending can sometimes work and reacting is the "lemon" of strategic management—at least in England (Andrews, Boyne, and Walker 2006). In the context of Texas school districts, it seems that defending is often a more successful strategy, though this depends upon the goal being pursued, with prospecting and reacting appearing to have benefits for "high-end" educational performance outcomes but costs for "lower-end" outcomes (Meier et al. 2007).

The difference between the findings for the English and Texas studies may reflect varying levels of goal ambiguity inherent in the separate organizational contexts, with English local governments providing multiple public services to the entire population, whereas Texas school districts provide only educational services to children. Nevertheless, similar findings to those observed for English local governments have been observed for the separate service departments within Welsh local governments (Andrews et al. 2012), which implies that the political context may actually be a more important influence than the organizational context on the strategy–performance relationship. These contextual variations aside, it is also highly likely that the full benefits of strategy are only realized when the strategy adopted by organizational leaders is aligned with the type of environment inhabited by an organization (Andrews 2008; Miles et al. 1978). Thus, to develop expectations about the likely moderating effects of strategy on the complexity–performance relationship, it is important to consider which strategies may fit best with an environment characterized by high or low environmental complexity.

Contingency theory suggests that an exploratory prospecting strategy would offer the best hope of enabling public organizations to respond effectively to client heterogeneity in ways that might enhance performance (Miles et al. 1978). By committing to a search for new approaches to service delivery, prospecting organizations are potentially more likely to seek out the views of different social groups and to involve them and other relevant stakeholders in the quest for service improvement. At the same time, complex environments may be a more suitable testing ground for organizations pursuing a prospecting strategy. For instance, learning for improvement may be more likely to occur where there are multiple channels through which knowledge about the alternative ways of doing things can be communicated (Greve 2003). Thus, a positive attitude toward innovation on the part of public organizations and a complementary diversity of viewpoints about what works will result in better organizational performance.

By contrast, a defensive focus on enhancing the efficiency of existing operations may impede responsiveness to diverse needs. In "sticking to the knitting," defending organizations may feel that they have little need to understand the diverse necessities of service users; and, being confident that they already know what works, these organizations will lack the incentive to develop the expertise to listen to service users (March 1991). In fact, a defending strategy should, in theory, fit best with an environment that is low in complexity, because such a context does not demand that an organization engage in risky exploratory learning, but rather that it can mine incremental rewards from the exploitation of its established knowledge base (March 1991).

Unlike prospecting and defending, a reacting strategy would probably worsen the complexity–performance relationship. This is because an inconsistent approach to dealing with the demands of a multitude of alternative external stakeholder groups would seem to undermine the possibility of developing a set of services that were tailored to the needs of any one particular group at any given point in time. Moreover, rather than anticipating the demands of citizens in advance, reacting organizations may well be more prone to doing too little too late, and only respond to changing needs when confronted with problems that have become so serious they can no longer be ignored.

In sum, it seems unlikely that a defending strategy would facilitate the kind of cross-organizational learning necessary to generate better outcomes where complexity is high. However, a prospecting strategy, when properly employed, appears likely to galvanize staff toward meeting multiple demands, and so will have a moderating effect on the negative complexity–performance relationship that is simply not observed for a defending strategy. The pervasive absence of a coherent approach to service delivery, in turn, may even result in a further performance penalty in the face of environmental complexity. That is, reacting organizations are simply doomed to fail in ever meeting any of the diverse needs to which they are inconsistently drawn to attempt to address, and so they may create additional problems that they are unable to devote time and energy to resolving.

## RESEARCH CONTEXT, DATA, AND MEASURES

To facilitate comparison of the analysis undertaken here with those in chapters 1 and 3 through 7, I now outline how the context in which my hypotheses are tested fits within the comparative public management framework developed in the introduction to this book. The units of analysis for the study presented in this chapter are single- and upper-tier local governments in England for the period 2001–2. These are elected bodies, with a Westminster-style cabinet system of political management, which is usually made up of senior members of the ruling political party. The politicians collectively decide policy on the basis of advice and guidance from professional local government managers, who are led by a chief executive officer. English local governments operate in specific geographical areas and receive approximately two-thirds of their income from the central government. Due to the unitary nature of the British state, "local government can be changed or even abolished at a stroke"; consequently, local authorities have fairly limited autonomy, for they "can only act within the bounds set by Parliament" (John and Copus 2011, 29–30). As a result, English local governments have become a kind of local service delivery agent for the central government (John 2014). Upper- and single-tier local governments, in particular, are multipurpose public organizations responsible for the delivery of a wide range of services, including education, social care, land use planning, waste management, public housing, leisure and culture, and welfare benefits.

During the study period, there were 148 of these organizations in England—32 London boroughs; 36 metropolitan boroughs; and 46 unitary authorities primarily found in urban areas that deliver all the services listed above; as well as 34 county councils in rural areas administering all but housing and welfare services. Needless to say, English local governments confront a diverse array of operating environments. At the time of the study, the demographic composition of the United Kingdom was undergoing considerable change, largely due to population growth and immigration, which contributed to a high level of environmental complexity and turbulence in local areas. Although some governments serve highly disadvantaged populations, this factor is taken into account in the grant allocation formula for English local governments. At the time of the study, public-sector expenditures were rising under Tony Blair's Labour Party national government. On the whole, then, these organizations were operating in a comparatively munificent resource environment. Likewise, despite considerable local variations in social capital, comparatively speaking the United Kingdom scores relatively well on indicators of social and political participation (Adam 2008). Thus, though the challenging political context may render an analysis of the moderating effects

**Table 2.1** The Public Management Context: English Local Government

| | | |
|---|---|---|
| *Political Context—Concentration of Power* | | |
| Separation of powers | **Unitary** | Shared |
| Federalism | **One level of government** | Multiple levels |
| Process | Corporatist | **Adversarial** |
| Performance appraisal | **Established** | No formal system |
| *Environmental Context* | | |
| Complexity | **Complex** | Simple |
| Turbulence | **Turbulent** | Placid |
| Munificence | **Rich** | Poor |
| Social capital | **Present** | Absent |
| *Internal Context* | | |
| Goals | Clear and consistent | **Multiple and conflicting** |
| Centralization | **Centralized, hierarchical** | Decentralized |
| Professionalization | **Professional** | Not professional |

of strategy on the complexity–performance relationship a tough test of the idea that "management matters," the considerable resources at the disposal of English local governments highlight that there may be considerable room for strategic maneuvering. The context in which these organizations operate is summarized in table 2.1.

## The Dependent Variable

English local governments are typically required to meet multiple and potentially conflicting organizational goals. Moreover, their achievements are judged by a diverse array of constituencies, such as taxpayers, staff, and politicians. The criteria, weighting, and interpretation of performance indicators are thus all subject to ongoing debate and contestation among key stakeholders (Boyne 2003). The analysis presented here focuses on the views of the primary external stakeholder on the service performance of English local governments: the UK central government.

At the time of the study, central government performance classifications were important (though contestable) means for assessing the achievements of English local governments. The central government provides the majority of their funding and monitors administrative accountability on behalf of citizens. During the study period, local government functions classified as "poor" could be externalized, new management imposed, or stricter regulation introduced, while those regarded as "excellent" could benefit from "lighter-touch" inspections and freedom from some central controls (Downe and Martin 2007). From this perspective, central–local relations in England during the study period were characterized by a strong emphasis on the development of appropriate managerial strategies, structures, and processes. The major external assessment of English local government performance carried out by central government inspectors was the Comprehensive Performance Assessment conducted by the Audit Commission (2002). This classified the service performance of local governments by making judgments about their achievements in six major service areas—education, social care, environment, housing, libraries, and leisure and benefits—together with their broader "management of resources."

In 2002 all the main strategic services provided by English local governments were given a score ranging from 1 (lowest) to 4 (highest), based mainly on achievements on statutory performance indicators that were independently audited and checked for accuracy, but also including inspections of service plans and standards. These service scores were weighted by the Audit Commission to reflect the relative importance and budget of the service area (children and young people and adult social care = 4; environment and housing = 2; libraries and leisure, and benefits and management of resources = 1). Finally, these weighted scores were summed to provide an overall service performance judgment, ranging from 15 (12 for county councils that do not provide housing or benefits services) to 60 (48 for county councils). Because these scores are not directly comparable across all types of authorities, each government's score is taken as a percentage of the maximum possible score. By providing an overall judgment on the achievements of local governments, the *core service performance* score therefore represents a good proxy for their ability to meet the multiple goals that they are required to accomplish.

## Environmental Complexity

The complexity that English local governments confront within their task environment may take a number of forms, but is principally a function of the divergent needs of the social groups to which they are obliged to provide key services. Several aspects of social heterogeneity may be relevant for local public services, but perhaps the most salient within the context of English local government is the degree of ethnic diversity within the areas that they serve. During the past decade, there have been heated debates about a so-called crisis of social cohesion in the United Kingdom, mostly prompted by the emergence of multiple ethnic identities in the wake of postcolonial immigration (Kearns and Forrest 2000). To measure ethnic diversity, the proportions of the sixteen ethnic subgroups identified in the 2001 decennial UK national census (e.g., black African and Chinese) for each local government area were squared, summed, and subtracted from 10,000. The resulting measure gives a proxy for "fractionalization" within an area, with a high score on the index reflecting a high level of diversity (see Trawick and Howsen 2006) and a correspondingly high level of environmental complexity.

## Organizational Strategies

Data on organizational strategies were derived from a survey of managers in English local governments undertaken in 2001. Survey responses were collected from senior and middle managers, as research indicates attitudes differ between these hierarchical levels (Payne and Mansfield 1973). The data were aggregated by creating mean scores for senior managers and middle managers in each government, adding these two scores together, and then dividing them by 2 to provide an organizational-level mean. In each participating organization, questionnaires were sent to at least three senior and four middle managers. In 2001 the total sample consisted of 120 organizations, with a 56 percent ($n$ = 1,259) informant response rate. *T*-tests on the independent and control variables for included or omitted governments revealed no statistically significant differences between the sample and the population, indicating that the sample is a representative one. Time-trend tests for nonresponse bias (Armstrong and Overton 1977) revealed no significant differences in the views of early and late respondents.

The survey asked informants to comment on the extent to which a range of key management practices were present in their organization, on a 7-point Likert Scale ranging from 1 (strongly disagree) to 7 (strongly agree). A *prospecting* strategy was operationalized through a measure of innovation because this is central to Miles and Snow's definition, which includes risk taking and proactive responses to changes in the external environment ("The authority/service is at the forefront of innovative approaches"). This implies innovations both in organizational form (e.g., partnerships with private or nonprofit organizations) and in policies or other practices (including specially designed services for minority ethnic groups).

To explore the extent to which local governments displayed *defending* characteristics, focusing upon tried-and-tested strategies in an existing market, informants were asked whether their approach to service delivery focused on their "core business" ("Focusing on key business areas is a major part of our approach to service delivery"). This captures the idea that although a defending strategy may involve smaller incremental innovations to existing processes, it does not entail the kind of radically innovative activity in new areas that typifies prospecting. *Reacting* organizations are expected to await instructions on how to respond to environmental change. We therefore asked our informants about the extent to which auditors and inspectors affected their approaches to service improvement ("Pressures from auditors and inspectors were important in driving performance improvement in our service"). All these measures of strategy are based on prior work (Miller 1986; Snow and Hrebiniak 1980).

Although, in theory, local governments can adopt multiple strategies simultaneously, in practice it is unlikely that this will occur to a very substantial degree, especially at the organizational level, where senior management is likely to share a common core strategic outlook. And, in fact, this is largely borne out for the data on organizational strategies in English local government. There is no correlation between prospecting and defending, and there is a negative correlation (–.21) between prospecting and reacting. That said, there is a small positive correlation (.19) between defending and reacting, pointing toward a potential complementarity between these two broad strategic stances, at least for English local governments.

## Control Variables

The potential effects of socioeconomic disadvantage among the local population on the performance of local governments are controlled by including the average ward score on the Indices of Multiple Deprivation from 2000. This is the population-weighted measure used by the UK central government to gauge levels of *deprivation* among the population. To compensate for high levels of deprivation, public organizations may be required to invest more heavily in core services to bring them up to an acceptable standard, and also to invest in specialist services to meet distinctive demands and thereby struggle to perform up to the same level as organizations serving less-deprived client populations.

Local governments serving larger populations may be able to garner scale economies by spreading fixed costs (i.e., the senior management team or information technology) across a wider range and higher quantity of service outputs (Stigler 1958). This, in turn, may free up resources that can be reinvested in service improvement. Population *size* was measured using figures from the 2001 national census. Public organizations in densely populated areas can reap scope economies by offering multiple services from the same site (Grosskopf and Yaisawamg 1990). Population figures were therefore divided by the area served by each local government to measure *density*. Finally, three dichotomous variables—coded 1 for London boroughs, metropolitan boroughs, and county councils each; and otherwise coded 0—were added to the model (with

**Table 2.2** Descriptive Statistics for 120 English Local Governments

| *Variable* | *Mean* | *Minimum* | *Maximum* | *Standard Deviation* |
|---|---|---|---|---|
| Core service performance | 65.70 | 36.67 | 88.33 | 9.32 |
| Ethnic diversity | 2,447.28 | 372.71 | 8,452.82 | 2,300.84 |
| Prospecting | 4.92 | 3.00 | 6.70 | .78 |
| Defending | 4.47 | 1.75 | 7.00 | .96 |
| Reacting | 4.93 | 2.67 | 6.50 | .77 |
| Deprivation | 27.29 | 4.89 | 58.22 | 11.84 |
| Population | 322,895.7 | 97,838 | 1,329,718 | 235,836.84 |
| Population density | 2,438.58 | 61.68 | 14,916.67 | 2,840.94 |

unitary authorities taken as the reference category). These dummy variables capture the potential effect of the different types of local governments on the relationships being studied, especially the functional and contextual differences between these groups. Descriptive statistics for all the variables used in the statistical modeling are shown in table 2.2.

## STATISTICAL RESULTS

Results for statistical estimates of variations in local government performance are shown in table 2.3. Four ordinary-least-squares regression models are presented. To illustrate the independent effects of environmental complexity and organizational strategy on performance, the first model incorporates all the independent and control variables. To facilitate analysis of the moderating role of organizational strategy on the complexity–performance relationship, Models 2 through 4 then present estimates of performance when variables interacting ethnic diversity with prospecting, defending, and reacting are added to Model 1. These interaction terms are entered separately in the models to reduce the impact of the multicollinearity generated when they are entered simultaneously.

The average variance inflation factor score for all the independent variables used in the model is about 3, indicating that the results are unlikely to be seriously distorted by multicollinearity (Bowerman and O'Connell 1990). Before the statistical models were run, skewness tests were carried out to establish whether each independent variable was distributed normally. High skew test results for population (1.92) and population density (2.09) indicated nonnormal distributions. To correct for positive skew, logged versions of these

**Table 2.3** Environmental Complexity, Organizational Strategy, and Performance

| *Variable* | *Model 1* | *Model 2* | *Model 3* | *Model 4* |
|---|---|---|---|---|
| Ethnic diversity (ED) | –.002* | –.008** | .002 | .003 |
| Prospecting | 3.616** | .615 | 3.535** | 3.806** |
| Defending | –.625 | –.626 | .927 | –.712 |
| Reacting | –2.605* | –2.704* | –2.463† | .185 |
| ED x prospecting | | .001** | | |
| ED x defending | | | –.001† | |
| ED x reacting | | | | –.001* |
| Controls | | | | |
| Deprivation | –.213** | –.240** | –.208** | –.232** |
| Population (log) | –2.678 | –.962 | –2.817 | –1.151 |
| Population density | .188 | –.002 | .300 | .169 |
| London | 5.700 | 6.739† | 6.136 | 5.105 |
| Metropolitan | 5.640* | 5.381† | 5.502† | 4.798† |
| County | 3.677 | 2.533 | 4.323 | 3.294 |
| Constant | 83.317** | 90.926** | 75.903* | 61.480* |
| *F* statistic | 4.08** | 7.08** | 4.87** | 4.76** |
| $R^2$ | .28 | .34 | .30 | .31 |
| N | 120 | 120 | 120 | 120 |

*Note:* Significance levels: †$p \leq 0.10$; *$p \leq 0.05$; **$p \leq 0.01$. Unstandardized coefficients are reported.

variables were entered in the models. Robust estimation of the standard errors corrects for the potential influence of heteroscedasticity.

The models provide a reasonable statistical explanation of variations in the performance of English local governments. In terms of the control variables, deprivation is associated with worse performance, with metropolitan borough councils performing better than other types of local governments. Turning to the main variables of interest, we can see that the first hypothesis is supported. As anticipated, environmental complexity is negatively related to local government performance; the coefficient for ethnic diversity is negative and statistically significant. This finding highlights that local governments serving ethnically diverse populations are likely to confront a variety of challenges in sustaining service standards, ranging from the development of specially designed services for different groups to managing intergroup relations in particularly diverse neighborhoods (Andrews et al. 2013). The results for the independent effects of strategy on performance confirm the findings of Andrews, Boyne, and Walker (2006); the coefficient for prospecting is positive and statistically significant, whereas the coefficient for reacting is negative and statistically significant. Although local government performance appears to be partly determined by the environment in which an organization operates, it does nevertheless seem that certain strategies are more successful than others. To understand whether some strategies are a better fit with a complex environment, it is necessary to include variables interacting organizational strategy and ethnic diversity in the model.

Table 2.3 highlights the situation that the inclusion of interactions between ethnic diversity and strategy makes a statistically significant addition to the explanatory power of the models predicting performance, especially in the case of the interaction between diversity and prospecting. In fact, the interaction between diversity and prospecting is positive and statistically significant, suggesting that prospecting may moderate the negative effect of complexity on performance. By contrast, the interaction of diversity with defending and with reacting stances is both negative and statistically significant. Thus, the estimates presented in table 2.3 suggest that there is support for the arguments about the interactive effects of complexity and strategy developed earlier in the chapter. Even so, to fully test these arguments, it is necessary to calculate the marginal effects on administrative intensity of varying levels of the moderator variable. Graphing the slope and confidence intervals of the marginal effects is the most effective way to present this information. Accordingly, figures 2.1 through 2.3 provide a graphical illustration of the moderating influence of organizational strategy on the relationship between ethnic diversity and performance.

Figure 2.1 highlights that prospecting is likely to have an important moderating effect on the relationship between ethnic diversity and local government performance. In particular, as the extent of prospecting rises from the minimum level of 3.0, the negative complexity–performance relationship becomes progressively weaker until it disappears at just over the mean level of prospecting (5.1). Just fewer than half (53) of the local governments were found to prospect to this extent or more, illustrating the fact that large numbers of these organizations are not realizing the benefits of an outward strategic outlook when managing a complex environment. Even so, prospecting local governments are not able to turn the benefits of the strategy into even better performance when confronting high levels of ethnic diversity—the lower confidence interval touches the zero line beyond the maximum point (7) of the Likert Scale.

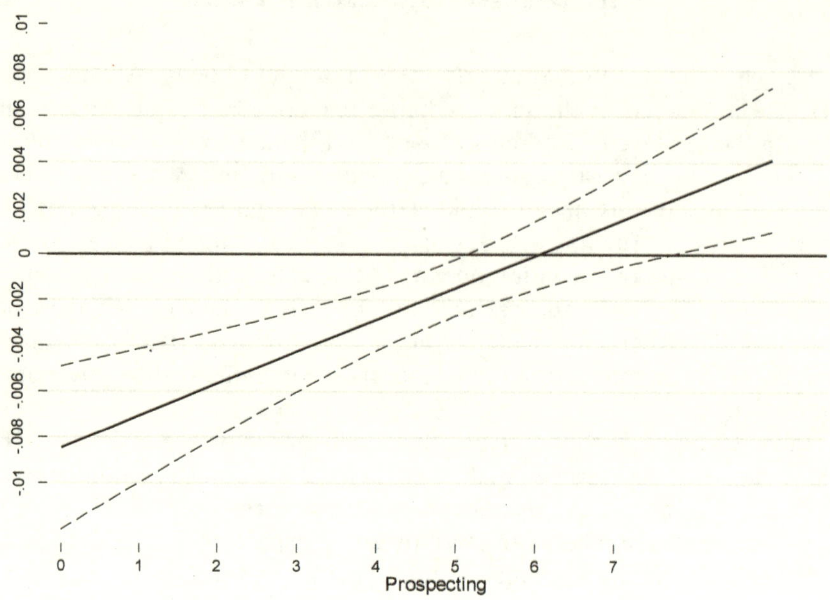


**Figure 2.1** The Marginal Impact of Prospecting on the Environmental Complexity–Performance Relationship

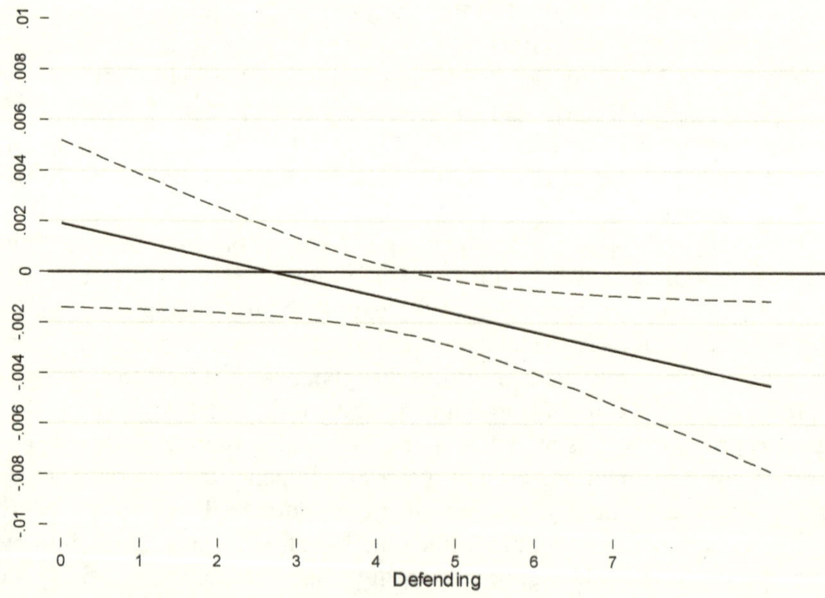


**Figure 2.2** The Marginal Impact of Defending on the Environmental Complexity–Performance Relationship

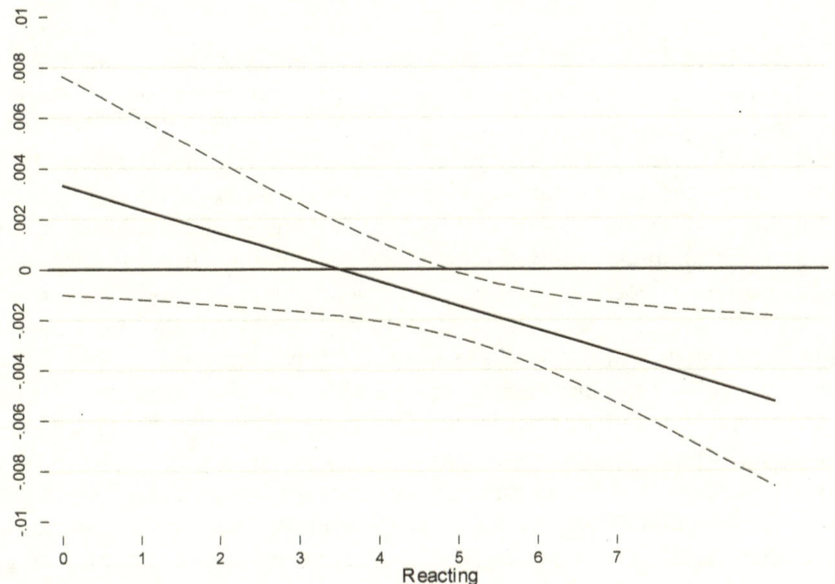


**Figure 2.3** The Marginal Impact of Reacting on the Environmental Complexity–Performance Relationship

By contrast, the interaction graph plotting the moderating effect of defending on the complexity–performance relationship indicates that when serving an ethnically diverse population defending at just below the mean level (4.5) and above is likely to result in even further performance decline. About half (59) the local governments defend to this extent, which suggests that a large proportion of organizations may be adopting an ill-suited strategy. A broadly similar set of marginal effects is found for the complexity–reacting interaction, with the problems posed by reacting in a complex environment appearing at just above the mean level (5.0). Nearly half the local governments react to this degree, indicating again that many organizations are adopting a poor strategic approach to providing services given the context that they confront.

In sum, the results presented in figures 2.1 through 2.3 provide strong support for the arguments about the interactive effects of strategy and environmental complexity developed above. A prospecting strategy moderates the negative relationship between ethnic diversity and performance, while a reacting strategy makes this relationship even worse. Somewhat surprisingly, a defending strategy also results in worse performance when local governments are operating in ethnically diverse areas.

## IMPLICATIONS

In this chapter, I have explored how organizational strategies matter for the management of environmental complexity in a set of public organizations—local governments in England—that are operating within a distinctive British public management context. Drawing on a contingency theory perspective, I hypothesized that an outward-looking prospecting strategy would offer these organizations a means for overcoming the challenges associated with providing services to an ethnically diverse client population. The theoretical arguments on the independent effect of complexity and the moderating effects of different strategies were largely confirmed through a statistical analysis of the performance of the local governments. Environmental complexity was negatively related to performance, but the adoption of a prospecting strategy moderated this negative effect. A reacting strategy was associated with even worse performance where complexity was high, as was a defending strategy. These findings from England confirm the arguments about the salience of environmental complexity found in the comparative public management framework developed in the introduction and have important theoretical and practical implications.

By theorizing and empirically exploring the separate and combined effects of environmental complexity and organizational strategy on performance, I have extended the existing literature on the influence of the environmental context on public services and how it can be best managed. Previous studies have largely been confined to the management of low munificence and high dynamism. Here, I assess the importance of organizational strategy as a tool for managing environmental complexity—a contextual factor at the heart of the comparative public management framework developed in the introduction, and one that has become increasingly salient in the English context. In confirming arguments derived from contingency theory, the findings have also confirmed the value of this perspective for managing and organizing public services—at least in terms of the management of environmental complexity. Prior research reveals mixed evidence on the potential for strategy–environment fit to result in better outcomes (Meier et al. 2010), but this study indicates that the arguments of contingency theorists may still have something to offer researchers interested in conceptualizing the interrelationships between strategy, environmental context, and performance.

Practically speaking, the findings suggest that organizations seeking to provide high-quality services to an ethnically diverse population should devote more time and resources to exploring new ways of doing things, and of anticipating and shaping the needs of client groups. For local governments, such activity could occur at multiple levels, ranging from ad hoc, street-level innovations implemented by frontline workers right through to the participation of senior managers in communities of practice through which new ideas and knowledge about service provision can be developed and disseminated. Contingency theorists also point toward the importance of environmental scanning when confronting a complex external context (Daft, Sormunen, and Parks 1988). The use of a wider range of techniques for better understanding changes in client needs and demands thus seems sure to play an important role in enabling public organizations to do a better job of responding to ethnic diversity.

Despite the strengths of the analysis I present, the findings nonetheless raise a range of further questions that are worthy of systematic analysis, drawing upon the comparative public management framework developed in the introduction. In particular, it is important to note that the research design could produce different results in different organizational and temporal settings, and across different national contexts. The findings presented here might simply reflect a particular moment in time within the English local government system—a system that is known to have a very distinctive political and environmental context (John and Copus 2011). In particular, English local governments are considerably larger than those in nearly all other developed countries, and so these organizations may confront a level of ethnic heterogeneity that is much greater than those local governments in other countries that serve much smaller and less diffuse populations. At the same time, one might argue that the measure of complexity actually captures turbulence within the environment, given the rapid expansion of ethnic diversity in the United Kingdom during the 2000s. In this respect, some of the arguments developed in the chapter and the findings may apply equally as well, if not better, in conditions of environmental dynamism than in a complex environment, which may be addressed through better tailoring of existing practices than the development of new ones. In addition to operating within a distinctive environmental context, the organizations analyzed in this chapter were subject to a far-reaching performance appraisal system. During the study period, the efforts of English local governments to develop innovative approaches to service delivery were supported (and resourced) by the central government, and were evaluated by regulatory bodies, making the study's findings potentially contingent on the intricacies of UK central–local relations in the 2000s.

It is a moot point whether the statistical relationships identified here would hold in smaller units of local government, in contexts where demographic change is less profound, and where performance management is weaker. Moreover, the analysis is undertaken in a time of fiscal plenty within the English public sector. Local governments in England are currently experiencing draconian budget cuts, which may well affect their ability to implement new and innovative initiatives to meet the needs of diverse client groups. In this respect, the development of new data sets on strategic management and performance that facilitated systematic cross-country comparisons of complexity, strategy, and performance would make a valuable contribution to our understanding of how the impact of environmental context might vary through time and space. In addition, a detailed qualitative investigation of the activities prospecting organizations actually undertake in order to respond effectively to diversity in the client population could furnish public managers and policymakers with a valuable store of knowledge about what works in managing a complex external environment. Such research could also evaluate the extent to which policy innovations might be particular to certain types of political or internal contexts.

To conclude, this study has confirmed that public management context matters for the performance of public organizations, but it has also affirmed that these organizations may be able to make positive choices that enable them to better manage the environmental context in which they find themselves. Future comparative research utilizing a longitudinal design could draw upon the approach adopted here to tease out whether there are positive reinforcement effects from successful environmental adaptation and how successful responses to complexity might diffuse across organizational populations, especially among those confronting different political and internal contexts.

# 3

# Do Public/Private Differences Matter?

## *Managerial Characteristics and Organizational Performance across Sectors of US Higher Education*

CLAIRE STIEG AND AMANDA RUTHERFORD

The identification of factors that distinguish public from private organizations has been both a broad theme and a controversy in public administration literature. Many policymakers, answering the calls for increased public accountability and performance-based metrics, argue that the two sectors are distinct, with varying goals and levels of effectiveness (Goodsell 2003). However, a number of scholars are wary of overemphasizing this structural divide (Rainey and Bozeman 2000; Pandey 2010; Andrews, Boyne, and Walker 2011). The difficulty of cleanly classifying organizations as public or private only emphasizes the need to theoretically consider and empirically measure the context of organizations (Rainey 2009). Regardless of these categorical overlaps, it is generally presumed that the public/private context influences how managers set goals, make decisions, and implement policies. The degree to which this public/private context affects management–performance linkages, however, has not been widely studied. Claims that the public sector lacks the efficiency and effectiveness of the private sector remain salient, despite convincing empirical research that provides substantial support for contradicting this popular notion (Haque 2001; Brewer and Brewer 2011; Meier and O'Toole 2011).

The purpose of this study is to step away from defining the structural differences of public and private organizations and to determine whether or not the context of these sectors leads to substantive effects on management–performance linkages (Pollitt and Bouckaert 2000; Hvidman and Andersen 2014). Even though the public management literature has often suggested that management matters for performance in a variety of contexts, we know very little about how the management–performance relationship is shaped by public or private organizations (see the introduction to this book). As defined here, "context" encompasses the situational opportunities and constraints that affect organizational behavior (Johns 2006). Examining the structural context of an organization and its effect on a manager's ability to influence outcomes allows us to further our understanding of whether differentiating between this specific classification is important for establishing a fully specified model of how and when management matters (Bozeman and Loveless 1987; Meier and O'Toole 2011).

This study uses cross-sectional time series data for four-year US institutions of higher education to determine the managerial–performance relationship across public and private organizations. This chapter first outlines prior research that has attempted to accurately define the public/private divide and situates this conversation in the context framework outlined in the introduction. This context is then linked to a review of research on the management–performance relationship and how this relationship may vary in public as compared with private organizations. After discussing public/private differences in the context of four-year higher education in the United States, analyses examine whether managerial characteristics can be linked to multiple performance indicators. Although various aspects of performance—including measures of equity, responsiveness, and quality—could be examined here, this study focuses on higher education student outputs, student access, and institutional resources. The findings suggest that a manager's socialization (measured as his or her propensity to value research) has a consistently positive effect on performance across both public and private organizations. Additionally, prior job experience has profoundly different effects on performance in the two settings.

## AN OVERVIEW OF THE PUBLIC/PRIVATE DIVIDE

Previous analyses of the distinctions between public and private organizations have been extensive, but this line of research often risks overgeneralizing the divide between the two contextual classifications (for comprehensive reviews, see Rainey, Backoff, and Levine 1976; and Perry and Rainey 1988). Observed variance between the two sectors in the level of operating efficiency and the availability of financial incentives has led to a consensus on the general ways in which public and private institutions differ (Perry and Rainey 1988). The private sector—with an emphasis on competition, customer satisfaction, and (greater) freedom from political persuasions—has long been compared to a seemingly more cautious, less innovative, and more restricted public sector. Environmental factors such as market exposure, legal constraints, and partial ownership by taxpayers are assumed to dampen cost reduction incentives and overall performance in public agencies (Rainey, Backoff, and Levine 1976; DeCanio 2013). However, previous research has noted that efforts to privatize and reinvent government and to introduce performance-based structures are largely a function of political rhetoric rather than concrete initiatives (Hodge 2000). It is challenging to demarcate a rigid definition that accounts for the overlap in structures, environments, and goals between the two sectors. As such, some scholars have proposed that there is some degree of "publicness," characterized by varying levels of political authority, in all organizations (Bozeman 1987).

Three features are commonly used to study the degree of publicness in organizations: government ownership, sources of funding, and regulating restrictions. Earlier research most commonly used ownership to classify organizations as public or private. Members of the general public collectively own public agencies, whereas entrepreneurs or shareholders own private firms (Boyne 2002). Government ownership diffuses responsibility and risk, and it is often associated with some type of public value that benefits the larger community (Antonsen and Jørgensen 1997). On one hand, there may be less of a personal incentive to improve the performance of a collective agency, leading to popular claims of inefficiency and increased red tape. On the other hand, the public interests that accompany public ownership can be an influential factor in employee motivation and satisfaction (Buchanan 1975). In contrast, private organizations value individuals' potential productive value with less regard for achieving some type of larger public good (Perry and Rainey 1988). This notion has contributed to the idea that private-sector firms operate more efficiently and achieve clearly defined goals, as compared with public agencies. Ownership, however, may not fully capture the structure of an organization, given that lines of ownership are often blurred due to contracting out and privatization (Besley and Ghatak 2001).

A second component used to delineate organizations is funding sources. Funding may often come in the form of taxpayer dollars or consumer fees. Public organizations are conventionally more dependent on resources derived from the political process and from taxpayers who have a diverse set of expectations. It is not uncommon, however, for organizations in the private sector to receive a substantial amount of public funds (Wamsley and Zald 1973). For example, private defense contractors and several research firms receive a sizable portion of their revenue from federal contracts. This can blur the lines between organizations that are traditionally thought of as public agencies and those that are considered private firms.

Funding that comes from government sources can generally be tied to increased regulation and oversight, but it can also provide incentives for managers to pursue equity and access—in other words, goals and outcomes that contribute to the public good. These nonmonetary goals can affect latent managerial values and, subsequently, decision making within public organizations (Dahl and Lindbolm 1953). Alternatively, under the assumption that private sources of funding come from a competitive market, there can be more opportunity to foster a reliable feedback system, in which shareholders and board members are able to oversee a firm's executives (Box 1999). The perceived efficiency and accountability of private-sector firms has generated many calls for the marketization of public agencies (Rainey and Bozeman 2000), though these efforts have often fallen short of expectations.

The third important indicator of publicness is the amount of regulation to which an organization is subject through state or federal oversight mechanisms. As mentioned above, government ownership and funding can often be associated with heavier regulations and restrictions. The presence of these regulations may burden an organization and restrict its ability to function efficiently (Meier and O'Toole 2011). With less regulation, the shareholders of organizations have more autonomy as to how they choose to define and accomplish their goals. More heavily regulated industries are subject to directives and additional pressure from political authorities and the general public. Consequently, the latter may have more varied and complex expectations. With different market influences and less regulation, organizations are more sensitive to economic risk, but they have more flexibility to be entrepreneurial and pursue change (Nutt 2006). This type of autonomy is not only expected to produce innovation, but is also theoretically linked to increases in organizational performance (Wagner 1983).

Beyond these three measures of publicness, research on goal ambiguity has often been used to differentiate public agencies from their private-sector counterparts. Because public organizations are linked to multiple stakeholder groups (state and federal politicians and numerous clientele groups), they must determine some process whereby they can prioritize a long list of organizational goals (Johnson and Lewin 1984; Pandey and Wright 2006). The presence of multiple, competing goals can subsequently lead to numerous kinds of ambiguity in organizations (Chun and Rainey 2005). These dimensions of ambiguity address whether an organization has defined its purpose, communicated its guidelines and specifications for goal completion, developed goal evaluation processes, and established priorities among multiple goals. Despite much research arguing that public agencies are held accountable for a larger number of goals, some surveys have shown that public managers do not perceive higher levels of goal ambiguity than their private counterparts (Rainey, Pandey, and Bozeman 1995). Rather, organizational constraints that are present in the public sector, including lower levels of technology and higher levels of red tape, are perceived to have a greater effect on managers than goal ambiguity.

Although efforts to distinguish public and private organizations continue to produce a wealth of research, many scholars caution against emphasizing stereotypes that may not be generalizable. What qualifies an organization as public is ambiguous, giving rise to measurement and methodological issues, such that causal inferences made about public organizations are often subject to debate (Bozeman 1987). Further, the spread of privatization, contracting out, and public–private collaborative systems continues to challenge the notion that public and private organizations are fundamentally different. However, though the degree of publicness in an organization is assumed to influence managerial discretion, it is likely to still be a factor in organizations that have little or no degree of publicness.

## ASSESSING PUBLIC AND PRIVATE ORGANIZATIONS WITHIN THE CONTEXT FRAMEWORK

The proposed framework in the introduction to this book provides a detailed approach to comparing organizations. However, this comparison may work better within the same sector as opposed to across sectors. This is due to the fact that the three primary ways in which public and private organizations are differentiated—ownership, funding source, and regulation—are not explicitly included in the framework. Ownership may be considered within discussions of the separation of powers and federalism, but sources of funding and regulation, which affect limitations on autonomy and decision making, are important contextual characteristics that may need to be added to the framework.

Figure 3.1 provides an overview of how US public and private organizations might be compared in the current framework. Here, we have placed public and private organizations on a continuum for each factor. Our assessments are those of average organizations, such that we admittedly are not scientifically precise in our placements; nor do we account for variance within each sector or variance over time. With regard to the separation of powers, the three branches of government influence both public and private organizations. Private organizations are placed closer to the unitary end of the scale, given that they are controlled perhaps to a lesser degree than their public counterparts by

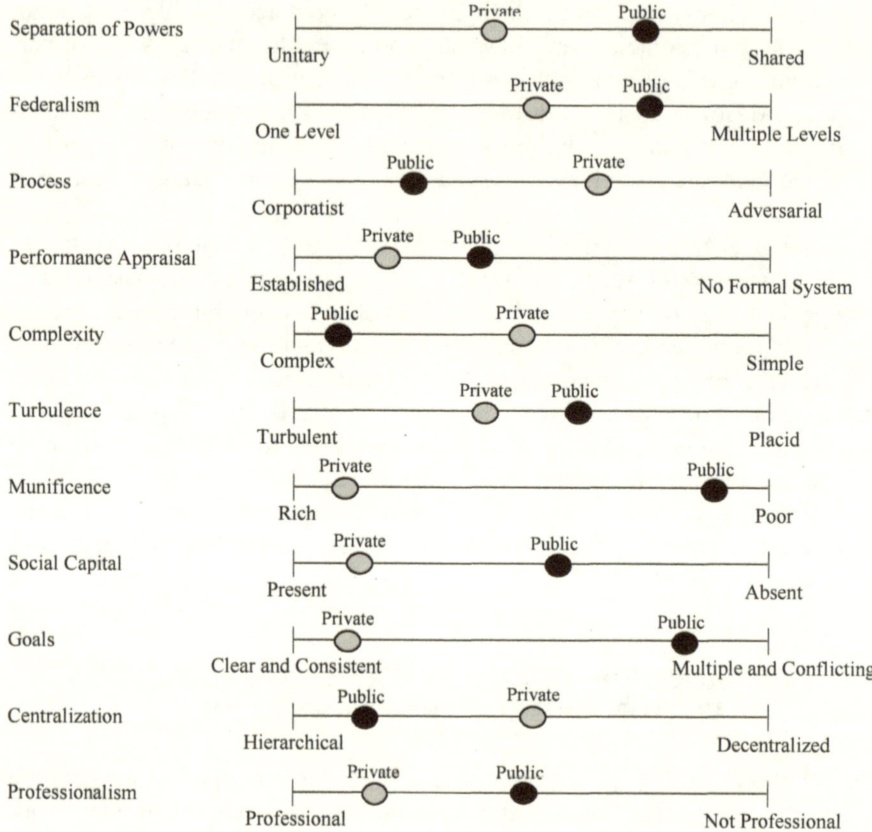


**Figure 3.1** Comparison of Public versus Private Organizations—Common Perceptions

these branches. The same may be true for federalism; though both public and private organizations answer to federal, state, and local regulations, private organizations are likely to face fewer restraints.

Next, process is often viewed as more corporatist within the public sector, given that public organizations must go through formal processes of creating new rules and regulations while considering a larger number of stakeholders. Private-sector organizations, conversely, may have more leverage to consider only select interests, given the market in which they are situated and the demand for their goods and services. Although the discussion of accountability in public organizations has been present since before the field of public administration was fully established, formal performance appraisal systems are relatively new (and will continue to become more prevalent over time, if current trends hold). However, private organizations are often perceived as having better performance appraisal systems in place, especially given the market functions whereby these organizations must compete to survive.

The environmental contexts of public and private organizations can also be differentiated with some degree of certainty. Public organizations are generally understood to be much more complex than private organizations. Their higher level of complexity is related to the nature of the problems these organizations are tasked with addressing, as well as the number of goals they are designed to achieve. Public organizations are, indeed, large systems of bureaucracy. Next, public organizations have been categorized as less turbulent than private firms, largely due to their autoregressive nature. In other words, public organizations are more sluggish and are less likely to change from one year to the next (though there are certainly exceptions to this generalization). In terms of munificence, public organizations are believed to reside in low-munificence environments that constrain managerial abilities to tap environmental resources. As hypothesized in the introduction, public organizations may be more inclined to buffer core competencies. Private organizations, conversely, have higher levels of munificence, whereby they can seek to be innovative. Further, if the environment of private firms lacks munificence, these firms may be unlikely to survive.

Third, the internal contexts of these two types of organizations can be considered. The first internal variable considered in the introduction, goals, is one of the largest points of variation between the two sectors. As mentioned above, public organizations are tasked with goals that are quite ambiguous and offer no clear direction. More often than not, these goals are conflicting, such that trade-offs create winners and losers. In terms of centralization, public organizations are seen as more hierarchical and rigid as compared with private firms. Although private firms generally maintain hierarchical structures, many have developed flatter organizations. Finally, professionalism can vary to a great degree, both within and across these sectors. However, popular notions might suggest that private firms have more professional employee groups, even though this may not always be empirically true.

Despite concerns about whether public and private organizations can be separated into distinct categories for each component of the proposed context framework, scholars have largely failed to determine if these perceived and real differences have any type of intervening effect on management–performance relationships. This study focuses on the ownership of an organization, due to the strong role it can play in formulating values and performance outcomes. In order to connect this measure of publicness to management, the next section considers this question: Do the characteristics of managers in public organizations influence performance differently than do those of managers in private organizations? In other words, do public/private structural differences moderate the effect of management on performance?

## THE MANAGEMENT–PERFORMANCE LINK

Numerous studies have indicated that management matters for an organization's performance (O'Toole and Meier 1999; Donahue et al. 2004; Boyne et al. 2006; Brewer 2005; Rainey 2009). Research suggests that a manager's leadership (Fernandez 2005), level of quality (Beam 2001; Johansen 2012), and ability to successfully network and collaborate (Esteve et al. 2013; Davis, Livermore, and Lim 2011) are generally linked to higher levels of performance. These studies, however, have often overlooked the individual characteristics of managers. In order to understand the processes that explain a manager's decision making, it is necessary to take into consideration the underlying causal mechanisms that shape managerial values. We argue that the personal skills and characteristics of managers (e.g., age, tenure, education, training, and gender) may provide some rationally bounded indication of an individual's underlying goals and values, which shape strategic decisions and, subsequently, performance outcomes in the organization.

Much research on the ability of managers to affect organizational performance implicitly relies on upper echelons theory (Hambrick and Mason 1984). This theory emphasizes the importance of top-level management in defining organizational outcomes and is based on two key assumptions: that agency executives make decisions based on their personal interpretations of the situation; and that these individual judgments are influenced by managerial experiences, values, and personalities. Managerial characteristics can act as proxies for values, priorities, and goals; by understanding these values and biases, we are better able to evaluate an organization's performance and direction (Hambrick 2007). Taking this approach to organizational performance is in contrast to making the assumption that organizations themselves are inertial and can only be influenced by changing pressures in the external environment (Hannan and Freeman 1977). If this assumption were true, management decisions would have little or no effect in organizations across multiple settings.

By focusing on tangible managerial characteristics, this study measures not only the effect of management on performance but also how an organization's structural context interacts with a manager's background. Characteristics considered here include managerial turnover, internal and external hires, length of tenure, and socialization. First, managerial turnover occurs when a new executive is hired to lead an agency. Much of the discussion on managerial turnover has been applied in the context of the private sector (see the summaries given by Brickley 2003 and Furtado and Karan 1990). Boards of directors and stockholders use reorganization and replacement as an opportunity to advance a corporation (Daily 1995). Studies focused on public organizations generally assume that turnover is an indication of ineffective leadership, and that a new manager may be able to transform the organization in order to improve outcomes (Hill 2005; Wright and Pandey 2009; Andrews, Boyne, and Walker 2011). In other words, a new manager can bring with him or her a new perspective that can revitalize performance through innovation and change.

However, new managers can also lead to a decline in performance. As the level of a position rises in an organization, the task complexity increases. Fewer managers at the highest levels have the skill set needed to administer change or maintain performance throughout an organization. Because the pool of potential hires with the necessary knowledge is small (Meier and Hicklin 2008), this greatly increases the cost of replacing top-level managers for organizations. If new top-level managers are unable to quickly adjust to their organization's environmental, political, and social contexts, they will be unlikely to improve its performance. In fact, as a new manager adapts to his or her new position, uncertainty may even cause a dip in organizational performance.

Within these two competing expectations related to a new manager's effect on performance, there is no theoretical reason to expect that the outcomes of this turnover should be significantly different in public and private organizations. Instead, the competing theories are applicable to both settings, given the need for top-level managers to sink or swim:

> H1. Managerial turnover and subsequent innovation will lead to positive effects on performance in both public and private organizations.
>
> H2. Managerial turnover and subsequent instability will lead to negative effects on performance in both public and private organizations.

Next, there has been some debate on whether internal hires are linked to higher or lower levels of organizational performance. An inside hire is more likely to understand the context in which the organization operates. Consequently, internal hires may require less adjustment time and be able to immediately focus on improving the organization. Outside hires may or may not be a good fit for the organization, depending on their prior experience and the structure of their previous organization (Petrovsky, James, and Boyne 2015). Alternatively, those internal hires who have been with an organization for an extended period may be less innovative and unwilling to make changes compared with external hires, who could negatively affect performance. If internal hires are more likely to encourage organizational inertia, the organization will not adapt appropriately to environmental changes.

Much like managerial turnover, there is no clear reason to believe that internal hires affect performance differently than external hires in public verses private organizations. Rather, hypotheses 3 and 4 reflect the possibility of competing effects of internal hires in both types of organizations. Given that the context framework does not directly deal with dynamic change but compares a snapshot of one or more organizations at one point in time, the internal context considered also does not provide clear direction:

> H3. Internal management hires positively affect organizational performance in both public and private organizations, due to there being little need for adjustment.
>
> H4. Internal management hires negatively affect performance in both public and private organizations, due to there being little desire to seek innovation and change.

The previous literature also found experience (tenure) to have important implications for managerial decision making and organizational performance. This research showed that longer tenure in top-level management increases managerial discretion, leading to improved outcomes (Finkelstein and Hambrick 1990). A longer tenure gives a manager more time to get adjusted, stabilize the organization, and establish strategic networks (Juenke 2005). Additionally, tenured managers are more likely to successfully resist external pressures and threats to the organization (Meyer 1975). Although the organization's momentum can overwhelm new managers, those with longer tenure are more capable of enacting change within it (Hill 2005).[1] Over time, a longer-serving manager is able to better influence the organization due to established relationships and a deeper understanding of the organization (Miller 1991). This effect, again, should not differ between public and private organizations. Within the context framework, managers with more experience may lessen the organization's turbulence and strengthen its munificence and social capital, which subsequently may improve its performance. But we do not have reason to expect that the size of this effect is different for public and private organizations (in other words, they may have different starting points, but the size of the change would be the same):

> H5. Higher levels of managerial experience will be associated with higher levels of organizational performance in public and private organizations.

Finally, the socialization of a manager may affect his or her cost/benefit assessments, which can lead to different approaches in defining organizational strategies (and thus, in organizational performance). Socialization is defined here as the process by which an organization's context, culture, and norms—including many of the contextual categories outlined in the context framework—shape a manager's individual values and expectations. In other words, a manager's experience within a certain organizational environment is likely to guide his or her evaluation of performance (Berlew and Hall 1966; Louis 1980). Socialization can therefore be used to test the transferability of skills along several dimensions. When a manager moves to a different organization, he or she may make a transition from one industry to another (e.g., health to education, or welfare to defense). Ultimately, the professional norms associated with a certain industry can lead to different approaches in policy implementation (Teodoro 2014):

> H6. A top-level manager who has a greater level of socialization within an industry will have a more positive effect on performance than nonindustry hires in both public and private organizations.

It is also possible for a manager to not move across industries but instead move upward within the same industry. A manager who is promoted to a more senior position experiences a shift in the complexity and magnitude of his or her duties, because top-level managers are tasked with overseeing a larger share of ambiguous and complex goals than mid-level or frontline managers (Van Maanen 1978). However, if the president of one organization becomes the president of another organization, the management skills used in the previous position should allow the manager to more quickly adapt to the role he or she is entering. This prior experience can affect the extent to which managers are prepared to respond to multiple goals and expectations from a number of stakeholder groups. Prior experience in a more challenging role should permit a manager to be better able to address the organization's performance needs (Fernandez 2005). If public organizations indeed face higher levels of goal ambiguity and complexity, as outlined in figure 3.1, it may be that managers who are hired from another public organization can be linked to higher levels of organizational performance than executives hired from private organizations, where goals are less ambiguous in scope:

> H7. A manager who has prior experience in a more complex, upper-level position will have a more positive effect on performance in public organizations than private organizations.

In sum, we expect management to generally have the same effect on performance in both public and private organizations—and this expectation, if true, would suggest that more caution should be taken when trying to distinguish the two sectors as being necessarily different. Socialization might provide one exception, as public organizations may be better off hiring individuals with experience in more complex roles such that they are more equipped to handle a multitude of unclear, competing goals in a public organization. In testing below whether the effect of management is similar or different across these sectors, the context framework may help to explain our findings.

## DISTINGUISHING PUBLIC/PRIVATE STRUCTURES IN THE CONTEXT OF HIGHER EDUCATION

Although the existing literature has offered a number of ways in which to delineate public and private organizations, this study focuses on differences as related to ownership. Higher education in the United States provides a context where both structural types exist in the same sphere and share similar goals, such that the two types of organizations can be directly compared. In other words, a four-year public institution of higher education will be more like a four-year private institution of higher education than it will be like another public organization in a separate policy arena.

The context of the institutions in this sample can be broadly described by the context framework, as displayed in figure 3.2. The political structure of higher education includes a system of shared powers, is multilevel, and is characterized by a nascent performance system that continues to evolve. The general environment of these organizations is complex, with many demands; is turbulent; and is poor in munificence in the face of declining state funding. Yet these institutions carry a notable level of social capital, and each has some weight with state legislatures (compared with baccalaureate institutions and two-year colleges). Within these organizations, multiple goals continually compete in decentralized systems whose staff members are trained to have a high degree of professionalism across all subunits.

When comparing public and private institutions, the largest differences may exist when considering federalism, turbulence, munificence, and social capital. These differences are due to the fact that public institutions are influenced more heavily by state regulations and demands as well as state funding. Because state funding is largely in flux, public institutions are experiencing higher levels of turbulence than their private counterparts. As for munificence, private organizations are often perceived as having additional resources (though this is generally only true for the most select private institutions).

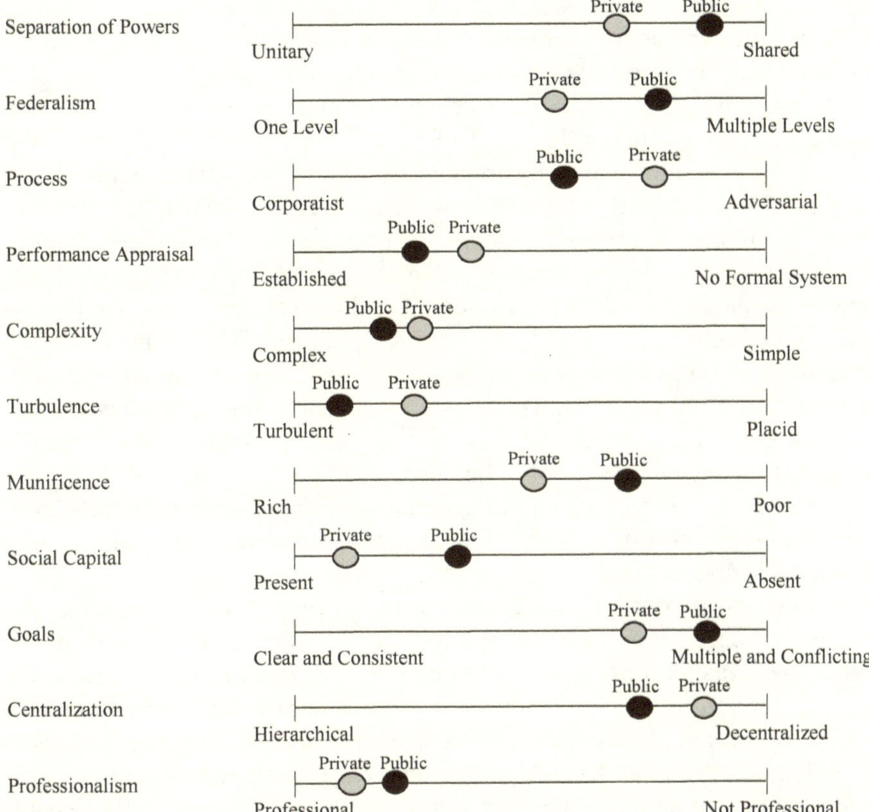


**Figure 3.2** Comparison of Public versus Private Higher Education—Common Perceptions

Private institutions are also seen as wielding higher levels of social capital and influence (this again may only apply to a certain group of private institutions that are not actually representative of all private institutions). That public and private higher education systems may not be entirely different among many of the contextual variables considered in the proposed framework again suggests that the relationship between management and organizational performance might not be significantly different across sectors in this study.

We can also consider similarities and differences between public and private institutions of higher education based on ownership, source of funding, and regulation. More differences stand out among these categories as compared with the context framework. Ownership in public and private universities across the United States has traditionally played a major role in defining these institutions' goals, values, and missions. Public universities rely on state funds and are subject to an array of procedural laws and regulations. Although they are frequently the recipients of private types of funding, including capital assets and athletic revenues, their primary revenue source has traditionally been state and local funds (Lowry 2009).[2] Additionally, state legislatures and the federal government heavily influence public universities' missions and expectations, because these institutions are charged with expanding opportunities and improving economic mobility for the general public (Scott, Bailey, and Kienzl 2006). The members of public universities' governing boards are frequently chosen based on their political affiliations, rather than their experience with higher education (Duderstadt and Womack 2011). This leads to a watchdog mentality that is philosophically different from the trustee mentality of private university boards. The state's higher education governance structure can control personnel decisions, accountability measures, and interactions with other political actors (Tandberg 2013). Ultimately, the politically charged environment in which public universities operate heavily influences policymaking decisions at both the state and organization levels (McLendon, Hearn, and Mokher 2009).

Private universities rely more heavily on tuition and fees, donations, and endowment income for revenue and receive little direct subsidies from the state. These institutions appoint their own boards of directors, allowing for more discretion in strategic decision-making processes. But private universities are not completely independent of public revenue sources, and most receive public benefits through endowment tax breaks, research grants, and student financial aid (Douglas and Lombardi 2006). There are still debates about the competitive and revenue-maximizing structures across university types, but the sector distinction largely has important implications for the level of control wielded over the institution and the type of funding sources available (Gander 1999; Lowry 2009). Ultimately, the ability to compare across organization types, with multiple measures of performance and a large data set, is extremely beneficial for reliable empirical analysis. In a competitive market—with decreasing resources, increasing demand, and shifting attitudes toward accountability—managers in the higher education setting face high levels of uncertainty in the external environment.

Another major advantage of studying the effect of management across public/private structural differences in the context of higher education is that the managers of these institutions come from a variety of backgrounds. Unlike many other industries, higher education does not have specified criteria to determine which individuals are eligible to assume an administrative role in a college or university (in other words, there are no specific requirements for a particular degree, type of certification, or other qualification). Other industries may have industry-specific skills that limit the pool of hires and the variation within top management. Presidents of universities, however, have come from political positions, private corporations, or other universities. This provides valuable insight into the experiences of managers across sectors.

## DATA AND METHODS

Data to test the influence of management on organizational performance in public and private institutions of higher education in the United States were collected from two sources. First, data on university presidents were gathered from colleges and universities rated by the Carnegie classification system as doctoral/research universities, research universities–high research activity, or research universities–very high research activity, across a twenty-one-year period (1993–2013).[3] The universe of these classifications consists of 292 institutions; data for 281 schools were coded because 11 schools do not provide over-time information on their president in a publicly accessible format. Data were collected on the length of managerial tenure, start and end dates of service, previous employment, educational background, and demographics, resulting in 5,685 institution-year observations.[4] These managerial data were then merged with institutional data from the Integrated Postsecondary Education Data System's Delta Cost Project, sponsored by the National Center for Education Statistics. Virtually all public, private nonprofit, and private for-profit colleges and universities in the United States are required to report data on a yearly basis in exchange for their receipt of federal funding (primarily in the form of student financial aid). Variables include a dichotomous variable for ownership (public vs. private), revenues and expenditures, staffing, and student enrollment profiles, among other variables. The descriptive statistics for the variables pertinent to this study are shown in table 3.1. Data from the National Center for Education Statistics were available through 2010 at the time of data collection, resulting in a period of 1993–2010 for this study. Because models are arranged to use managerial characteristics in time $t$ to predict performance in time $t$+1, we lose one year of observations in our specification. Next, because institutional data were self-reported, a small percentage of nonsystematic missing observations are present. Finally, the analyses provided here exclude any institution-years in which an organization had an interim president in office (191 of the total 5,685 cases). Interim presidents maintain and oversee the institution until the next president is hired and are generally not tasked with changing the organization in any meaningful way. With all factors considered, the tables include up to 3,600 institution-years, for 281 total institutions between 1994 and 2010.[5]

**Table 3.1** Descriptive Statistics for Institutions of US Higher Education

| *Variable* | *Mean* | *Standard Deviation* | *Minimum* | *Maximum* |
|---|---|---|---|---|
| 150% graduation rate | 61.369 | 18.296 | 11.188 | 97.926 |
| Degrees per 100 full-time-equivalent students | 26.323 | 5.981 | 4.769 | 109.43 |
| Share of low-income students | 0.097 | 0.063 | 0 | 0.797 |
| Average institutional award (logged) | 8.549 | 0.837 | 5.198 | 10.452 |
| Federal grants and contracts (logged) | 17.348 | 1.747 | 7.537 | 21.265 |
| Gifts, investments, and endowment earnings revenue (logged) | 16.913 | 1.805 | 8.357 | 22.861 |
| First year of presidency | 0.147 | 0.354 | 0 | 1 |
| Experience (years) | 5.973 | 5.4 | 0 | 34 |
| h-index | 10.269 | 12.229 | 0 | 96 |
| Most recent position–other university | 0.63 | 0.483 | 0 | 1 |
| Most recent position–outside higher education | 0.099 | 0.298 | 0 | 1 |
| Most recent position–dean | 0.144 | 0.351 | 0 | 1 |
| Most recent position–vice president / provost | 0.425 | 0.494 | 0 | 1 |
| Most recent position–professor | 0.065 | 0.247 | 0 | 1 |
| Most recent position–other | 0.03 | 0.17 | 0 | 1 |
| Percent black students | 10.003 | 15.774 | 0 | 98.103 |
| Percent Hispanic students | 5.323 | 7.254 | 0 | 63.496 |
| Percent part-time students | 25.716 | 14.213 | 0.076 | 83.574 |
| Enrollment (logged) | 9.529 | 0.872 | 4.828 | 12.25 |
| Sticker price (logged) | 8.878 | 0.903 | 6.122 | 10.629 |
| Percent full-time faculty | 52.508 | 19.589 | 2.439 | 100 |
| State performance funding policy | 0.19 | 0.392 | 0 | 1 |
| Change in state unemployment rate | 0.031 | 0.195 | –0.413 | 1.184 |

## Measuring Organizational Performance

Objectively defining, measuring, and assessing performance is simultaneously one of the most important and most challenging tasks in organizations. Organizations are often held responsible for meeting multiple goals, and each organization may place a different emphasis on the many goals they are expected to address. Despite a long history of autonomy from regulation and oversight, higher education is no exception in discussions of performance accountability. Policymakers at the federal and state levels as well as governing boards have developed numerous accountability policies, which include pay-for-performance and performance-accountability mechanisms whereby institutions must meet performance goals in order to receive state allocations (Rutherford and Rabovsky 2014). These environmental shifts have demanded much attention from administrators in both public and private colleges and universities. Many scholars of higher education now believe that access, affordability, and quality are positioned on an "iron triangle," whereby a change to improve one axis will inevitably affect the others in a negative way (Rodriguez and Kelly 2014). In the present study, multiple indicators related to student performance, student access, and institutional resources are examined in order to paint a complete picture for how and when management is similar or different in public and private organizations.

## Student Performance

Student outcomes related to attaining an academic degree are among the most salient performance indicators debated in scholarly and popular discussions of accountability in higher education. We use two indicators of completion—graduation rates and degree production. The graduation rate—calculated as the percentage of first-time, full-time students who graduate within six years of enrolling at the same institution—is perhaps the most commonly used assessment of overall student performance (Rabovsky 2012). Unfortunately, this rate excludes a number of student groups, such as transfer students and part-time students, and can be strategically manipulated by either decreasing the size of the freshman class or raising admission standards to admit students who are more likely to graduate within six years. The number of baccalaureate degrees conferred per 100 full-time-equivalent students (commonly referred to as degree production) provides an alternative means for measuring performance and takes account of several student groups that are excluded in the graduation rate (the two measures have a correlation of .37). Although data on degree production were collected across the entire span of our sample, the graduation rate has only been reported since 2001.

## Student Access

Higher education in the United States was once available only for students from the highest echelons of society. However, the importance of creating equal educational opportunities for students from all backgrounds was spurred by the GI Bill and the creation of aptitude tests, and was secured as part of the national dialogue on education with the passing of the Higher Education Act of 1965. Policies at the federal and state levels continue to provide financial assistance for low-income students, and institutional-level awards often provide additional funds (though institutions have been much criticized for tailoring scholarships to the middle and upper classes through merit aid, as opposed to providing more need-based aid). Despite ongoing debates regarding access and affordability, the US Department of Education collects little information on access across socioeconomic tiers. We are, however, able to tap data on performance related to access through the share of low-income, dependent undergraduate students at each institution and the size of the average institutional award at each college and university. The share of low-income, dependent undergraduate students is measured as the share of undergraduate students who applied for financial aid whose total annual family income is reported to be below $15,000. This variable is a conservative measure of low-income students, given that an institution may have some low-income students who do not apply for financial aid. Further, $15,000 is a very low family income; these students are essentially living in poverty. Still, the higher the share of these low-income, dependent students, the more accessible the institution will be for students enrolling in higher education. Second, institutional assistance for students is collected through the average amount of institutional grants received by full-time, first-time, degree-seeking undergraduates. Although this measure may include awards based on residency, academic programs, and even athletic teams, it may indicate the willingness of institutional administrators to provide additional dollars to students.

## Institutional Resources

In light of declining state allocations to higher education and a recent recession, maintaining or increasing resources and revenues is especially important for keeping an organization stable. Presidents and vice presidents at both public and private institutions are often directly responsible for raising funds for a variety of causes (e.g., infrastructure, scholarship, and expansion). Two indicators of resources that may be directly influenced by managerial strategies and actions include (1) federal grants and contracts and (2) revenue from private gifts/grants/contracts, investment returns, and endowment earnings. Revenue from federal grants and contracts will be larger when a university president places a priority on acquiring national grants, which are seen as means of improving the institution's financial stability, reputation, and scholarly output. Gifts/grants/contracts, investment returns, and endowment earnings are commonly based on building relationships with alumni constituency groups and raising private money. This strategy is targeted to very specific audiences and can generate funds for a variety of purposes (scholarships, infrastructure, beautification, etc.) that are deemed essential for meeting the institution's goals.

## Managerial Characteristics

The primary focus of this study is to determine whether managerial–performance relationships are similar or different across structural or contextual differences that may exist in the public/private organizational divide. To compare management across these settings, we include variables for presidential turnover, the total years of a president's term (or experience), the president's h-index (which is defined below), whether the president's prior organization was outside higher education, and whether the president's prior organization was another institution of higher education (making the excluded category an internal hire). Each of these measures is interacted with a dichotomous measure of whether the organization is private to determine the similarities and differences of management across the two structures.

To test hypotheses 1 and 2, presidential turnover is measured as a dichotomous variable noting a president's first year in office. Following the notion that new managers can institute needed change and innovation, presidential turnover may be associated with higher levels of performance. Conversely, new presidents may also be linked to lower levels of performance due to a break in stability. A new president may need a significant amount of time to adjust to a new organization or a new position, and will need sufficient time to build relationships that will help him or her to make informed decisions to improve the institution.

Dichotomous variables are included for whether the president's most recent managerial role was not with an institution of higher education or was with another institution of higher education (as opposed to being an internal hire); these variables allow for a direct test of hypotheses 3 and 4. For example, some individuals in our data set become presidents after serving as a governor, a lawyer, the chief executive of a private business, or the director of a nonprofit organization. These individuals may have a different effect on performance compared with presidents hired from another higher education role because of differing values, norms, and expectations for what the institution can or should do.

Total tenure, measured as the number of years an individual has served as president of the institution, captures the president's more gradual adjustment to the organization over time. Following hypothesis 5, this may be associated with an increase in performance as the president gains more power and expands his or her network. Conversely, longer tenures may possibly become associated with stagnant or lower levels of performance if inertia and an unwillingness to challenge the status quo become the norm.

Additional variables are included in each model to tap various types of managerial socialization (hypothesis 6). First, a president's h-index is used as proxy for his or her prior socialization experiences and propensity to value research.[6] In other words, presidents with higher h-indexes are assumed to have a specific approach to managing institutions of higher education than president with low indexes. The higher the h-index, the more a president may focus on core institutional functions related to classroom instruction and research, which can influence a number of revenues and expenditures. Presidents with a high h-index are also more likely to have spent more time in and around higher education or a related research institution, which can provide a unique perspective on which goals to pursue and how to realize these priorities.

Beyond the use of dichotomous measures to determine the degree to which an individual is an inside or outside hire, additional analyses are conducted of presidents who have a background in higher education (they are either hired from the same institution or another college). Within this group, we can test for whether transitioning from a set of job categories has a positive or negative effect on performance. We control for whether the most recent position held by the current president was a vice president or provost, dean, professor, or some other position, with president being the excluded category. It may be that those who were most recently a president are more likely to adjust to another presidential position. However, it might also be the case that universities look for talented provosts, deans, or professors who may be able to address the needs of their university well, even without full knowledge of what the role of a presidency requires.

## Control Variables

Task complexity is captured through three measures of diversity in the student enrollment profile: the percentages of black students, of Hispanic students, and of part-time students. Each of these variables serves as an indicator of at-risk and vulnerable student populations that often require additional support and resources from the institution. Many of these students must find employment while attending school, and many have greater support demands from family and friends (London 1993; Thayer 2000). They may take longer to graduate, and may not attend school in a continuous manner. Institutions with large at-risk populations must develop methods (e.g., summer programs, learning communities, and counseling services) to help these students progress toward graduation.

To assess whether turbulence in the external environment affects organizational strategy, we control for the presence of a state performance-funding policy and the year-to-year change in state unemployment. Policymakers largely tout performance-funding policies as a mechanism by which universities seek to improve students' performance. Though research is at best mixed on whether these policies work to improve student outcomes, many recognize that the presence of these policies is likely to generate some type of response or reaction from university presidents (e.g., Rutherford and Rabovsky 2014). Second, state unemployment rates provide a measure of competition for state allocations. During lean economic years, higher education is one of the first budget categories cut, while more funding is focused on welfare programs (see the recent discussion of the balance wheel hypothesis by Delaney and Doyle 2011). Rises in unemployment rates are also associated with increases in enrollments in higher education (Betts and McFarland 1995); these changes in enrollments create a need to alter institutional strategies.

Finally, we control for additional resources to avoid producing underspecified models with spurious results. Student access is measured using logged in-state tuition and fees (the "sticker price"). Total student enrollment (logged) captures institutional size and represents the traditional mechanism though which colleges and universities have received funding from state policymakers. The percentage of full-time faculty may influence the demands of faculty constituent groups at a university in terms of benefits, spending, and student support.

Beyond including theoretically important variables to avoid model underspecification, analyses must also appropriately address model specifications that capture over-time changes, and thus they require giving attention to the presence of serial autocorrelation and heteroskedasticity. As such, all models include panel-corrected standard errors with panel-specific corrections for AR1 autocorrelations to address the nature of the time series–cross-sectional data (Beck and Katz 1995).[7]

## FINDINGS

Table 3.2 presents findings for the effect of management on student performance outcomes. Private institutions have both higher graduation rates

(7–8 percent higher) and degree production (4–5 degrees per 100 full-time-equivalent students higher). Considering the general differences between public and private institutions, joint *F*-tests for all interactive variables proves significant only for degree production. However, several more nuanced relationships are also important to note for all four student outcome models. In the context of both public and private institutions, presidents with higher h-indexes appear to do better (see Model 2 and Model 1, respectively). These presidents may have a certain outlook on how to raise graduation rates that

**Table 3.2** The Effect of Management on Student Performance

| | *150% Graduation Rate* | | *Degrees per 100 Full-Time Students* | |
|---|---|---|---|---|
| *Variable* | *Model 1* | *Model 2* | *Model 3* | *Model 4* |
| Private institution | 8.2819* (2.0202) | 7.3804* (2.2813) | 4.8302* (0.7295) | 5.5483* (0.9059) |
| First year of presidency | 0.0817 (0.3148) | 0.2270 (0.3494) | –0.1557 (0.1144) | –0.1965 (0.1222) |
| Experience (years) | 0.0316 (0.0467) | 0.0867+ (0.0487) | –0.0254 (0.0167) | –0.0216 (0.0183) |
| h-index | 0.0096 (0.0205) | 0.0475* (0.0214) | –0.0043 (0.0083) | 0.0047 (0.0079) |
| Most recent position–other university | 0.3072 (0.5744) | –0.4124 (0.6703) | 0.2016 (0.1832) | 0.2444 (0.1946) |
| Most recent position–outside higher education | –0.3929 (0.8793) | | –0.5181+ (0.3025) | |
| First year x private institution | –0.0056 (0.7304) | 0.0166 (0.7319) | 0.0308 (0.2898) | –0.0565 (0.2905) |
| Experience x private institution | 0.0384 (0.1004) | 0.0319 (0.0972) | 0.0607+ (0.0327) | 0.0491 (0.0333) |
| H-index x private institution | 0.0799* (0.0327) | 0.0536 (0.0357) | –0.0035 (0.0123) | –0.0057 (0.0139) |
| Other university x private institution | –0.9432 (1.2649) | –0.4949 (1.4060) | –0.4163 (0.4661) | –0.9156+ (0.5148) |
| Outside higher ed x private institution | 0.8121 (2.2241) | | 2.0191* (0.8278) | |
| Most recent position–dean | | –2.2760* (1.0775) | | 0.1494 (0.3486) |
| Most recent position–vice president / provost | | –1.5908* (0.5328) | | –0.3633+ (0.2147) |

**Table 3.2** *(continued)*

| *Variable* | *150% Graduation Rate* Model 1 | *150% Graduation Rate* Model 2 | *Degrees per 100 Full-Time Students* Model 3 | *Degrees per 100 Full-Time Students* Model 4 |
|---|---|---|---|---|
| Most recent position–professor | | 0.7984<br>(1.0980) | | 0.1924<br>(0.2982) |
| Most recent position–other | | –5.0063*<br>(1.8898) | | –0.3526<br>(0.4183) |
| Dean x private institution | | 2.5578+<br>(1.4923) | | –1.5188*<br>(0.6700) |
| Vice president / provost x private institution | | 0.8153<br>(1.2619) | | –0.3259<br>(0.5550) |
| Professor x private institution | | –1.6365<br>(2.3482) | | –1.7917+<br>(0.9476) |
| Other x private institution | | 1.1675<br>(3.7230) | | –0.7559<br>(1.2940) |
| Percent black students | –0.2634*<br>(0.0248) | –0.2618*<br>(0.0248) | –0.0569*<br>(0.0077) | –0.0581*<br>(0.0076) |
| Percent Hispanic students | –0.1714*<br>(0.0483) | –0.1632*<br>(0.0491) | 0.0567*<br>(0.0184) | 0.0486*<br>(0.0181) |
| Percent part-time students | –0.5567*<br>(0.0315) | –0.5890*<br>(0.0293) | 0.0726*<br>(0.0133) | 0.0801*<br>(0.0120) |
| Enrollment (logged) | 5.4228*<br>(0.6497) | 5.6966*<br>(0.6168) | 0.4386+<br>(0.2591) | 0.5895*<br>(0.2655) |
| Sticker price (logged) | 6.8651*<br>(0.7680) | 6.9988*<br>(0.7583) | 1.3025*<br>(0.2634) | 1.5596*<br>(0.2468) |
| Percent full-time faculty | –0.0020<br>(0.0122) | 0.0137<br>(0.0129) | –0.0041<br>(0.0044) | –0.0052<br>(0.0044) |
| State performance funding policy | –1.4843*<br>(0.5694) | –1.4259*<br>(0.5747) | –0.2947<br>(0.2088) | –0.3587+<br>(0.2008) |
| Change in state unemployment rate | 0.1736<br>(0.5021) | 0.0478<br>(0.5321) | 0.0607<br>(0.2186) | 0.1715<br>(0.2262) |
| Constant | –39.4155*<br>(9.2249) | –42.3480*<br>(8.8239) | 7.5516*<br>(3.3847) | 3.9196<br>(3.3180) |
| *N* | 2,007 | 1,803 | 3,575 | 3,219 |
| Joint *f*-test for interactions | .24 | .51 | .03 | .07 |
| $X^2$ | 1,845.970 | 2,134.914 | 833.815 | 943.408 |
| $R^2$ | .81 | .84 | .69 | .72 |

$+ p < 0.10$, $* p < 0.05$.

could be informed by their research background or interactions with students. In terms of prior position, presidents who were most recently employed as a president appear to do best in public institutions; with the exception of prior professors, all other positions are negatively related to graduation rates when compared with those hired from other president positions. The same is not true for private institutions; only presidents who were previously deans have a significant relationship with graduation rates, as compared with individuals who were most recently presidents. Further, the relationship is positive, indicating that these individuals do better raising performance, despite having little experience in a president's office.

Although degree completion also measures student success, the findings in Models 3 and 4 differ somewhat from the graduation rate. A president's h-index is not meaningful, and prior position matters little for public institutions. Instead, prior position seems to have a stronger effect in private universities, where those who were previously vice presidents / provosts or deans do worse than those who were previously presidents. Also of interest, presidents hired from another university seem to hurt degree production (Model 4), whereas those hired from outside the higher education industry improve this performance indicator. Finally, experience appears to help private university presidents, further adding to the implication that managerial characteristics appear to matter more in private institutions compared with public institutions in terms of degree performance.

From table 3.2, findings reveal that individuals who have served as presidents and who have some level of a research background may best manage public institutions; for private institutions, a mix of backgrounds may actually help presidents improve performance. Do these initial findings hold across other performance indicators? Table 3.3 displays results for student access measures. With the exception of Model 3, public and private institutions tend to have similar shares of low-income students and average institutional awards. Joint *F*-tests for all interactions broadly support these similarities, because they are insignificant for low-income students and strong but not significant for institutional award models.

The effects of individual managerial characteristics, however, vary across the two types of organizations. Presidents who are hired from other colleges or universities are negatively related to the share of low-income students in public institutions; but the same relationship does not apply to the context of private institutions. Much like table 3.2, no one appears to perform better than managers who were most recently presidents in public institutions, but background is slightly less important in private institutions, where deans and provosts tend to provide higher levels of access for low-income students compared with prior presidents. For institutional awards, presidents hired from

**Table 3.3** The Effect of Management on Student Access

| Variable | *Share of Low-Income Students* | | *Average Institutional Award (logged)* | |
|---|---|---|---|---|
| | *Model 1* | *Model 2* | *Model 3* | *Model 4* |
| Private institution | –0.0018<br>(0.0114) | –0.0219<br>(0.0151) | 0.2925*<br>(0.1279) | 0.0416<br>(0.1115) |
| First year of presidency | 0.0014<br>(0.0034) | 0.0015<br>(0.0038) | 0.0129<br>(0.0220) | 0.0177<br>(0.0232) |
| Experience (years) | 0.0004<br>(0.0004) | 0.0004<br>(0.0004) | 0.0026<br>(0.0031) | 0.0058+<br>(0.0033) |
| h-index | 0.0000<br>(0.0002) | 0.0001<br>(0.0002) | –0.0006<br>(0.0014) | 0.0013<br>(0.0012) |
| Most recent position–other university | –0.0089*<br>(0.0034) | –0.0129*<br>(0.0038) | 0.0771*<br>(0.0315) | 0.0466<br>(0.0378) |
| Most recent position–outside higher education | –0.0160*<br>(0.0045) | | –0.0360<br>(0.0555) | |
| First year x private institution | –0.0031<br>(0.0051) | –0.0040<br>(0.0055) | –0.0186<br>(0.0386) | –0.0182<br>(0.0385) |
| Experience x private institution | –0.0005<br>(0.0005) | –0.0005<br>(0.0006) | –0.0003<br>(0.0048) | –0.0002<br>(0.0049) |
| h-index x private institution | 0.0000<br>(0.0002) | –0.0000<br>(0.0003) | 0.0042*<br>(0.0016) | 0.0026+<br>(0.0015) |
| Other university x private institution | 0.0057<br>(0.0065) | 0.0105<br>(0.0077) | 0.0180<br>(0.0579) | 0.0218<br>(0.0591) |
| Outside higher ed x private institution | 0.0110<br>(0.0088) | | 0.0184<br>(0.0917) | |
| Most recent position–dean | | –0.0104+<br>(0.0057) | | –0.0927<br>(0.0590) |
| Most recent position– vice president / provost | | –0.0063<br>(0.0045) | | –0.0598+<br>(0.0337) |
| Most recent position–professor | | –0.0082<br>(0.0092) | | –0.0042<br>(0.0677) |
| Most recent position–other | | –0.0290+<br>(0.0169) | | –0.2391+<br>(0.1384) |
| Dean x private institution | | 0.0212*<br>(0.0093) | | 0.1263+<br>(0.0729) |
| Vice president / provost x private institution | | 0.0144*<br>(0.0067) | | 0.0519<br>(0.0612) |
| Professor x private institution | | 0.0107<br>(0.0136) | | –0.1063<br>(0.0893) |

**Table 3.3** (*continued*)

| | *Share of Low-Income Students* | | *Average Institutional Award (logged)* | |
|---|---|---|---|---|
| *Variable* | *Model 1* | *Model 2* | *Model 3* | *Model 4* |
| Other x private institution | | 0.0239<br>(0.0195) | | 0.0650<br>(0.1989) |
| Percent black students | 0.0017*<br>(0.0002) | 0.0017*<br>(0.0002) | 0.0019<br>(0.0015) | 0.0017<br>(0.0015) |
| Percent Hispanic students | 0.0025*<br>(0.0003) | 0.0026*<br>(0.0003) | –0.0041<br>(0.0028) | –0.0037<br>(0.0030) |
| Percent part-time students | 0.0004*<br>(0.0001) | 0.0004*<br>(0.0002) | –0.0076*<br>(0.0012) | –0.0071*<br>(0.0012) |
| Enrollment (logged) | –0.0085*<br>(0.0037) | –0.0106*<br>(0.0043) | 0.0720*<br>(0.0257) | 0.0289<br>(0.0259) |
| Sticker price (logged) | –0.0173*<br>(0.0050) | –0.0151*<br>(0.0056) | 0.6349*<br>(0.0663) | 0.7474*<br>(0.0387) |
| Percent full-time faculty | –0.0001+<br>(0.0001) | –0.0001<br>(0.0001) | 0.0007<br>(0.0007) | 0.0009<br>(0.0007) |
| State performance funding policy | –0.0030<br>(0.0038) | –0.0037<br>(0.0043) | –0.0438<br>(0.0291) | –0.0568+<br>(0.0300) |
| Change in state unemployment rate | –0.0169*<br>(0.0050) | –0.0161*<br>(0.0054) | 0.0853*<br>(0.0305) | 0.0532+<br>(0.0303) |
| Constant | 0.3065*<br>(0.0497) | 0.3172*<br>(0.0566) | 2.1037*<br>(0.6111) | 1.6048*<br>(0.4201) |
| *N* | 2,463 | 2,217 | 2,439 | 2,187 |
| Joint *f*-test for interactions | .77 | .51 | .18 | .13 |
| $X^2$ | 342.158 | 309.482 | 3,226.801 | 3,759.328 |
| $R^2$ | .32 | .31 | .94 | .95 |

$+ p < 0.10$, $* p < 0.05$.

other institutions again have a negative effect for public institutions but no effect in private organizations; the notion that prior position matters for public organizations but is less significant in private organizations (with the exception of deans) is also supported. Unlike Models 1 and 2, Models 3 and 4 provide some support that presidents with higher h-indexes in private institutions are more attuned to the importance of access, at least via institutional awards to help lower the cost of attendance.

Next, the effect of management on resources is shown in table 3.4. Resources are a means to improving performance at institutions of higher education, and they are thus seen as an indicator of whether a president is doing his or her job well (in other words, presidents are expected to raise funds for the institution and are evaluated based on the related numeric). Private universities, overall, have lower levels of federal grants and contracts but are able to attain higher levels of gifts, investments, and endowment earnings (joint *F*-tests strongly support the former and are more mixed on the latter). A president's h-index

**Table 3.4** The Effect of Management on Institutional Resources

| | *Federal Grants and Contracts (logged)* | | *Gifts, Investments, and Endowment Earnings Revenue (logged)* | |
|---|---|---|---|---|
| *Variable* | *Model 1* | *Model 2* | *Model 3* | *Model 4* |
| Private institution | –0.9645*<br>(0.1473) | –1.1842*<br>(0.1874) | 1.4340*<br>(0.2115) | 0.8183*<br>(0.2457) |
| First year of presidency | –0.0081<br>(0.0167) | –0.0082<br>(0.0181) | 0.0338<br>(0.0450) | 0.0450<br>(0.0476) |
| Experience (years) | 0.0018<br>(0.0023) | 0.0028<br>(0.0025) | 0.0057<br>(0.0060) | 0.0054<br>(0.0065) |
| h-index | 0.0040*<br>(0.0013) | 0.0044*<br>(0.0014) | 0.0059*<br>(0.0025) | 0.0082*<br>(0.0026) |
| Most recent position—other university | –0.0069<br>(0.0322) | –0.0035<br>(0.0336) | –0.0609<br>(0.0564) | –0.1705*<br>(0.0639) |
| Most recent position—outside higher education | 0.0918*<br>(0.0406) | | –0.0093<br>(0.0928) | |
| First year x private institution | 0.0063<br>(0.0562) | 0.0397<br>(0.0605) | –0.1667<br>(0.1084) | –0.1350<br>(0.1128) |
| Experience x private institution | 0.0014<br>(0.0066) | 0.0042<br>(0.0081) | –0.0130<br>(0.0102) | –0.0031<br>(0.0114) |
| h-index x private institution | 0.0039+<br>(0.0022) | 0.0043<br>(0.0028) | 0.0030<br>(0.0047) | –0.0025<br>(0.0051) |
| Other university x private institution | 0.1961*<br>(0.0995) | 0.2770*<br>(0.1215) | 0.0526<br>(0.1485) | 0.1981<br>(0.1675) |
| Outside higher education x private institution | –0.3552*<br>(0.1345) | | –0.0250<br>(0.2026) | |
| Most recent position—dean | | –0.0258<br>(0.0528) | | –0.2418*<br>(0.1054) |
| Most recent position—vice president / provost | | –0.0125<br>(0.0393) | | –0.3159*<br>(0.0743) |
| Most recent position—professor | | –0.0018<br>(0.0626) | | –0.2666*<br>(0.1231) |

**Table 3.4** (*continued*)

| | *Federal Grants and Contracts (logged)* | | *Gifts, Investments, and Endowment Earnings Revenue (logged)* | |
|---|---|---|---|---|
| *Variable* | *Model 1* | *Model 2* | *Model 3* | *Model 4* |
| Most recent position—other | | –0.0555<br>(0.1304) | | –0.4800*<br>(0.2205) |
| Dean x private institution | | 0.1596<br>(0.1394) | | 0.4016*<br>(0.2013) |
| Vice president / provost x private institution | | 0.2877*<br>(0.1189) | | 0.5814*<br>(0.1735) |
| Professor x private institution | | –0.0088<br>(0.1854) | | 0.2588<br>(0.2940) |
| Other x private institution | | 0.1718<br>(0.3337) | | 0.3593<br>(0.3387) |
| Percent black students | 0.0054*<br>(0.0025) | 0.0062*<br>(0.0026) | –0.0156*<br>(0.0025) | –0.0154*<br>(0.0026) |
| Percent Hispanic students | –0.0005<br>(0.0031) | 0.0003<br>(0.0032) | –0.0078+<br>(0.0042) | –0.0049<br>(0.0044) |
| Percent part-time students | –0.0248*<br>(0.0021) | –0.0242*<br>(0.0023) | –0.0329*<br>(0.0024) | –0.0312*<br>(0.0025) |
| Enrollment (logged) | 1.4250*<br>(0.0642) | 1.4237*<br>(0.0658) | 1.4343*<br>(0.0510) | 1.4087*<br>(0.0549) |
| Sticker price (logged) | 0.5590*<br>(0.0533) | 0.5652*<br>(0.0524) | 0.5072*<br>(0.0823) | 0.5890*<br>(0.0699) |
| Percent full-time faculty | 0.0039*<br>(0.0009) | 0.0036*<br>(0.0009) | 0.0038*<br>(0.0015) | 0.0052*<br>(0.0015) |
| State performance funding policy | –0.0396<br>(0.0359) | –0.0387<br>(0.0350) | –0.0082<br>(0.0591) | –0.0347<br>(0.0627) |
| Change in state unemployment rate | 0.0602<br>(0.0397) | 0.0662<br>(0.0425) | –0.4806*<br>(0.0832) | –0.4894*<br>(0.0870) |
| Constant | –0.5485<br>(0.7490) | –0.6056<br>(0.7521) | –0.9319<br>(0.8165) | –1.2022<br>(0.7905) |
| *N* | 3,563 | 3,212 | 3,421 | 3,081 |
| Joint *f*-test for interactions | .00 | .02 | .61 | .09 |
| $X^2$ | 1,115.746 | 1,237.025 | 1,661.234 | 1,654.383 |
| $R^2$ | .96 | .96 | .90 | .91 |

$+ p < 0.10$, $* p < 0.05$.

appears to be strongly related to both revenue performance indicators for public institutions but has only limited support (Model 1) in private institutions. Presidents hired from outside the higher education industry are positively and significantly related to federal grants and contracts for public institutions but have the opposite effect in private institutions. Instead, presidents hired from another institution of higher education are most successful in attaining these grants and contracts for private institutions. In terms of prior positions, only prior vice presidents / provosts in private institutions are significantly different than prior presidents.

Interestingly, for the gifts, investments, and endowment earnings measure, the management characteristics that are significant essentially flip. Little matters in terms of whether the president was hired from another institution or from outside higher education. Prior position, however, is much more important. Prior presidents are related to significantly higher revenues than any other category for public institutions, whereas deans and vice presidents and provosts are related to higher levels of this revenue than prior presidents in private institutions. These differentiations are likely due to the skills learned in prior positions that shape decision-making abilities once the individual assumes the president position.

Finally, across all models, it is important to note that the presence of state performance policies is consistently related to lower performance. Although this may be related to institutional strategies, it may also be the case that states with lower performance are those that have implemented these types of accountability policies. Across all models, enrollment, the sticker price, the number of full-time faculty, and changes in unemployment rates at the state level are related to performance in expected directions.

## IMPLICATIONS

The effects of managerial characteristics have been examined across a number of performance indicators for public and private doctoral and research institutions in the United States. These analyses have found some similarities across the two types of structural contexts considered here, whereas other relationships appear to differ in the two settings. Presidential turnover has no effect on performance for either type of institution, indicating that new presidents neither cause instability nor generate innovation in the short term—efforts that push in both directions may result in a null effect overall. Experience, when significant (twice for public institutions and once for private institutions), is positively related to performance; this factor thus seems to be beneficial but is not necessarily the most important managerial characteristic. A president's h-index is also positively related to performance where significant, though this type of socialization appears to have more meaning in public institutions (five of twelve models) than in private institutions (three of twelve models). This difference is notable, given that the mean and standard deviation values for this variable in public and private institutions are largely similar (mean = 10.22 and s.d. = 12.21 in 3,896 public institution-years; mean = 10.34 and s.d. = 15.24 in 1,736 private institution-years). A slightly longer tail for maximum values generates a larger standard deviation for private institution presidents.

The sector from which the president is hired (internal, external–other university, external–outside higher education) has very mixed findings for both public and private institutions. It may be that this trait is very individual-specific or that the trait is observed on a smaller scale. For example, individuals hired from other institutions that are small are likely to be very different from those hired from other institutions that are large. Similarly, among those hired from outside higher education, former politicians have a different outlook than former agency heads or military personnel.

The most recent position of those within higher education has a much different effect in public institutions compared with private institutions. Public institutions have higher levels of performance across the indicators tested in this study when the current president has served as a president elsewhere. This could show some level of external experience or socialization vis-à-vis the office of the president. However, this same trend is not detected for private institutions, where presidents who were promoted directly from a dean's office or from a vice president / provost position occasionally generate higher levels of performance than prior presidents. This is possibly related to the ability of private institutions to be more competitive in salary and/or reputation. These institutions are likely to have the ability to hire the best managers in the higher education market. For example, it is more common for administrators to move from private institutions into Ivy League schools or for administrators to move among Ivy League schools than it is for Ivy League administrators to move to public institutions (but see Stripling 2014 about how this trend appears to be changing).

Theoretically, these findings indicate that managers may have very similar effects in public and private institutions across some dimensions (experience, h-index), and very different effects across others (primarily the socialization gained in the prior position). Overall, the analyses conducted for this study do not provide evidence that public/private structural differences necessarily create systematic variance in management–performance links. This highlights the limitations of oversimplifying the distinctions between public and private organizations; though trying to define accurate and parsimonious differences is theoretically important, the observed differences are very complex and may not be the mechanisms that drive the performance differences that exist between the two types of organizations. As public and private organizations continue to take on characteristics (though privatization, contracting, and reliance on government aid) that make differentiation even more difficult (through phenomena like isomorphism), previously observed differences in management–performance linkages will erode further.

However, we must be careful to note that this study also does not provide strong causal evidence that management is the same across both types of organizations. The effect of managerial characteristics should be tested in additional settings (either other countries or other policy realms) to determine the extent to which findings in the case of higher education in the United States can be extended elsewhere. Practically, these findings are informative in terms of hiring processes in universities. Public institutions should consider the prior experiences of their candidates carefully, because those with prior experience as a university president may indeed be better equipped to address the more complex and ambiguous goals that public institutions are tasked with fulfilling.

The goal of this book is to propose and test a new framework focused on organizational context. Perhaps one of the best characteristics of this framework is that it can force scholars to think about either how similar or different the organizations they wish to study are for a variety of characteristics. This exercise can help scholars to develop more informed theories and hypotheses, for they will have a higher awareness of the degree to which context may or may not play a role in their research. Here, by noting both the common differences between public and private organizations generally and public and private institutions of higher education specifically, we were able to determine more precisely where we expect the effect of management on performance to be similar or different between the sectors. For some contextual components, differences across the sectors were not so large as to intervene in this relationship (at least given our measurement and approach in this study). For other categories, differences were more apparent.

Our use of this framework also revealed areas where it might be improved. Though the framework does address goal complexity, the most common characteristics by which to distinguish public and private organizations—ownership, funding sources, and regulations—are not fully addressed in the current framework but could easily be incorporated into future iterations. In addition to considering the framework's completeness, we also found it useful to treat the contextual variables as continua rather than dichotomous categories to better compare our organizations of interest. In taking this approach, scholars should have more flexibility in determining how and why organizations differ and can identify areas where additional research and empirical analysis are warranted.

## NOTES

1. Though not tested here, it is possible that a long-serving leader may become resistant to change, resulting in a decline in performance. This may point to a nonlinear relationship between managerial experience and performance.
2. Though not the focus of this study, the reliance of public universities on government funding is largely changing due to a rapid decline in state appropriations per student in recent years.
3. By president, we mean the individual who serves as the executive manager of a university campus, not the manager of a university system with multiple campuses. For example, data are coded for each University of California campus, not for the University of California system. Notė that some university systems (e.g., Colorado's) use the term "chancellor" for executives at the institutional level and "president" for those at the system level. In these cases, chancellors were coded as "presidents."
4. It needs to be noted that we could not code all twenty-one years for a selected number of institutions due to the occasional lack of information provided through publicly available websites.
5. It is also possible to generate analyses based on a continuous ownership variable. In this context, the percentage of revenue from state allocations may indicate how public an institution is in a given year (this also links to the discussion of privatization in higher education given recent declines in allocations).When we use this continuous variable, similar overall findings generally hold while some individual, model specific relationships shift slightly.
6. The h-index is a measure of academic reputation that is designed to be comparable across disciplines. An index of ten means that the individual has ten publications, with each cited a minimum of ten times. While the h-index may be influenced by publishing norms across disciplines, it can certainly separate nonacademic from academics.
7. Two-way fixed-effects models (not shown here) produce findings that are not significantly different from those shown here. We also tested models with a lagged dependent variable; though the inclusion of this variable often explains a larger share of variance and can mask other relationships, our findings are similar to those shown here.

# 4

# The Better You Look, the More You See

## *Nonlinear Effects of Managerial Networking Hidden in the Research Setting of Dutch Primary Education*

RENÉ TORENVLIED AND AGNES AKKERMAN

In the last fifteen years, the field of public management has witnessed a steady accumulation of systematic research on the link between management and performance (Akkerman and Torenvlied 2011; Boyne et al. 2005; Heinrich and Lynn 2000; Forbes and Lynn 2005; O'Toole and Meier 1999). O'Toole and Meier launched a research agenda founded on a model of public management that has been successfully applied, tested, and further developed in different specifications. Public management, according to their model, is a set of management activities that provides organizations with the necessary internal stability to improve upon their past performance, buffer themselves against turbulent shocks in their environment, and tap resources from the organizational environment.

Studies of Texas school districts revealed that both *internally* and *externally* oriented management activities make an important difference for organizational performance. In testing the essential version of the public management model, O'Toole and Meier (2011) present strong evidence for the presence of the effects of internal management and managerial networking on the performance of Texas school districts. They find that internal management, especially the presence of highly qualified personnel, has a strong positive effect on performance and can compensate for the negative effect of instability.

Further, some of the concepts found to affect performance are contingent on other variables. For example, the nonlinear relationship between managerial networking and performance is positive and highly significant for school districts with more central staff (O'Toole and Meier 2011, 123).

If a theoretical model is parsimonious, and the hypotheses derived from this model are sufficiently general, then its external validity should be able to be determined through careful replication. Replication is important, because it reveals the boundary conditions under which the assumed mechanisms operate and produce the hypothesized effects (Boyne 1996; King 1995; Popper 1968). The main empirical setting in which O'Toole and Meier's model of public management has been put to a full, integral test is the domain of public education—more specifically, the performance of school districts in the State of Texas. Elements of the public management model have also been tested indirectly and separately in other research settings. For example, the impact of internal management has been tested in the context of local service provision by English local governments (Andrews et al. 2005; Meier et al. 2007), and in Colombian local governments (Avellaneda 2009b). Nicholson-Crotty and O'Toole (2004) tested an integral version of the public management model for police organizations and also find positive effects of internally and externally oriented managerial activities on police performance.

Recently, data on Dutch primary education were collected to replicate and extend the Texas school district studies. Strong effects of managerial networking, it turned out, seemed to be absent in this particular research setting (O'Toole et al. 2013). Meier and colleagues (2015) report no effects of managerial networking on school performance in the research setting of Danish primary education. Thus, in replicating existing US public management studies in European research settings, we seem to obtain test results that vary substantially. These findings challenge the plausibility of our core assumption: that some universal mechanisms exist which link management to organizational performance.

The mixed test results of the general model of public management in different research settings give rise to the question of how context affects our understanding of the mechanisms that drive the relation between management and organizational performance. In the remainder of this chapter, we address this question on the basis of a replication of the O'Toole–Meier management model in Dutch primary education.

## PUTTING CONTEXT IN PERSPECTIVE

A common approach to modeling context in social science research assumes that the context of a research setting triggers specific mechanisms, which affect the behaviors of social actors and the outcomes stemming from these behaviors (Pawson and Tilley 1997). Indeed, many public management studies assume that context fundamentally alters the impact of managerial activities on organizational performance (Meier et al. 2015; O'Toole and Meier 2015; Pollitt 2012). Qualitatively oriented scholars produce "thick descriptions" of diverse, complex administrative situations. Quantitatively oriented scholars build context-specific parameters into their statistical test models. And yet such contextual relativism may be discomforting (see Blatter and Haverland 2014), because universal explanatory models have been the key to much of the progress made in public management research in recent years. If we assume a priori that inconclusive, unexpected, and contradictory results could be fully explained by an idiosyncratic research context, our models would have no external validity at all.

Now, let us suppose that a *general*, *parsimonious*, and *plausible* model of public management predicts specific effects that can be empirically detected in one research setting. Then we should search for these same fundamental effects in other research settings as well. For such a search, two complementary research strategies are available. First, we would need to use appropriate conceptualizations and apply well-tailored measurement instruments for the key variables in the explanatory model to fit the new research setting. The modeling context, then, refers to an appropriate conceptualization and measurement of model variables in a new research setting. For example, a survey question should be specified so that it can measure the theoretical construct of a model variable in the new research setting in order to be able to compare it with the same theoretical construct from the original context.

The second research strategy for modeling context is to include (new) conditioning variables in the model, thus parametrizing the predicted effects between research settings. This approach is taken in the comparative public management framework that is presented in the introduction. Below, we describe how the context of the Netherlands fits the comparative public management framework. We also show how institutional differences *within* the research setting fit the comparative public management framework. Here, these institutional differences refer to a school's denominational or religious identity. In the research setting of the Netherlands, this is the distinction of schools that have a specific religious or cultural background from schools that do not (also see a similar division of context in studies on US charter schools, e.g., Roch and Pitts 2012). In Dutch education, schools are allowed to adopt a denominational identity, such as Catholic, Protestant, Islamic, Hindu, Jewish, or Waldorf. On the basis of this identity, schools have discretion in accepting or rejecting students.[1] Many schools, however, have no specific denomination. These nondenominational schools are required to accept all pupils who register.

In the present chapter we show that, when properly specified, not only do differences in context matter *between* research settings but they also matter *within* research settings. We combine both approaches to modeling the context in order to replicate the effects found in other research settings—effects predicted by the general model of public management proposed by O'Toole and Meier. We combine survey data on 1,348 school principals with performance data on their schools, resulting in 422 valid cases. Our analyses show that at both denominational and nondenominational schools, the nonlinear effects of managerial networking on performance are present, as predicted by the model of public management. We detect these effects, however, only when we specify denominational identity as a context variable within the research setting. We show that nondenominational schools benefit from networking with local government, whereas denominational schools benefit from networking with professional organizations for youth care. These professionals are concerned with students who are more at risk to cause problems in their school.[2] Without the proper contextual specification within the research setting (in terms of having a denominational identity), these universal effects would have remained undetected. Thus, we show that a more appropriately specified research setting enables us to see more in terms of predicted, universal effects.

## A MODEL OF PUBLIC MANAGEMENT

The core assumption of the theoretical model of public management and performance is that, in essence, public organizations are inertial systems (O'Toole and Meier 2011). This is because organizational missions are quite slow to change, reflecting the incremental decision processes in political systems. Public organizations, therefore, are characterized by several forms of stabilizing features. Externally, public organizations are embedded in well-defined hierarchical settings and operate in stable interorganizational networks. Internally, public organizations typically employ standard operating procedures—routines, rules, and standardized solutions or tools for getting things done in daily practice. As a consequence, bureaucratic organizations are designed to produce consistent, stable, and (hence) highly predictable outcomes (O'Toole and Meier 2011, 28–29). The current performance of a public organization (denoted by $O_t$,) therefore is strongly affected by its past performance (denoted by $O_{t-1}$).

However, this model of public management and performance is not deterministically defined by an organization's past performance. In the first place, *(de)stabilizing factors* (denoted by $S_0$) may vary between organizations. For example, these can include rapid technological changes in production modes, policy changes that affect an organization's mission and/or production modes, or high personnel turnover rates. This variation over time in the organization's internal stability is likely to generate variation between organizations in the extent to which current performance is related to past performance.

In the second place, organizations experience *external shocks* from the environment (denoted by $X_t$). These shocks often have strong effects on organizational performance. For example, policymakers could impose severe budget cuts on the organization or rapid changes in clientele demand may occur. On one hand, such shocks are likely to have profound negative effects on the organization's performance. On the other hand, opportunities in the organization's environment may arise that could positively affect performance. This variation over time in the impact of specific environmental shocks may also create variation between organizations in their current performance.

Having defined the effects of organizational stability and environmental shocks on current performance, we turn to the effects of public management activity. With regard to *internal management activity* ($M_1$), Meier and O'Toole (2011, 133) consider different management activities that maintain organizational stability ($S_0$)—public managers frame the goals and mission of the organization, define incentive structures within the organization, and initiate stabilizing procedures. In addition, public managers buffer personnel instability through active human resources policies, thereby attracting capable employees. Personnel instability can involve the turnover rates of both top-level managers and frontline professional workers (O'Toole and Meier 2011, 137). Stability in top-level management is important because managers need time to get acquainted with the organization and its environment (assuming that managerial skills improve over time). It also takes time for the organization's stakeholders to become familiar with a public manager's norms, values, and management style. This familiarity with the public manager builds trust, which further eases the effective use of a manager's authority (Barnard 1938). The effective use of managerial authority further benefits from the administrative intensity of the organization. Administrative intensity becomes managerial capacity when it enables the manager to seize opportunities beyond the scope of the internal organization and when it reinforces the effects of internal management activities. Indeed, administrative intensity reduces the diminishing returns in the nonlinear relation between networking and performance (O'Toole and Meier 2011, 118–24).

In analyzing *managerial networking activity* ($M_2$), Meier and O'Toole (2011) specify how public managers cope with external shocks. These shocks are either exacerbated or mitigated by an external stability parameter ($S_e$), which in turn is affected by managerial networking activity. Public organizations are often encouraged, or even required, to operate in collaborative settings with external entities over which they exercise little or no authority. Public managers' investment in network relations helps them to anticipate and buffer their organization from external shocks. However, the networked environment of public organizations does not only help to combat turbulence but also provides these organizations with valuable resources. External organizations and actors in the network of the public managers are often a rich source of support in the form of the provision of funds, staff, information, advice, and ideas (Meier and O'Toole 2003). Managers who actively network are able to tap these resources from their network by devoting substantial time and energy to their external network nodes (it is important to note that these effects can take a nonlinear form; see Hicklin, O'Toole, and Meier 2008).

On the basis of the assumptions and mechanisms described above, O'Toole and Meier (2011) define the relations between the key variables of public performance and management in the following, parsimonious model:

$$O_t = \alpha + \beta_1 (S_o + M_1)\, O_{t-1} + \beta_2 M_2 (X_t / S_e) + \varepsilon_t \qquad (1)$$

The model states that current organizational performance, $O_t$, is an additive function of (1) past performance, $O_{t-1}$, which is affected by organizational stability, $S_o$, and is stabilized by internal management activity, $M_1$; and (2) the public manager's ability to buffer external shocks, $X_t$, with managerial networking activity, $M_2$. These external shocks are moderated by environmental stability, $S_e$. Finally, an error component, $\varepsilon_t$, is included that captures random fluctuations in current performance.

In this chapter, we use a reduced version of the general model by dropping the interaction term of internal management and past performance as well as the interaction term of managerial networking and external shocks (which was studied more closely in the Dutch research setting by Bekerom, Torenvlied, and Akkerman 2014). This reduced model, specified in equation 2, reflects multiple testable hypotheses—with positive signs for parameters $\beta_1$ through $\beta_5$—as listed in equation 2 just below. Finally, we add the nonlinear effects of internal management (moderated by administrative intensity) and managerial networking as separate hypotheses:

$$O_t = \alpha + \beta_1 S_o + \beta_2 M_1 + \beta_3 M_1 A + \beta_3 O_{t-1} + \beta_4 M_2 - \beta_5 M_2^2 + \varepsilon_t \qquad (2)$$

H1a. *The main effects of public management.* Organizational stability, internal management, and managerial networking activity all positively affect primary school performance—while controlling for a positive effect of past performance.

H1b. *The nonlinear effect of internal management.* The positive effect of internal management on primary school performance is reinforced by administrative intensity.

H1c. *The nonlinear effect of managerial networking.* The effect of managerial networking on school performance is nonlinear, reflecting diminishing returns of networking activity on primary school performance.

Here we take a transposition approach to modeling context.[3] We show how a simple, moderating (dummy) variable—denomination—reveals how different indicators for the same model variables have a specific effect on performance. We frame this as the *denominational context hypothesis* and further substantiate this hypothesis in the next section:

H2. *The effect of denominational context.* The denominational identity of a primary school moderates the impact of specific indicators for public management activities on primary school performance.

## THE RESEARCH SETTING: DUTCH PRIMARY EDUCATION

The setting of the present study is formed by the Dutch system of education, and the managers in our research context are the principals of primary schools. In the Netherlands, 6,864 primary schools are responsible for the education of more than 1.5 million students between the ages of four and twelve. Dutch primary schools have two main responsibilities: (1) to qualify pupils by promoting their cognitive skills in language and arithmetic; and (2) to socialize pupils by promoting their social and moral development in citizenship behavior (Dutch Education Council 2009). School principals must translate these broad responsibilities into their school's educational program. In addition, they coach teachers; develop plans for pedagogical quality, student care, and quality control; and monitor pupil performance. These principals also have considerable administrative duties associated with the school's day-to-day management. They are responsible for planning activities, human resources management, and developing and maintaining buildings. The principal is the main representative of the school and maintains relationships with many organizations and actors in the school's environment—including the parent committee, the school board, the local government, public libraries, youth care, the Dutch Inspectorate of Education, and test suppliers.

Dutch primary schools are subject to Dutch education law, which is partly a national concern and partly decentralized to local governments. There is no financial sponsoring of education from the private sector; all schools are entirely government funded, by a block grant from the Dutch Ministry of Education, Culture, and Science. These grants are based primarily on school size, defined as the number of students who attend the primary school. The block grants are, however, also partly dependent on pupil weights, in which specific categories of pupils are weighted more heavily than others; these categories are related to parental background characteristics, such as educational level and immigrant background. Thus, pupil characteristics at least partly affect the size of a school's budget. In addition, primary schools are allowed to request voluntary parental contributions, to be designated for extracurricular activities such as school outings, additional teaching materials, and festivities. Accountability for these additional expenses occurs through the parents' council.

All schools are assessed on the same final attainment levels. Most prominent is Cito, a standardized, independent national examination that provides information about both pupils' educational progress and the school's performance (the Cito test is described in more detail below). The Cito attainment levels have driven the standardization of educational programs offered by primary schools and make it possible to compare and monitor performance for all primary schools. The Inspectorate of Education produces risk analyses for each primary school and uses these analyses to determine a specific oversight arrangement for each school.

Additional compliance standards for performance management include the documentation of student achievements, the school's social climate, and the application of educational programs. The inspectorate's reports on many of these indicators are made available online, making all evaluations easily accessible to the general public. The inspectorate's benchmarking activity has direct consequences for the popularity of primary schools because parents are, in principle, free to choose which primary school their children attend. Schools that fail to comply with the performance standards are subjected to an intensive supervision program and an annual evaluation (which is also made public). Schools that continue to fail ultimately risk losing their funding.

Dutch primary education is embedded in a relatively homogeneous institutional environment (Torenvlied and Akkerman 2012), comprising national rules, regulations, and procedures, as well as sector-wide collective bargaining agreements that set minimum standards and job classifications for personnel policies at school (Franssen, Pastors, and Van Rooijen 2010). Local government further shapes the conditions for the provision of education by making budgetary allocations for school improvements, infrastructure, and public space and safety issues.

## Comparison of the Texas and Dutch Contexts

The model of public management reviewed above is formulated in a parsimonious fashion and at a high level of generalization. Hence, any application of the model should draw considerable attention to the importance of the environmental context (Torenvlied et al. 2012). Table 4.1 provides an overview of the context of primary education in the Netherlands in terms of the comparative public management framework proposed in the introduction. The second column of table 4.1 provides information about the "between-system" comparison for the context of Dutch primary education and the context of the Texas school district system, the relevant context for most past studies. In terms of population, Texas is the second-largest of the fifty US states, with about 25 million residents. The Netherlands is a small European country with a population of approximately 17 million. As of 2013, the State of Texas has 1,266 school districts with 9,225 public and private schools. The Dutch primary school system has 6,864 denominational and nondenominational schools (Common Core of Data 2016). The managerial level of the Dutch school principal is below that of the top managerial level of a US school district superintendent. The Dutch school directors' management activities are much closer to the day-to-day provision of education and the direct supervision of school teachers. US school district superintendents have a stronger strategic and political component embedded in their management activities. However, many of their tasks and responsibilities are quite comparable, as related to daily school management, external relations, curriculum development, the procurement of funding and subsidies, and human resources policies. The Texas and Dutch education systems are also alike in that they are experiencing an overlap of goals and policies in their sector from fields other than education, such as public safety and health.

Although many of the management activities of school district superintendents and school principals are quite comparable, there are clearly also some differences. For example, school operations take place on a much larger scale in Texas than in Dutch primary schools. The largest school district in Texas, the Houston Independent School District, has an enrollment of 203,000 students; and the largest school in Texas, Skyline High School in Dallas, has nearly 4,900 students (American School and University 2015; Molina 2014). The largest primary school in the Netherlands, conversely, opened its doors in August 2011 with an enrollment of 1,050 students. There are other key differences—for example, in the governance structure of the provision of education. Texas school district superintendents are top managers who often supervise many different schools and report to a single board that covers a school district. Dutch primary schools, conversely, are each governed by a

**Table 4.1** The Public Management Context: Dutch Primary Education

| *Context* | *Between-System Dutch Primary Education (Ref.: Texas School Districts)* | *Within-System Denominational Schools (Ref.: Nondenominational)* |
|---|---|---|
| *Political context—Concentration of Power* | | |
| Separation of powers | Unitary | Unitary |
| Federalism | Multiple levels | No difference |
| Process | Corporatist | Corporatist |
| Performance appraisal | Established | No difference |
| *Environmental Context* | | |
| Complexity | Within-system variation | Less complex |
| Turbulence | Within-system variation | Less turbulent |
| Munificence | Modest | Richer |
| Social capital | Present | Stronger |
| *Internal Context* | | |
| Goals | Clear / consistent | Clear / consistent |
| Centralization | Decentralized | No difference |
| Professionalization | Professional | No difference |

school board—though, like those in Texas, these boards vary considerably in their level of professionalization and in the number of schools for which they are held accountable.

With respect to financial resources, there is much less discretion in the Dutch system than in the Texas system. In the Netherlands, primary schools only have the right to ask for minor, voluntary contributions from parents. In Texas, by contrast, school districts collect property taxes for the provision of their (public) services among a wider, local public. Hence, we may expect Texas school district superintendents to have incentives to be more active networkers for financial resources compared with Dutch primary school principals. Finally, there are also marked differences in the educational system's broader organization. Dutch parents rely heavily on school care services to provide activities for their children, both before and after school hours. There is quite a demand for school care services because Dutch primary education has no school bus system; instead, all parents are required to bring their children to school in the morning, pick them up for lunch at noon, bring them back, and finally pick them up in the afternoon.

Finally, three more differences need to be noted. First, Dutch education is highly unionized, whereas teachers' unions in Texas are weak or nonexistent (though they do exist elsewhere in the United States). Second, religious schools are generally not included as part of the public education system in Texas. And third, Texas schools are far more diverse in terms of race, ethnicity, and income than are Dutch schools, given the overall populations of these two geographic regions.

### Nondenominational and Denominational Schools

Dutch primary schools vary with respect to their denominational identity and educational philosophy. This variation developed from the principle of "freedom of education," which is embodied in the Dutch Constitution. This principle embraces the freedom of Dutch citizens to found schools, to determine the principles of faith for their schools, and to organize teaching (De Vijlder 2000, 1). Since the beginning of the nineteenth century, any community, parent, or other initiator has been allowed to establish a primary school on the basis of its own initiative. Almost 70 percent of all primary schools in the Netherlands are denominational. Roughly 29 percent have a Roman Catholic identity, 26 percent have a Protestant identity, and 11 percent have another denominational identity (Islamic, Hindu, Jewish, or Waldorf) (Center on International Education Benchmarking 2009). In the Netherlands, parents are free to choose which primary school their children will attend. However, primary schools with a denominational identity have the right to refuse children—for example, because they have limited capacity for students. Primary schools also have some discretion to apply selection criteria (i.e., the geographical distance of students' homes from school). Denominational primary schools may also give priority to pupils with a particular religious background. Nondenominational schools, however, are obliged to accept all students, regardless of their religious background.

The third column of table 4.1 provides information about the within-system comparison between denominational and nondenominational schools in terms of the proposed context framework. Denominational schools are more unitary and more corporatist compared with nondenominational schools, which must be responsive to more heterogeneous public interests. Due to the fact that denominational schools can be more selective, they have less environmental complexity and turbulence than nondenominational schools. And because of their ties to special interest groups and religious organizations, denominational schools generally have more access to resources and stronger social capital. Finally, the goals of denominational schools are clearer and more consistent than the goals of nondenominational schools, because the latter schools must serve pupils from more heterogeneous backgrounds.

All Dutch primary schools are governed by a school board that shares the school's denomination. About 30 percent of all the 1,069 school boards in the Netherlands are responsible for a single school, but most school boards govern more than one school (sometimes even more than sixty schools) (Dutch Ministry of Education, Culture, and Science 2014, 48). Nondenominational school boards are, traditionally, closely tied to the local municipal government (until recently, the alderman for education had a formal position on the school board). Denominational school boards have a composition that reflects their particular background (representatives from religions are not uncommon). Formally, the school board is accountable for the school's internal organization, personnel and employment policies, and financial management, and is ultimately held responsible for the school's performance (Turkenburg 2008). However, school boards often delegate much of their authority and discretion to the school principal. These principals make important decisions about the school budget, educational curriculum, and personnel processes. They maintain direct contacts with the parents' council and other key actors; they are essentially the school's primary representative in all external relations.

## DATA AND MEASUREMENT

To test the model of public management in the context of Dutch primary education, we use a pooled data set of primary schools. The first component of the pooled data set is information from a survey of Dutch primary school principals. More specifically, for the Dutch School Networks & Learning Project, we conducted a nationwide survey among principals of Dutch primary schools. The survey data were collected in early 2010 using an internet survey. Principals of all 6,896 Dutch primary schools were invited by mail and email to participate in the survey. The invitation included a personal link to the project website. A reminder was sent after two weeks. After six weeks, the response rate was 19.55 percent ($n$ = 1,348). This rate is comparable to response rates reported by other studies of Dutch school principals, and is substantial given the work pressure on school principals and the prevalence of survey research in this sector. A nonresponse analysis shows that schools in the sample do not differ with respect to a large number of relevant characteristics (Torenvlied and Akkerman 2012).

The second component is a data set from the Dutch Inspectorate of Education, which provides information about various indicators of school performance for many different years, as well as a wide range of control variables. We selected the year 2010 for further analysis because the survey, held in the spring of 2010, asked the school principals explicitly about their activities in the previous year. The two data sets were matched using the unique identification school number assigned by the Dutch Ministry of Education, Culture, and Science. This number is a four-digit code that allows the ministry to identify primary schools as separate educational units. The data set also contains an identification number for school boards, which enables us to cluster schools by board. Below, we discuss the construction of the different measures in the analysis.

Any proper application of the public management model in a specific research setting (here, Dutch primary education) requires that we balance two demands: first, to replicate the existing measures developed in the context of Texas education to allow for comparisons across contexts; and, second, to carefully retain the construct validity of the existing measures that were developed in the US setting. The latter demand may result in slight modifications of existing measures.

Hence, the measurement of the variables in the model of public management aims to capture the constructs used in Texas school district studies as much as possible, given the context of the Dutch provision of primary education. Most of the measures we use in the present study are direct translations of the measures used in the Texas school district studies. Thus, when we observe differences in results between the two settings, these differences most likely arise from differences in the mechanisms that operate within these settings and not from differences in the framing and conceptualization of measures used.

## Organizational Performance ($O_t$)

The dependent variable in this study is the school's average student score on the standardized test taken in the second half of the eighth (and final) grade of primary education. Roughly 75 percent of all primary schools participate on a voluntary basis in the Cito test (the test is named after the independent institute that develops, supplies, and administers the scores). The Cito test score is based on three subtests: language (100 questions), arithmetic (60 questions), and study competences (40 questions). Students' scores on these 200 questions are transformed to a scale that ranges from 501 to 550. In 2009, approximately 154,000 students participated in the test, and the average score was 535.5 (Cito 2009). In 2010, 137,000 student participants resulted in an average score of 535.8 (Cito 2010).

The Cito scores are very important in the Dutch system of education.[4] Secondary education is split between different subcategories—special education, vocational education, and higher secondary education—as well as many different sublevels within these categories. Pupils are referred to a specific level of higher secondary education by their teacher in collaboration with representatives from schools in secondary education. The referral of pupils to secondary education is based, to a large extent, on their individual Cito test score.[5] Some secondary schools even apply a strictly defined minimum Cito score in their admittance decisions.

The Cito test has not been without controversy and challenges. Standardized tests clearly do not measure all the relevant aspects of an educational system. Thus, some primary schools use intelligence tests as the basis for pupil referral. In addition, all primary schools are allowed to exempt specific, well-defined categories of pupils from the test: (1) pupils with severe language problems who have been living in the Netherlands for less than four years and (2) pupils with an indication for special secondary education and sometimes for lower levels of vocational secondary education.

Despite this room for discretion, average Cito test scores (corrected for pupil characteristics) are considered to be an authoritative indicator for school performance by the Dutch Inspectorate of Education, as well as by most teachers and parents. The inspectorate uses students' average test scores, among other indicators, to distinguish between insufficient, (very) weak schools on one hand and average or strong schools on the other hand. Information about Cito test scores is important in the news and is reported online with freely accessible average test scores by school. However, in order to use a school's average Cito score for analysis, explicit consent must be obtained from each school. As such, we asked school principals to indicate whether they allowed the use of their school's average Cito score data.[6]

The Cito scores are very comparable to the standardized test scores used in Texas. High-stakes testing is present in both contexts, and these tests can influence the future education prospects for individual students. Average test scores in Texas are also publicly available, though no consent is needed to link tests to specific schools in analyses. Both tests allow for similar exemptions from the test (e.g., special education), and both are well publicized.

## Organizational Stability ($S_0$)

O'Toole and Meier (2011, 140) conceptualize organizational stability in terms of personnel stability. We specify managerial stability as a measure of personnel stability because no authorized data are available for teacher or staff turnover. Managerial stability is captured as tenure, or the number of years that the school principal has worked as head of the specific school. This measure of tenure also taps the concept of experience; we thus control for the age of the school principal, to single out at least some of the variance that can be ascribed to overall experience, separate from experience as principal of the current school.

### Internal Management ($M_1$)

We use three variables to capture internal management: team involvement, human resources rule restrictions, and quality of human capital. Team involvement measures managerial activities intended to involve the school team in various aspects of decision making. We measured team involvement using ten items, each of which covers a specific aspect of daily decision making in a school. These indicators were derived from in-depth interviews with school principals, board members, and representatives from the Inspectorate of Education. The items consist of identity and external communication, school housing and maintenance, financial matters, personnel and employment policy, quality of education, pupil results and performance monitoring, pupil care, educational quality, external relations, and scheduling and other practicalities. Involvement was measured using a 6-point Likert Scale, asking principals how frequently (daily, weekly, monthly, quarterly, yearly, or never) their team discusses each aspect of the school. An unrotated factor analysis reveals the existence of one factor on which all items load positively and strongly, with an eigenvalue of 3.62. Factor scores were saved using the Bartlett method.

Next, rules restrictions capture a different aspect of internal management (O'Toole et al. 2013). This variable was measured using the statement "The formal pay structures and rules make it hard to reward a good teacher," a standard approach for understanding personnel red tape (Rainey, Pandey, and Bozeman 1995; Torenvlied and Akkerman 2012). School principals were asked to indicate their level of agreement with this statement on a 4-point Likert Scale. The third internal management variable pertains to the quality of human capital. This variable should tap the successful attraction and development of human capital within the organization, resulting in high-quality teachers (O'Toole and Meier 2011, 153). In the context of the Texas school districts, O'Toole and Meier (2011, 153) have asked superintendents to rate the quality of their principals' management skills and professional development and of experienced teachers and to indicate their level of agreement with the statement "Our people can make any program work."[7] We adapted this approach for the management level of school principals, and we asked principals to rate the quality of their team of teachers on a 0–10 scale (O'Toole et al. 2013). The measures from both surveys are unrelated ($\rho = -0.03$), suggesting that different forces shape the internal management of primary schools.

Finally, administrative intensity captures the managerial capacity of the organization. Administrative intensity is conceptualized as the percentage of all personnel who have a managerial or administrative function.

## Managerial Networking ($M_2$)

We follow O'Toole and Meier's (2011) measurement of managerial networking activity as captured by the frequency of relations with external organizations.[8] A detailed list of external organizations with which school principals network was determined through interviews with key informants in the education sector, school principals, and members of school boards. This procedure resulted in a list of forty-one external organizations and actors (Torenvlied and Akkerman 2012). Managerial networking variables were measured by asking each school principal "How frequently do you interact with this type of organization?" for each of these organizations and actors (also see Meier and O'Toole 2003; O'Toole and Meier 2011). Responses could span a 6-point scale, with categories ranging from never (0) to yearly (1), several times per year (2), monthly (3), weekly (4), and daily (5).

To measure managerial networking, we selected three sets of organizations that represent *national* and *local* government actors as well as organizations focused on high-risk students (i.e., those who may cause problems and/or have a problematic background). National government actors and organizations consist of the financial agency DUO (Dienst Uitvoering Onderwijs, Office of Education), which is the semiautonomous government agency responsible for budgeting and finance; the Dutch Ministry of Education, Culture, and Science, which is the national government department responsible for formulating educational policies and programs; test suppliers, those corporations that develop standardized tests for primary education; and the Inspectorate of Education, the office responsible for monitoring school performance and auditing the schools on a wide variety of performance indicators. All organizations in the "intensity of national networking scale" are involved in the process of assigning accountability to schools with respect to their specific pupil achievements, educational climate, and financial management. We use a nonparametric variant of item-response theory to test the strength of the managerial networking scales (for the advantages of using this theory for the analysis of networking scales, see Torenvlied et al. 2012; and Zhu, Robinson, and Torenvlied 2014). The homogeneity index—*H*, for the national networking scale—is 0.46, indicating that the scale is of intermediate strength. We computed a sum scale, standardized with respect to the number of items on the scale.

Local government actors and organizations consist of the members of the city council, who are the representatives in the local political arena; the aldermen, or chief administrators in local government; and the municipal department of education, which is the main local government agency responsible for implementing education policies in the local domain. The items on local networking activity form together a strong scale ($H = 0.51$). Similar to the national actors, we computed a standardized sum scale (the sum divided by the number of organizations on the scale).

The school director's frequency of contact with four additional organizations aims to tap youth care networking—the attendance officer, the police, the provincial authority's youth services, and municipal youth care services. The aim of this construct is to tap the networking activities of school directors seeking to resolve problematic behaviors of students, such as dropping out of school, violent or criminal behavior, and additional social issues associated with these behaviors. The four networking frequency items together form an intermediate strong youth care scale ($H = 0.40$).

## Control Variables

We use a number of control variables that aim to tap differences in the pupil population, school characteristics, characteristics of the school team composition, and characteristics of the school principal.

*Pupil population.* The percentage of disadvantaged pupils includes students who carry a "pupil weight," which indicates the existence of a problematic background of the student.[9] This is similar in nature to O'Toole and Meier's (2011) controlling for complexity that may negatively affect the system.

*School (team) and principal characteristics.* We control for size by including the number of pupils, the number of teachers, and the number of teacher assistants in the school. In measuring the composition of the school team, we include the number of female teachers and the average age of school personnel. We also include three characteristics that may lead to variance in school principals—the number of hours per week a school principal spends on his or her job as a school principal, the age of the school principal, and the school principal's gender.

## Denomination and School Characteristics

Table 4.2 provides an overview of the dependent and independent variables in the present study for nondenominational and denominational schools. For both the performance variable (mean Cito test scores for 2010) and the one-year performance lag, nondenominational schools perform significantly worse. In terms of the internal characteristics of the organization, there are no notable differences between schools. Tenure ranges from zero to 40.5 years, while, on average, principals tend to work about eight years for their school. For the schools in our sample, administrative intensity has a mean value of roughly 9 percent but also includes large variation, with some schools having

**Table 4.2** Means and Standard Deviations for Dutch Schools

| *Variable* | *All Schools in Sample* (*N* = 430) | | *Nondenominational Schools* (*N* = 139) | | *Denominational Schools* (*N* = 291) | | *Significance Level*[a] |
|---|---|---|---|---|---|---|---|
| *Performance indicator* | | | | | | | |
| Cito test score ($O_{2010}$) | 535.23 | (4.23) | 533.86 | (4.99) | 535.88 | (3.64) | *** |
| Cito test score ($O_{2009}$) | 534.80 | (4.31) | 533.71 | (4.24) | 535.33 | (4.25) | *** |
| *Internal organization* ($S_o$) | | | | | | | |
| Tenure | 8.16 | (8.07) | 7.98 | (8.04) | 8.25 | (8.09) | |
| Administrative intensity | 9.32 | (5.00) | 9.47 | (5.06) | 9.24 | (4.98) | |
| *Internal management* ($M_1$) | | | | | | | |
| Team involvement factor | 0.01 | (0.91) | 0.15 | (0.93) | −0.09 | (0.89) | *** |
| Human resources rules | 3.23 | (0.82) | 3.31 | (0.77) | 3.20 | (0.84) | * |
| Quality of human capital | 7.64 | (0.76) | 7.60 | (0.83) | 7.65 | (0.72) | |
| *Managerial networking* ($M_2$) | | | | | | | |
| Local | 2.11 | (0.73) | 2.25 | (0.80) | 2.05 | (0.69) | *** |
| National | 2.46 | (0.61) | 2.46 | (0.62) | 2.46 | (0.61) | |
| Youth care | 2.68 | (0.67) | 2.90 | (0.71) | 2.57 | (0.63) | *** |
| *Director characteristics* | | | | | | | |
| Director = female | 1.35 | (0.48) | 1.37 | (0.48) | 1.34 | (0.47) | |
| Age | 51.68 | (7.66) | 52.23 | (6.66) | 51.42 | (8.10) | |
| Hours spent in job | 0.45 | (0.12) | 0.43 | (0.14) | 0.46 | (0.11) | *** |
| *School characteristics* | | | | | | | |
| Number of pupils | 2.39 | (1.36) | 2.29 | (1.28) | 2.43 | (1.39) | |
| No. of teachers | 19.78 | (9.82) | 19.75 | (9.95) | 19.79 | (9.77) | |
| No. of teacher assistants | 11.72 | (8.15) | 10.54 | (8.28) | 12.28 | (8.05) | ** |
| % female teachers | 80.54 | (9.35) | 80.72 | (8.93) | 80.45 | (9.56) | |
| Average age personnel | 43.07 | (4.51) | 43.69 | (4.34) | 42.77 | (4.56) | ** |
| % disadvantaged | 17.67 | (18.53) | 22.80 | (21.00) | 15.20 | (16.70) | *** |

[a]Differences in mean scores between nondenominational and denominational schools; two-tailed *$p < .10$; **$p < .05$; ***$p < .01$.

management or administrative functions that account for 30 percent of their total of employees.

With respect to team involvement, nondenominational schools appear to involve their team much more than denominational schools. There are no differences in perceived burden from rules or the perceived quality of human capital, indicating that most school principals are generally quite satisfied in this regard. The managerial networking variables were standardized with respect to the number of organizations included in the scale, and mean values represent the averages of these standardized scores. In general, average networking activity varies significantly between nondenominational and denominational schools. Principals of nondenominational schools are significantly more active in networking with both local government actors and youth care agencies.

Finally, we checked for differences in the structural characteristics of these schools. Principals of denominational schools spend more time on the job, albeit the difference is small. Denominational schools do not differ from nondenominational schools along some dimensions of size (number of pupils and number of teachers), but they do have more teacher assistants. Finally, the context of denominational schools is much less complex than that of nondenominational schools (in terms of the percentage of disadvantaged pupils), reflecting the selection mechanisms that draw students to nondenominational schools.

We present the correlations between the most salient dependent and independent variables in table 4.3, splitting the sample between nondenominational and denominational schools. As expected, past performance and current performance are highly correlated. The networking variables and team involvement are related, but not too strongly ($\rho$ varies between .14 and .35). Most other correlations (not reported in table 4.3) are generally low.

**Table 4.3** Correlations of Performance and Management Variables

| *Variable* | *Cito* | *2* | *3* | *4* |
|---|---|---|---|---|
| *All schools* ($n$ = 430) | | | | |
| 1. Performance 2009 | 0.55 | | | |
| 2. Team involvement | 0.04 | 1.00 | | |
| 3. Local government networking | –0.01 | 0.26 | 1.00 | |
| 4. National government networking | 0.01 | 0.25 | 0.24 | 1.00 |
| 5. Youth care networking | –0.22 | 0.20 | 0.35 | 0.23 |
| *Nondenominational schools* ($n$ = 139) | | | | |
| 1. Performance, 2009 | 0.50 | | | |
| 2. Team involvement | 0.06 | 1.00 | | |
| 3. Local government networking | 0.00 | 0.23 | 1.00 | |
| 4. National government networking | 0.09 | 0.16 | 0.20 | 1.00 |
| 5. Youth care networking | –0.30 | 0.25 | 0.35 | 0.24 |
| *Denominational schools* ($n$ = 291) | | | | |
| 1. Performance, 2009 | 0.56 | | | |
| 2. Team involvement | 0.08 | 1.00 | | |
| 3. Local government networking | 0.04 | 0.25 | 1.00 | |
| 4. National government networking | –0.04 | 0.30 | 0.27 | 1.00 |
| 5. Youth care networking | –0.10 | 0.14 | 0.31 | 0.24 |

## FINDINGS

To test our model, we employ a strategy similar to that used in the early Texas school district studies, when the first wave of school principal data was available (Meier and O'Toole 2003). We first apply a "simple model" cross-sectional design and, subsequently, include a (lagged) performance variable for performance in the previous year. We conduct each analysis for all schools combined as well for the split samples that contrast nondenominational schools with denominational schools. The analyses are ordinary-least-squares regressions, with robust standard errors clustered by school board.

### Effects of Internal Management on Performance

Table 4.4 presents the test of the internal organization and internal management portions of the public management model. The analyses in Model 1 replicate the results of a previous test (O'Toole et al. 2013), which shows that stringent human resources rules negatively affect school performance, and that team involvement positively affects school performance, though this relationship is conditional on high levels of administrative intensity. The interaction effect remains when controlling for past performance in Model 4. When the sample is split, however, these results change. Managerial stability appears to contribute only to the performance of nondenominational schools. This result is similar to that of Roch and Pitts (2012), who show that representation by teachers and administrators has a much smaller effect on charter schools than on traditional public elementary schools in Georgia. These charter schools might resemble Dutch denominational schools, given that both systems rely on specific values to generate stability rather than traditional experience.

With respect to the internal management variables, the interactive relationship between team involvement and administrative intensity disappears. The negative effect of human resources rules is stronger for nondenominational schools than for denominational schools. Remarkably, we observe a negative interactive effect between the quality of human capital and administrative intensity for nondenominational schools. Nondenominational schools with high-quality teachers tend to perform worse if administrative intensity is relatively high. Finally, the current performance of nondenominational schools appears to be unaffected by their past performance. Yet there is a strong bivariate correlation between the past and present performance of nondenominational schools (rho = 0.50; see table 4.3). Hence, the covariation between past and present performance must be explained away by school characteristics and management variables.[10]

These models appear to yield specific results in our two contexts. Nondenominational schools are unaffected by past performance, benefit from

**Table 4.4** School Performance and Internal Management: Cito Scores Split by Denominational Nature

| | *Simple Model* | | | *Autoregressive Model* | | |
|---|---|---|---|---|---|---|
| | | *Denomination* | | | *Denomination* | |
| *Variable* | *(1) All* | *(2) No* | *(3) Yes* | *(4) All* | *(5) No* | *(6) Yes* |
| *Lagged dependent variable* | | | | | | |
| Performance, 2009 | | | | 0.29*** | 0.16 | 0.35*** |
| *Internal organization* | | | | | | |
| Managerial stability | 0.01 | 0.11** | –0.01 | 0.02 | 0.11** | –0.00 |
| Administrative intensity | 0.04 | –0.00 | 0.06 | 0.03 | 0.01 | 0.03 |
| *Internal management* | | | | | | |
| Team involvement | –0.04 | 0.09 | 0.10 | –0.06 | 0.06 | 0.10 |
| Human resources rules | –0.58** | –1.04** | –0.42* | –0.43** | –0.91* | –0.29 |
| Human capital quality | 0.02 | –0.14 | 0.05 | –0.10 | –0.20 | –0.09 |
| *Interaction terms* | | | | | | |
| Involvement x intensity | 0.07** | 0.07 | 0.06 | 0.06** | 0.05 | 0.06* |
| Human capital x intensity | –0.01 | –0.02** | 0.00 | –0.00 | –0.02** | 0.00 |
| *Controls* | | | | | | |
| Director = female | 0.53 | –0.14 | 0.85* | 0.49 | –0.17 | 0.81** |
| Director age | 0.02 | –0.02 | 0.03 | 0.01 | –0.02 | 0.01 |
| Hours spent on job | 0.02 | –2.81 | 1.77 | 0.08 | –2.82 | 2.05 |
| No. of pupils | 0.24 | 1.27 | –0.81** | 0.04 | 1.19 | –1.12** |
| No. of teachers | –0.00 | –0.19* | 0.16*** | 0.01 | –0.19* | 0.18*** |
| No. of teacher assistants | –0.02 | –0.03 | –0.03 | –0.02 | –0.03 | –0.04 |
| % female teachers | –0.08*** | –0.06 | –0.10*** | –0.07*** | –0.04 | –0.09*** |
| Average age of personnel | –0.02 | –0.11 | –0.00 | –0.04 | –0.12 | –0.01 |
| % disadvantaged pupils | –0.12*** | –0.11*** | –0.11*** | –0.08*** | –0.09** | –0.06*** |
| Constant | 544.00*** | 553.58*** | 541.27*** | 388.19*** | 465.33*** | 356.85*** |
| $R^2$ | 0.36 | 0.44 | 0.33 | 0.41 | 0.45 | 0.43 |
| *N* | 430 | 139 | 291 | 430 | 139 | 291 |

*Note:* Two-tailed $^{*}p < .10$; $^{**}p < .05$; $^{***}p < .01$. Computed on the basis of robust standard errors clustered in school boards. All analyses control for principal's gender, age, hours spent in the job, number of pupils, number of teachers, number of teacher assistants, percentage of female teachers, average age of personnel, and percentage disadvantaged pupils.

managerial stability, and suffer from human resources rules and administrative intensity—the latter if teacher quality is relatively high. Denominational schools are only affected by past performance; internal organization or internal management variables do not generally matter for schools in this context.

## Effects of Managerial Networking on Performance

Table 4.5 focuses on the internal organization and management portion of the public management model. Previous analyses (O'Toole et al. 2013) revealed the negative effect of a single networking factor. In the present analysis, we distinguish between local government, national government, and youth care networking (Torenvlied and Akkerman 2012). In addition, we include a squared term to check for a nonlinear effect (see Hicklin, O'Toole, and Meier 2008). Model 1 shows that none of the networking dimensions significantly affect school performance when all schools are included in the analysis. The same result holds for Model 4 when lagged performance is added to the model. A comparison with the estimates of Models 1 and 4 in table 4.4 shows that inclusion of the managerial networking variables does not alter the effects of internal organization and management variables on school performance.

The results again change considerably when the sample is split between nondenominational and denominational schools. For nondenominational schools (Model 2), principals' networking activity with local government has a positive and significant effect on the average Cito test scores of pupils. The effect is nonlinear; there is a significant decreasing marginal benefit from networking with the local government. This nonlinear effect of government networking holds in the presence of lagged performance (in Model 5) and for all specifications of control variables (not reported in table 4.5). The estimates of internal organization and management variables also remain the same, as a comparison with table 4.4 reveals. Figure 4.1 enables us to visually inspect the nonlinear effect of local government networking on school performance. The upper panel of figure 4.1 presents the plot of cases for local networking intensity versus average Cito test scores, as well as a quadratic line, fit with a 95 percent confidence interval, for nondenominational schools. Clearly, no effect is present. When we plot networking activity against the *residual* of average Cito test scores, controlling for the percentage of disadvantaged pupils (task difficulty), the nonlinear effect is clearly visible (see the lower panel of figure 4.1). Networking is associated with highest performance for a value of 2.5 (between monthly and weekly). Beyond this point, more intensive local government networking is associated with lower values of school performance.

Model 3, presented in table 4.5, shows whether managerial networking affects denominational schools. Here, principals' networking activity with youth care organizations has a positive and significant nonlinear effect on the average Cito test scores of pupils. There is a significant decreasing marginal benefit from networking with youth care organizations, which is robust, to the introduction of a control for lagged performance (Model 5). Figure 4.2

**Table 4.5** School Performance and Managerial Networking: Ordinary-Least-Squares Regression of 2010 Cito Scores, Split by Denominational Nature for Simple and Autoregressive Model

| | *Simple Model* | | | *Autoregressive Model* | | |
|---|---|---|---|---|---|---|
| *Variable* | *(1) All* | *(2) No* | *(3) Yes* | *(4) All* | *(5) No* | *(6) Yes* |
| *Lagged dependent variable* | | | | | | |
| Performance, 2009 | | | | 0.29*** | 0.16 | 0.34*** |
| *Managerial networking* | | | | | | |
| Local government | 1.25 | 4.11** | −1.68 | 1.29 | 4.11** | −1.41 |
| —squared | −0.22 | −0.83** | 0.45 | −0.26 | −0.85** | 0.35 |
| National government | −1.28 | 2.06 | −2.17 | −1.08 | 1.97 | −1.70 |
| —squared | 0.22 | −0.35 | 0.33 | 0.18 | −0.35 | 0.25 |
| Youth care | 1.61 | −2.11 | 4.42** | 1.65 | −2.20 | 3.53** |
| —squared | −0.34 | 0.31 | −0.84** | −0.31 | 0.34 | −0.62** |
| *Internal organization* | | | | | | |
| Managerial stability | 0.01 | 0.12** | −0.01 | 0.01 | 0.11** | −0.00 |
| Administrative intensity | 0.03 | 0.01 | 0.04 | 0.02 | 0.02 | 0.03 |
| *Internal management* | | | | | | |
| Team involvement | −0.01 | 0.17 | 0.14 | −0.04 | 0.14 | 0.12 |
| Human resources rules | −0.58** | −1.09** | −0.36* | −0.44** | −0.96* | −0.25 |
| Human capital quality | 0.01 | −0.15 | 0.05 | −0.09 | −0.21 | −0.07 |
| *Interaction terms* | | | | | | |
| Involvement x intensity | 0.07** | 0.06 | 0.06 | 0.06** | 0.04 | 0.05 |
| Human capital x intensity | −0.00 | −0.02** | 0.00 | −0.00 | −0.02** | 0.00 |
| Constant | 542.48*** | 550.41*** | 540.41*** | 388.13*** | 464.45*** | 361.13*** |
| $R^2$ | 0.37 | 0.46 | 0.35 | 0.42 | 0.47 | 0.45 |
| *N* | 430 | 139 | 291 | 430 | 139 | 291 |

*Note:* Two-tailed $^{*}p < .10$; $^{**}p < .05$; $^{***}p < .01$. Computed on the basis of robust standard errors clustered in school boards. All analyses control for principal's gender, age, hours spent in job, number of pupils, number of teachers, number of teacher assistants, percentage female teachers, average age personnel, and percentage disadvantaged pupils.

shows the nonlinear effect of youth care networking on school performance for denominational schools. The upper panel of figure 4.2 presents the plot of cases for youth care networking intensity versus average Cito test scores, as well as a quadratic line fit with the 95 percent confidence interval—for non-denominational schools. Clearly, a nonlinear effect is present, which remains if we plot networking activity against the *residual* of average Cito test scores, controlling for the percentage of disadvantaged pupils (the lower panel of figure 4.2). Networking, again, is associated with the highest performance

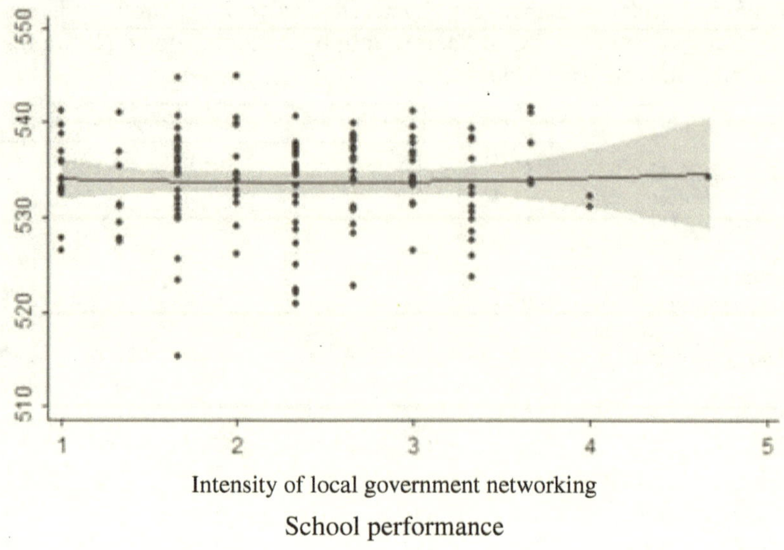


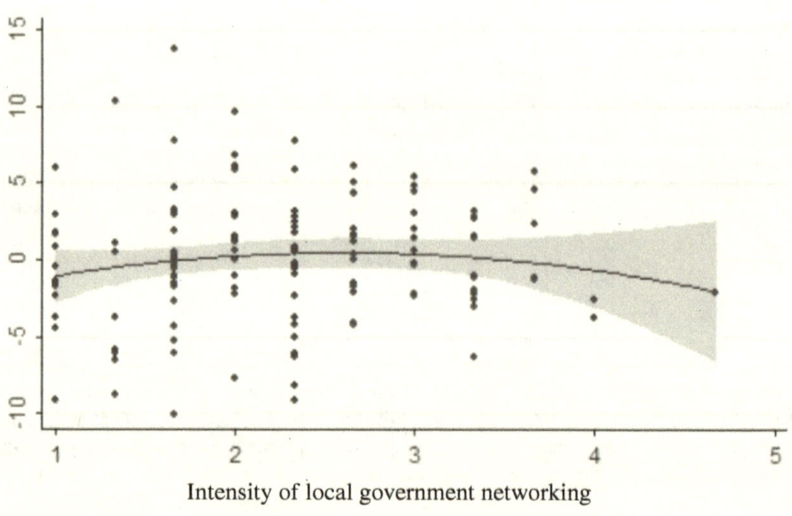


**Figure 4.1** Connecting Local Government Networking to School Performance and Residual School Performance

*Note:* Residual school performance controls for the percentage of disadvantaged pupils.

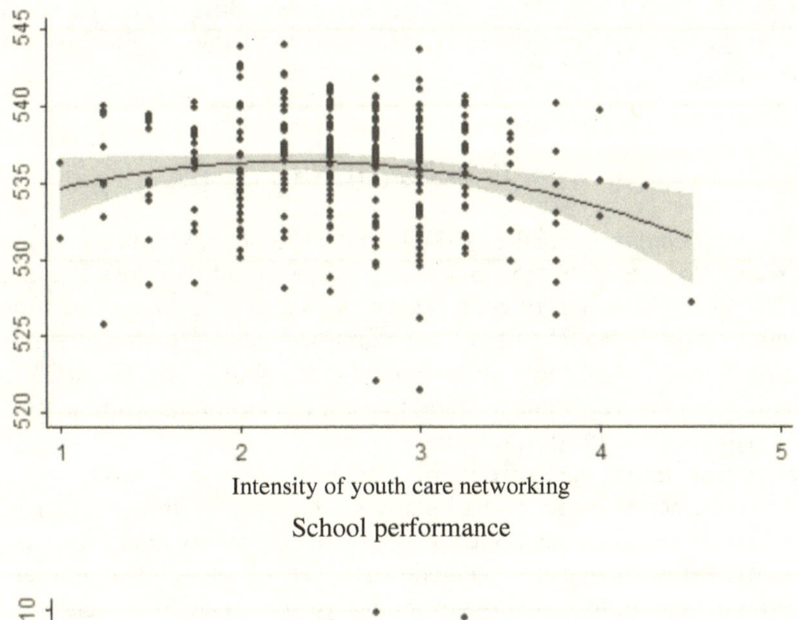


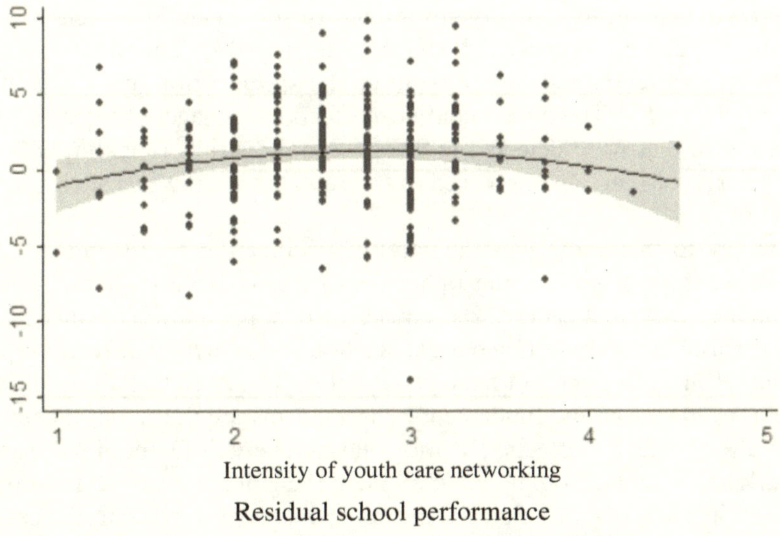


**Figure 4.2** Connecting the Intensity of Youth Care Networking to School Performance and Residual School Performance

*Note:* Residual school performance controls for the percentage of disadvantaged pupils.

for a value of 2.5 (between monthly and weekly). Beyond this point, more intensive youth care networking is associated with lower values of school performance.

## IMPLICATIONS

In the novel *Glamorama* (Ellis 1998) the main character, Victor, finds himself lost in a world of fashion models—losing all control of time, place, and context. Dropping the names of celebrities turns out to be a superficial survival strategy in fashion model culture, and Victor's challenge is to seek a deeper meaning for his inexplicable observations. In academics, we are like Victor, as we search for a deeper understanding of our models of the world in the face of contradictory and inexplicable observations.

Despite an initial lack of empirical support, we found strong evidence for the fundamental mechanisms linking management with performance, as postulated by the O'Toole–Meier model of public management. In a previous study, we replicated the interaction effect between external shocks and managerial networking on organizational performance in Dutch primary education (Bekerom, Torenvlied, and Akkerman 2014). The present chapter reports on a different test, which required the specification of a moderating, contextual variable. The direct, nonlinear effects of managerial networking on performance that were detected in Texas school districts (Hicklin, O'Toole, and Meier 2008) are also observed in the research setting of Dutch primary education.

The key to this study was the careful specification of institutional context *within* the research setting rather than parametrizing the entire context of Dutch primary education. The choice of denomination as a moderating context variable was based on our expectation that critically different aspects of internal management and managerial networking were important in each context, even though the fundamental mechanisms are the same. Indeed, we observe the predicted effects, albeit on substantively different dimensions of networking for nondenominational and denominational schools. For nondenominational schools, principals' contacts with local governments are crucial; this likely stems from their public orientation and their obligation to accept all registered pupils in the municipality. Principals of denominational schools who focus more on youth care professionals perform better. On the basis of the comparative public management framework, the introduction to this book predicted that complexity (hypothesis 5) and turbulence (hypothesis 9) would reinforce the relationship between managerial networking and performance. This is exactly what we observe, for both nondenominational schools and denominational schools, although the dimensions of complexity and turbulence are different. The comparative public management framework predicts that nondenominational schools, with more turbulent and complex environments, will perform worse than denominational schools. Interestingly, we observe the opposite in this setting.

The empirical test of this public management model in a Dutch setting provides strong support for the general model of public management. On the basis of this study, we need not reconsider the fundamental mechanisms of public management and performance. Thus, the present study further bolsters the model of public management by testing it in a European research setting and at a level of management below the top management level to which it has been applied in previous studies (Nicholson-Crotty and O'Toole 2004; O'Toole and Meier 2011).

The present study also has its limitations. The most important limitation is that the study is confined to a cross section of data. Thus, the present study is comparable to the earlier studies of the Texas school districts. The autoregressive model specifications deal with these issues only to some extent. Additional surveys will provide new and exciting data that will enable us to specify longitudinal models of management and organizational performance.

Additional careful replications of this model of public management in other contexts are still needed. Holding the education sector constant allows us to study the effects of variation between countries or between sectors within education. Holding the country constant allows us to study the effects of variation between sectors within countries in the study of management and performance. These replications will require a great deal of attention to measurement and conceptualization issues. The present study shows how important it is to distinguish between different substantive dimensions of managerial networking, as these dimensions have mattered differently in different contexts. Finally, we should devote more attention to the theoretical underpinning of contextual effects within the framework of comparative public management. Here, a promising avenue for research builds on the work of Pawson and Tilley (1997), who developed a heuristic for realistic evaluation, probing into the specific mechanisms that are triggered in specific contexts. By following their heuristic, we will be able to better understand why some managerial strategies work well in one context but fail in another.

## NOTES

1. The crucial distinction between denominational and nondenominational is the school identity. School identity is not the same as an adopted educational philosophy such as Montessori or Jenaplan. Hence, mixed categories exist combining

a specific identity with a specific educational philosophy. For example, there are nondenominational, Catholic, and Protestant schools with a Montessori or Jenaplan educational philosophy. Waldorf schools have their own identity and the discretion to accept pupils on the basis of their identity.

2. In other publications (Torenvlied and Akkerman 2012), we refer to these as child protective organizations, because they work at the intersection of child protection and youth care.
3. In the introduction, O'Toole and Meier propose the inclusion of a contextual term, C, which interacts with all the parameters and terms in the estimation model, radically expanding the range of potential model predictions. This context variable is assumed to cover three dimensions: political, environmental, and internal.
4. More precisely, the student's percentile score is used rather than the Cito test score to take into account cohort and year effects. Two other performance indicators used by the inspectorate are derived from the Cito test scores—the percentage of correct answers to the language and arithmetic questions, respectively. These two derived indicators are highly correlated with the Cito test scores ($\rho$ = 0.87 and 0.88 respectively; $n$ = 817) and generally capture the same construct. Rich assessment data from inspector reports are not available annually, except for underperforming schools.
5. The system of referral has changed as of 2014. The Cito test scores are now mandatory for all schools, to monitor school performance, but the tests are taken too late to be used for referral, which now relies on pupil progress and school career more than the final test.
6. Out of 1,284 primary schools in the data set, 726 principals gave permission to use their Cito test scores (57 percent). This is almost exactly the percentage one expects when we have a consent rate of 75 percent out of the 75 percent of schools using the Cito test scores. We tested whether the permission produced any response biases. Indeed, $t$-tests show that principals of larger schools and principals assigning their team a higher grade were significantly more likely to give permission to use their Cito test scores. Schools with permission and without permission, however, do not differ significantly on the evaluation of school results by the Dutch inspectorate of education. Because the inspectorate's evaluation is an alternative (though rough) indicator for school performance, the response in permission is not likely to be strongly driven by school performance.
7. O'Toole and Meier (2011, 154) also included an item "I am quite likely to recommend a subordinate for a superintendent position in another district." This item has a relatively low factor loading compared with the other items.
8. This assumption is strong, because interaction frequency does not fully capture the richness of network ties that may exist between organizations, nor does the interaction frequency provide information about who initiated the contact. The Texas school data reveal, however, that taking the initiative in networking and managerial networking activity are highly correlated variables (Goerdel 2006).
9. The percentage of disadvantaged students is based on pupil weights. Students are assigned specific weights if both parents have only attended elementary school

(0.25); they live in a foster home (0.4); both parents work in a circus or fair (0.7); one or both parents live at a trailer park (0.7); they have a non-Dutch cultural background; if the father or mother (care taker) has finished a lower professional education at most; or if the highest-earning parent is employed in a profession in which he or she does physical or hand labor, or is unemployed (0.9 if one of these conditions is satisfied).

10. The lagged variable taps stability in school performance over time. A post hoc explanation for the result is that there is more stability in the performance of nondenominational schools than in the performance of denominational schools. The data show that changes in test scores between 2009 and 2010 are on average 0.16 (standard deviation = 4.66) for nondenominational schools and 0.55 (standard deviation =3.73) for denominational schools.

# 5

# Loyal Agents or Saboteurs?

## *Performance-Increasing Policies and Public Service Motivation among Hospital Workers in Denmark*

MADS LETH JAKOBSEN, ANNE METTE KJELDSEN,
AND THOMAS PALLESEN

Achieving performance increases in public organizations is a challenging task (O'Toole and Meier 2015; Wilson 1989). Using the comparative public management framework set out by O'Toole and Meier in the introduction to this book, it is possible to distinguish between the management challenges in improving performance that arise from the internal and external environmental factors in which an organization is situated. Regarding the challenges from the external context, organizations often struggle to meet the demands of several stakeholders, including multiple political principals, partner organizations, and the public they are intended to serve (Rainey 2009). Understanding an organization's external context is, therefore, one of a public manager's primary tasks. The external context may be complex, turbulent, and difficult to handle, but skillfully navigating the environment is a path to gaining increased political support and the additional resources needed to achieve an organization's goals (Meier and O'Toole 2008).

Other challenges stem from the internal context of organizations. Increasing performance is a key goal for any public organization, but it is not always the most important metric of success for its employees (Johansen and Zhu 2014). This relates to the employment structure in public organizations. The vast majority of public-sector employees are often (semi)professionals, such as doctors, nurses, or teachers, occupational groups that possibly pose a challenge when attempting to increase performance because they tend to have altruistic values and ideas about policy goals and implementation that may conflict with the goals and policies intended to increase performance. As such, public-sector personnel are generally considered to be motivated by public service values; this is generally termed public service motivation (PSM). In this chapter, we use the comparative public management framework to scrutinize the possible managerial challenge of increasing performance in a public organization, where the internal context is characterized by different policy goals relating to performance and predominantly (semi)professional employees motivated by delivering public service. Thus, in terms of the comparative public management framework, we are effectively studying the impact of different policy goals (policies aimed at increasing performance) in one interesting context (Denmark).

The PSM literature has focused on the positive consequences of PSM for organizational and individual performance, employee job satisfaction, and commitment (Perry and Hondeghem 2008; Perry, Hondeghem, and Wise 2010). Agency problems—where public service providers shirk or commit sabotage—should be limited if employees are motivated to help others and contribute to society (Gailmard 2010; Le Grand 2010; Moynihan 2010). But while PSM is likely to curb shirking, it is a priori more difficult to make sense of why it should always curtail sabotage. High-PSM employees are energized by altruistic values and motives that can easily conflict with the organization's current policies and practices. For instance, performance policies aimed at containing costs and curbing the service levels desired by high-need clients are likely to run against such values, thereby limiting the opportunities available to employees to do good for others and society. In such a case, high-PSM employees could easily become highly motivated saboteurs of such change policies.

Specifically, this chapter examines the relationship between PSM and employee support for performance policies in public organizations—a topic that has received only limited attention in the PSM literature (Wright, Christensen, and Isett 2013, 738). The existing research also produces a mixed picture. Some studies find a positive relationship between PSM and employee support for strategic service-oriented change policies directed at performance development. This relationship, however, appears to disappear for short-term austerity reforms involving savings, layoffs, and mergers (Lee, Cayer, and Lan 2006; Naff and Crum 1999; Paarlberg and Lavigna 2010; Paarlberg 2007; Wright, Christensen, and Isett 2013). In this chapter, we therefore distinguish between two types of performance policies (i.e., two different policy goals) as varying internal characteristics of the management context: (1) an austerity-reform policy involving savings, layoffs, and mergers; and (2) a strategic service-oriented policy. This leads to the following research questions: (1) Does higher PSM lead to higher support for a public organization's performance policies? (2) Does the relationship between PSM and employee support for performance policies vary across different types of performance reforms?

The relationship between PSM and support for performance policies is vital for public managers seeking organizational change. Employee support, motivation, cooperation, and commitment are key requisites for the successful implementation of such policies. We argue that the impact of this support must, however, be considered jointly with employee power. Managers hope to work with supportive, loyal employees who will use their energy and power to advance the policy; and managers dread strong saboteurs who are nonsupportive, yet still motivated and efficacious. This may have even larger consequences if these potential saboteurs are actively taking part in the organization's management structure, such that they could potentially use their energy and position to work against the policy. Hence, the chapter's third research question: Is there a systematic relationship between PSM, employee self-efficacy, participation in leadership tasks, and support for performance policies that leads to either strong saboteurs or strong loyalists?

## THE THEORETICAL FRAMEWORK

Public service motivation is "an individual's orientation to delivering service to people with the purpose of doing good for others and society" (Hondeghem and Perry 2009, 6). Thus, PSM can be described as a pro-social form of motivation based on a desire to fulfill tasks by contributing to others and to society in general, which is a key component in the motivation of most employees working to provide public services (Kjeldsen and Andersen 2013). The most common conceptualization of PSM consists of four subdimensions that reflect how an employee is energized: serving the public interest, self-sacrifice, compassion, and an attraction to making public policy (Perry 1996; Vandenabeele 2008).

Policies to change performance in times of austerity represent key challenges for public managers, who simultaneously face pressures to improve organizational performance and to cope with economic crises. More specifically, the promotion of performance management as a key element in public management has generated attention concerning the need for public organizations to strategically develop their service production (Moynihan 2008), while economic crises have often produced austerity change policies that make curbing public spending a key political priority (Lodge and Hood 2012).

We distinguish between two types of performance policies as varying the internal management characteristics of an organization: strategic service-oriented change policies, and austerity reform policies. Strategic service-oriented change policies can be defined as "the broad way in which an organization seeks to maintain or improve its performance" (Boyne and Walker 2004). Such change policies are directed at the performance of an organization and can be pursued through strategies such as prospecting, defending, and reacting. For organizations producing public services, such strategies would often be congruent with the values of high-PSM employees. Austerity reform policies contrast with service-oriented changes as they prioritize cost reductions and savings. More specifically, they include cost-cutting measures such as layoffs, budget reductions, and the merger of units, including the physical relocation of employees (Wright, Christensen, and Isett 2013, 741). Such reforms may conflict with the values of high-PSM employees who seek to continue to provide services to meet the needs of others to the highest degree.

## PSM AND SUPPORT FOR PERFORMANCE-INCREASING POLICIES

The preferences of public-sector employees are at least two-dimensional. They have preferences related to effort—that is, to shirk or work—and to how the policy goals are implemented—that is, to sabotage or be loyal (Brehm and Gates 1997). Managers face the complex task of motivating employees to work in a manner that is loyal to the goals of the organization.

The PSM literature generally views the PSM–employee behavior relationship (i.e., shirking or working) in a positive light; in general, scholars expect a positive relationship to exist between PSM and both individual and organizational performance (Brewer 2008, 137; Steen and Rutgers 2011, 344). PSM should, for instance, solve moral hazard problems. If work is directed at doing good for others and society, PSM should reduce shirking and sabotage by motivating employees and rendering them supportive of the policy (Gailmard 2010, 40). If the management uses high-powered incentive systems, PSM also mitigates the risk of opportunistic behavior, such as gaming and creaming (Moynihan 2010, 29). A similar positive view also exists when considering organizational change policies. In relation to the Reinventing Government movement, Moynihan and Pandey (2007) found a positive relationship between employee PSM and a reformist orientation focused on empowerment and the reduction of constraints on service production. Others have also found positive relationships between PSM and organizational commitment and perceptions of change (Naff and Crum 1999; Leisink and

Steijn 2009). Furthermore, Wright, Christensen, and Isett (2013) have found that high levels of self-sacrifice are positively related to support for austerity reforms; the authors report that employees with high levels of self-sacrifice see such reforms as opportunities to make sacrifices for the greater good.

There is, however, also a more negative view of the PSM–employee behavior relationship. Following Gailmard (2010, 40), public employees attracted to making public policy are inclined to try to shape organizational policies based on their own values. Research also shows that high-PSM employees sometimes work toward the goals that they consider desirable from a professional or personal standpoint, as opposed to the goals set by management (Andersen, Kristensen, and Pedersen 2013; Andersen and Serritzlew 2012; Kjeldsen 2012; Steen and Rutgers 2011). The positive relationship between PSM and whistle-blowing—a form of sabotage, from a managerial perspective—points in the same direction (Brewer and Selden 1998). Hence, if PSM is negatively related to the managers' policy intentions, it contributes to motives for sabotage (Maesschalck, Van der Wal, and Huberts 2008, 170; Steen and Rutgers 2011, 354–55).

In one of the few empirical studies on the relationship between PSM and employee support for performance-increasing policies, Wright, Christensen, and Isett (2013) find a weak relationship between PSM and employee support for austerity-like change policies. It does not fully corroborate the negative theories but provides a clear contrast to the positive connotation associated with PSM. The key issue seems to be what type of change policy is being implemented. A central argument in the PSM literature is that PSM will be positively related to performance policies that improve public service delivery (Naff and Crum 1999; Moynihan and Pandey 2007; Wright, Christensen, and Isett 2013, 738). Wright, Christensen, and Isett (2013, 739), for instance, argue that "PSM increases commitment to change because it makes employees more supportive of the interests, values, or beneficiaries that these changes are intended to help advance." Employees evaluate and determine their support for performance-increasing policies based on whether the policy helps other individuals and society in general. Hence, only those change policies that support employees' respective conceptions of doing good will be supported; if the policies are not perceived to support a greater good, employees could be opposed to such change.

This argument is also supported by Yang and Kassekert (2010), who find that performance reforms targeted at service improvement are positively correlated with job satisfaction, while the outsourcing and removal of employee protections are negatively correlated with job satisfaction. Job satisfaction and PSM are highly correlated among public-sector employees (Bright 2008; Kjeldsen and Andersen 2013; Naff and Crum 1999). Likewise, the relationship between PSM and performance policies is expected to differ, depending on whether the policies enhance or constrain the employees' ability to do good for others and society. It is reasonable to assume that for employees in vocations providing welfare services, performance austerity policies will generally be perceived as conflicting more with PSM values than policies aimed at improving service performance. We thus propose that whether PSM plays a positive role in managing the implementation of performance policies depends on the internal management context of the public organization vis-à-vis the policy's goal. More specifically, we expect (H1) a positive effect of PSM on support for service-oriented performance-increasing policies; and (H2) either no effect or a negative effect of PSM on support for performance-increasing austerity policies.

## THE MANAGEMENT PERSPECTIVE: TYPES OF EMPLOYEES

Fernandez and Rainey (2006) identify six key factors behind successful organizational change policies in public organizations: ensure the need, provide a plan, build internal backing, provide resources, institutionalize change, and pursue comprehensive change. Employee perceptions and support are central for at least three of these factors: ensuring a need for change, the building of internal organizational backing, and the institutionalization of the change policy in everyday organizational practices (Fernandez and Rainey 2006, 69–72). The importance of employee support for the outcome of organizational change policies is also widely recognized in the literature (Bordia et al. 2004; Isett, Morrissey, and Topping 2006; Kelman 2005; Isett et al. 2013). For a leader trying to implement a policy involving organizational change, it is paramount to know which employee types are present in the organization. The key question is whether employees support or oppose the new policy, but the importance of attitude depends on the employees' capacity and position to change the course of events. Hence, the manager must consider whether the supporters have the capacity and position to affect the policy implementation or whether those who oppose the policy will have a significant influence on change.

We define capacity as internal political self-efficacy, or the "beliefs about one's own competence to understand, and to participate effectively in politics" (Niemi, Craig, and Mattei 1991, 1407).[1] Such self-efficacy increases the persistence and effort of the individual employee to overcome any challenges they are facing (Bandura 1986; Earley and Lituchy 1991). This concept can be used to evaluate an employee's capacity to influence the implementation of performance policies. Hence, if employees are highly motivated and support performance policies, they are more likely to work to achieve the policy goals and have a higher level of internal political efficacy.

From a managerial perspective, the best employees are very strong loyalists who support the performance policy, have high levels of PSM, and have the capacity to implement the policy effectively. Conversely, the worst employees are very strong saboteurs who are not supportive of the policy regarding organizational change and are highly motivated to hinder the implementation of the policy. Between these two extremes exist a number of mixed types, as displayed in table 5.1. For instance, an organization may have strong saboteurs (or loyalists) who disagree (agree) with the reform goal and have high political efficacy; but due to their limited role in the management of the organization, they have lower levels of impact compared with employees with stronger leadership participation. Others may be saboteurs who do not support the reform but who have little to no influence due to low levels of political efficacy and little or no participation in management. Finally, the organization can also include weak loyalists who support the performance policy but are not strong agents for policy change in the organization due to their low level of PSM and internal political efficacy and little or no leadership experience.

On the basis of the expectation that PSM increases support for strategic service-oriented policies but not for austerity policies, we expect a configuration of employee types that is more preferable by the manager in relation to a strategic service-oriented change policy than in relation to an austerity reform policy. Employees with high levels of PSM should, on average, be less supportive of performance austerity reforms than strategic service-oriented change policies, because the former conflict more with their opportunity to do good for others and society than the latter. Still, there can be many high-PSM employees who are nonsupportive of the strategic service-oriented change policy. If they have high efficacy and participate in the organization's management, they would be very strong saboteurs. We expect these employee types to be more frequent in relation to austerity change policies than strategic service-oriented change policies.

The likelihood that employee capacity will have an observable effect on the implementation of performance reforms is, however, also likely to depend upon the employees' organizational positions. Insights from organizational psychology show that the ability to distribute leadership effectively among employees is an important prerequisite for achieving organizational reforms, such as performance policies; and, conversely, that successful organizational reform policies depend on the support of employees who participate in the organization's leadership (Harris 2008; Wegge et al. 2010). Participation in managerial tasks is correlated but not entirely congruent with formal

**Table 5.1** Distinguishing Different Types of Agents

| | | *Change policy support high* | | *Change policy support low* | |
|---|---|---|---|---|---|
| | | *PSM high* | *PSM low* | *PSM high* | *PSM low* |
| *IPE high* | *DL high* | Very strong loyalists | | Very strong saboteurs | |
| | *DL low* | Strong loyalists | | Strong saboteurs | |
| *IPE low* | *DL high* | | Weak loyalists | | Weak saboteurs |
| | *DL low* | | Very weak loyalists | | Very weak saboteurs |

management positions in the organization. There is an overlap between the two types of leadership, but "distributed leadership" is a broader concept because it includes the de facto managerial functions that many formally rank-and-file employees perform on a day-to-day basis—functions that are essential for a successful reform outcome.

## THE CONTEXT OF DANISH HOSPITALS

To examine the configuration of different types of employees in relation to a varying internal management context characterized by the different types of performance-increasing policies, we use a case from Danish hospitals. Applying the comparative public management framework (see the introduction to this book) to this case, table 5.2 shows that, in terms of the external political context, Danish public hospitals are publicly owned, funded, and governed by democratically elected boards in five regions. The main task of these regional boards is specialized health care service delivery. In solving this task, the boards engage in corporatist decision-making processes with the formal involvement of different external stakeholders, such as patient associations and unions. In the present study, these characteristics are treated as constants, along with the characteristics of the larger environmental context of Danish public hospitals. Internally, hospital services are hierarchically organized; personnel such as doctors, nurses, radiologists, and others have a high degree of discretion in performing daily health care routines and tasks but ultimately report to the regional board.

In this study, we examine the efforts to change performance at the Hospitalsenhed Midt (Hospital of Central Jutland), which has recently been subjected

**Table 5.2** The Management Context of the Danish Hospital Sector

| *Context Variable* | *The Danish Hospital Context* |
|---|---|
| *Political context—Concentration of Power* | |
| Separation of powers | Unitary system with parliamentary rule |
| Federalism | Multiple levels—hospitals governed by democratically elected regional boards but financed by central government taxes and funds |
| Process | Corporatist decision-making processes with formal involvement of unions and patients associations |
| Performance appraisal | Established appraisal system across all public-sector organizations |
| *Environmental Context* | |
| Complexity | Simple context with few, powerful actors that are engaged in the corporatist decision-making processes |
| Turbulence | Moderately turbulent due to unforeseen patient flows and treatment development |
| Munificence | Highly munificent environment |
| Social capital | High level of social capital present |
| Development | Stable, developed context |
| *Internal Context* | |
| Goals | Multiple and conflicting goals (e.g., patient satisfaction vs. paternalistic approach, or budget keeping vs. best and rapid treatments) |
| Centralization | Hospitals are formally hierarchically organized, but discretion lies with the health professionals |
| Professionalization | High degrees of professionalization |

to two performance-increasing policies—an austerity reform, including mergers and savings; and a strategic service-oriented reform policy for the new hospital unit. These two policies are the central characteristics of varying policy contexts for managing to improve performance that will be subject to empirical investigation in relation to PSM, self-efficacy, and participation in leadership tasks among the hospital staff.

## The Austerity Reform

The recent global financial crisis had a major impact on the Region of Central Denmark and its largest regional hospital, Hospitalsenhed Midt. In the fall of 2010, the politically elected regional board predicted a major financial shortfall and instructed its senior administrative team to develop a savings plan to reduce the region's health care budget by DKK 200 million in 2011 and a total reduction of DKK 500 million between 2012 and 2014 (in total, approximately $120 million) (Region Midtjylland 2011). On top of spending cuts already scheduled for 2011, the plan aimed to cut regional health care spending by 10 percent, primarily by amalgamating two hospitals and centralizing several medical specialties with a number of medical, administrative, and technical support functions in fewer locations.

After the plan was announced, there was a one-month interim period that included public hearings. The regional board received more than 100 written responses to the plan from, among others, the affected hospitals, medical boards, local governments, and employee organizations and unions. The central messages repeated in many of these responses were deep concern or outright rejection of the proposed centralization of hospitals and medical specialties and strong criticism of the plan's consequences for employees, patients, and localities. Nevertheless, the regional board decided to proceed with the main blueprint of the administrative plan; the hospitals were merged, and the mergers of medical specialties and support functions were set in motion within two months. Thousands of employees were replaced or laid off in the process.

In essence, the reform was a modern, austerity type of performance reform, initiated by top-down decision making and characterized by substantial spending cuts aimed at increasing productivity. Even though the reform intended to cut spending without reducing the quality of care, the negative responses of the affected hospitals, medical boards, and hospital employees (and their unions) suggest that the content of the reform not only affected employee and local interests in a narrow sense but also seriously jeopardized how the employees perceived their respective abilities to do good for others and society. As such, the reform is likely to conflict with PSM values—and especially to provoke resistance or a lack of acceptance from the employees holding these attitudes.

### The Service-Oriented Reform

After the merger, the Hospitalsenhed Midt's senior management team launched a service-oriented performance strategy for the hospital, prioritizing the delivery of high-quality specialized services to patients. The paramount goal of this reform was for the hospital to be patients' preferred health care provider (Region Midtjylland 2011).

The hospital aimed to reach these goals based on values of timeliness, assertiveness, and confident dialogues and professional development. It emphasized a coherent and optimal flow of patients, patients' involvement and empowerment, an effective and attractive workplace, efficient management, high productivity within the budget, and strong professional communities. In 2013 the hospital's management team, in collaboration with the managers of multiple clinical departments and centers, decided to emphasize the hospital's focus on strong professional communities and organizational and management development in conjunction with the establishment of a new center for acute care within the hospital.

This strategic service-oriented, performance-increasing plan emphasized specialized, high-quality health care services focusing on patients' needs and interests. In contrast to the austerity plan, we argue that this type of strategic service-oriented plan is more aligned with PSM values and less likely to provoke resistance or a lack of acceptance from employees holding such attitudes.

## DATA AND MEASURES

The data for this study come from a survey distributed to all Hospitalsenhed Midt employees in October 2012 ($n$ = 4,575). The survey was distributed in three different ways: by e-mail to those hospital staff members who have regular access to e-mail during working hours, by personal password on the survey webpage for those staff members with no regular access to e-mail during working hours, and in paper form for those staff members with no work e-mail account (e.g., support staff and cleaning personnel). In total, we received 2,217 responses, corresponding to a 48.5 percent response rate. After reviewing the data and deleting incomplete answers and duplicates, we arrived at a valid and effective sample of 1,263 respondents. An overview of the sample can be seen in table 5.3.

We measure support for the performance policies through employees' subjective evaluation of reform goal support. Support for the austerity reform policy is measured using four questions, with Likert Scale responses (ranging from 5 = "strongly agree" to 1 = "strongly disagree"). We asked about general attitudes toward the reform (e.g., "The merger has important advantages"), and to what extent respondents view the reform as the right and necessary step for the hospital management to take, given the hospital's current situation. If an employee has a positive perception of the reform and views it as an appropriate and necessary means for tackling the current situation, we take this as an indicator of policy support. An exploratory factor analysis showed that a valid, one-dimensional scale could be formed, with a Cronbach's alpha

**Table 5.3** An Overview of the Study Sample

| *N = 1,263*<br>*Variable* | *N* | *Percent* |
|---|---|---|
| **Gender** | | |
| Male | 154 | 12.2 |
| Female | 1,109 | 87.8 |
| **Age (years)** | | |
| Mean | 44.42 | |
| Standard deviation | 10.15 | |
| **Organizational tenure (years)** | | |
| Mean | 7.58 | |
| Standard deviation | 7.55 | |
| **Affected by the merger (changed hospital)** | | |
| Yes | 167 | 13.2 |
| No | 1,096 | 86.8 |
| **Occupational group** | | |
| Nurse | 498 | 39.4 |
| Service / cleaning / assistant staff | 59 | 4.7 |
| Social and health care / nursing assistant | 76 | 6.0 |
| Medical secretary | 134 | 10.6 |
| Kitchen staff | 15 | 1.2 |
| Hospital porter | 16 | 1.3 |
| Radiographer | 10 | 0.8 |
| Young physician | 56 | 4.4 |
| Chief physician | 71 | 5.6 |
| Bioanalyst | 82 | 6.5 |
| Physiotherapist | 78 | 6.1 |
| Occupational therapist | 43 | 3.4 |
| Administrative staff | 66 | 5.2 |
| Technical staff | 20 | 1.6 |
| Midwife | 28 | 2.2 |
| Other functionary | 11 | 0.8 |

reliability measure of $\alpha = 0.856$. This measure was then rescaled to range from 0 to 100, where 100 represents the highest possible level of perceived policy support. Descriptive statistics and definitions for all the measures used in the study can be found in tables 5.4 and 5.5.

Support for the strategic service-oriented performance policy was measured using a scale previously tested by Bohn (2010). It consists of three 5-point Likert Scale items (e.g., "I would be surprised if Hospitalsenhed Midt exists in its current form in five years") that were originally developed to measure the resilience dimension of perceptions of organizational efficacy.

**Table 5.4** Descriptive Statistics and Pairwise Correlations

| | *N = 1,263* | *Mean* | *Standard Deviation* | *Minimum* | *Maximum* | *1* | *2* | *3* | *4* | *5* | *6* | *7* |
|---|---|---|---|---|---|---|---|---|---|---|---|---|
| 1 | Support—austerity | 47.04 | 16.63 | 0 | 100 | 1,000* | | | | | | |
| 2 | Support–strategic | 67.35 | 19.82 | 0 | 100 | 0.179* | 1,000* | | | | | |
| 3 | PSM | 70.83 | 15.33 | 0 | 100 | 0.028* | 0.109* | 1,000* | | | | |
| 4 | Internal political efficacy | 37.91 | 22.09 | 0 | 100 | 0.027* | –0.130* | 0.136* | 1,000* | | | |
| 5 | Gender (male = 1) | 0.12 | 0.33 | 0 | 1 | 0.037* | –0.033* | 0.049* | 0.217* | 1,000* | | |
| 6 | Age | 44.42 | 10.15 | 20 | 69 | –0.091* | –0.019* | 0.155* | 0.069* | 0.052* | 1,000* | |
| 7 | Tenure (in years) | 7.58 | 7.55 | 0 | 40 | –0.066* | 0.031* | 0.060* | –0.020* | –0.037* | 0.474* | 1,000* |
| 8 | Merger (affected = 1) | 0.13 | 0.34 | 0 | 1 | 0.007* | –0.001* | –0.034* | 0.027* | 0.024* | –0.168* | –0.162* |

*Note:* * $p < 0.05$, correlations (Pearson's *r*).

**Table 5.5** The Survey's Operationalization of Core Concepts

| *Measure* | *Items* |
|---|---|
| Goal support—strategic (Source: Bohn 2010) | • Hospitalsenhed Midt has no hope of surviving a year or two<br>• I would be surprised if Hospitalsenhed Midt exists in its current form in five years<br>• Because Hospitalsenhed Midt is likely to fail, I would never recommend a friend to work here |
| Goal support—reform | • The merger has important advantages<br>• The merger was necessary<br>• Things could not continue the way they were<br>• The merger makes good sense in our situation |
| PSM (Sources: Andersen and Serritzlew 2012; Brewer and Selden 2000; Alonso and Lewis 2001) | • I am often reminded by daily events how dependent we are on one another<br>• Making a difference in society means more to me than personal achievements<br>• It motivates me to help improve public services<br>• I consider public service my civic duty<br>• I am prepared to make enormous sacrifices for the good of society |
| Internal political self-efficacy (Sources: Lassen and Serritzlew 2011; Niemi, Craig, and Mattei 1991) | • I consider myself to be well qualified to participate in the management of Hospitalsenhed Midt<br>• I feel that I have a pretty good understanding of the most important management issues concerning Hospitalsenhed Midt<br>• I feel that I could do as good a job in the hospital management as most other people |

In this study, resilience is used as an indicator of the goal alignment between principal and employee. If an employee is invested in the future of the current organization, then their sense of direction for the organization is aligned with the goals set by management (assuming that the manager is working hard to sustain the organization and sets out a sustainable course of action). A confirmatory factor analysis supported a valid and reliable scale, with a Cronbach's alpha measure of $\alpha = 0.769$, and the final scale ranging from 0 to 100 (100 again indicating the highest possible level of organizational change strategy support).

PSM was measured using a well-established short form of the Perry (1996) scale: the MPS96 measure (Alonso and Lewis 2001; Brewer and Selden 2000; Wright and Pandey 2008). It consists of five Likert-type items reflecting an employee's motivation to do good for others and society through public service delivery. A confirmatory factor analysis of the scale showed that item 1—"Meaningful public service is very important to me"—had to be dropped for the scale to fit our hospital sample data. Furthermore, one item was added to the scale—"It motivates me to help improve public services"—which was inspired by Kim and colleagues' (2013) scale to enable the PSM measure to better reflect the attraction to the aspect of the concept pertaining to making public policy. We have a 5-item scale ranging from 0 to 100, with 100 being the maximum level of PSM, with a Cronbach's alpha of $\alpha = 0.795$.

Political self-efficacy was operationalized using a well-established and previously validated measure in both international and Danish contexts (Lassen and Serritzlew 2011; Niemi, Craig, and Mattei 1991). Our measure of internal political self-efficacy has been adjusted to fit the context of this study, in the sense that we ask about the competence to understand and participate in the management of the hospital (instead of the larger political process in a country). After performing a confirmatory factor analysis, the final scale consists of three of the 5-point Likert Scale items proposed by Niemi, Craig, and Mattei (1991). Like the other scales, an additive index ranging from 0 to 100 was formed ($\alpha = 0.773$).

Finally, participation in hospital management (i.e., the variable Distributed Leadership) is measured using a 10-item Likert-type scale of self-reported engagement in various hospital management tasks (e.g., "Have you been involved in coordinating different functions in your department?" measured on a 5-point scale, where 5 = "very much"). The final measure of this variable was constructed as a reflective index, which was rescaled to range from 0 to 100 with a reliability of $\alpha = .92$. A factor analysis for the full measurement model, including all the scales described above, provides strong support that each measure represents a distinct latent variable, bolstering both convergent and discriminant validity of the model used here.[2]

We include a number of control variables that can affect both PSM and support for performance policies. First, employee gender (male = 1) and age are added to the model, because male and female employees of different ages may have different levels of PSM and varying levels support for the policies. Second, employees' tenure (years) captures the fact that people are likely to become more socialized over time to fit the values and goals of the organization (Cable and Parsons 2001; Cooper-Thomas, Van Vianen, and Anderson 2004; Kjeldsen 2012). Third, the extent to which the respondents were physically affected by the reform (i.e., they had to switch hospitals) may be linked to both the positive and negative consequences of their PSM and support. Finally, we include occupational groups (see table 5.3), because PSM and support could be related to professional norms and status.

## FINDINGS

It is important for managers pursuing a policy change to know which employee type(s) they may confront in their organization. Tables 5.6 and 5.7 show the distribution of employee types related to their support for, respectively, the austerity reform policy and the service-oriented policy.

In relation to the austerity reform policy, the distributions given in table 5.6 show that the share of potential saboteurs in Hospitalsenhed Midt is substantial. Nearly three-fourths of all employees do not support the reform, and two-thirds of employees are high-PSM individuals critical of the reform. This may have negative implications for the hospital manager and for the regional politicians who initiated the performance policy process. It indicates that high-PSM employees are not necessarily a benefit to an organization pursuing austerity reforms when in a difficult situation. Furthermore, taking into account the employees' political efficacy (their capacity to divert the hospital policies), the gray-shaded areas in table 5.6 indicate that there are more than twice as many potential saboteurs as loyalists. Narrowing down to the potentially very strong saboteurs (those who also participate in management tasks and who are, therefore, in a position to actually sabotage the reform), there are equal numbers of saboteurs and loyalists. Nevertheless, this does not substantively change the general picture of very low support for the austerity reform among high-PSM hospital staff. The difference in the proportions of

**Table 5.6** The Distribution of Hospital Staff in Support of an Austerity Reform Policy

<table>
<tr><td colspan="2" rowspan="2"></td><td colspan="2">Change Policy Support High</td><td colspan="2">Change Policy Support Low</td></tr>
<tr><td>PSM high</td><td>PSM low</td><td>PSM high</td><td>PSM low</td></tr>
<tr><td rowspan="2">IPE high</td><td>DL high</td><td>35<br>(2.8%)</td><td>3<br>(0.2%)</td><td>34<br>(2.7%)</td><td>0<br>(0.0%)</td></tr>
<tr><td>DL low</td><td>49<br>(3.9%)</td><td>5<br>(0.4%)</td><td>133<br>(10.5%)</td><td>1<br>(0.1%)</td></tr>
<tr><td rowspan="2">IPE low</td><td>DL high</td><td>35<br>(32.8%)</td><td>3<br>(0.2%)</td><td>86<br>(6.8%)</td><td>5<br>(0.4%)</td></tr>
<tr><td>DL low</td><td>219<br>(17.3%)</td><td>12<br>(21.0%)</td><td>592<br>(46.9%)</td><td>51<br>(4.0%)</td></tr>
<tr><td colspan="2">Total (N = 1,263/100%)</td><td>338<br>(26.8%)</td><td>23<br>(1.8%)</td><td>845<br>(66.9%)</td><td>57<br>(4.5%)</td></tr>
</table>

*Note:* The cutoff point for low versus high on the 0–100 scales for Reform Support, PSM, Internal Political Efficacy, and DL is 50. The difference in the proportions of very strong and strong loyalists and very strong and strong saboteurs is significant at $p < 0.01$ (the gray areas).

**Table 5.7** The Distribution of Hospital Staff in Support of a Service-Oriented Change Policy

| | | *Change Policy Support High* | | *Change Policy Support Low* | |
|---|---|---|---|---|---|
| | | *PSM high* | *PSM low* | *PSM high* | *PSM low* |
| ***IPE High*** | *DL high* | 51 (4.0%) | 2 (0.2%) | 18 (1.4%) | 1 (0.1%) |
| | *DL low* | 109 (8.6%) | 5 (0.4%) | 73 (5.8%) | 1 (0.1%) |
| ***IPE Low*** | *DL high* | 100 (7.9%) | 4 (0.3%) | 21 (1.7%) | 4 (0.3%) |
| | *DL low* | 601 (47.6%) | 46 (3.6%) | 210 (16.6%) | 17 (1.3%) |
| **Total (*N* = 1,263/100%)** | | **861 (68.2%)** | **57 (4.5%)** | **322 (25.5%)** | **23 (1.3%)** |

*Note:* The cutoff point for low versus high on the 0–100 scales for Reform Support, PSM, Internal Political Efficacy, and DL is 50. The difference in the proportions of very strong and strong loyalists and very strong and strong saboteurs is significant at $p < 0.01$ (the gray areas).

very strong loyalists and very strong saboteurs is significant at $p < 0.01$ (the gray areas).

Turning to table 5.7 and support for the strategic service-oriented performance policy, the distribution in the table indicates that, because the policy did not require any downsizing or restructuring, more members of the hospital staff are efficacious and loyal employees. For this policy change, the manager now faces almost twice as many strong loyalists as strong saboteurs. In contrast to the austerity reform, high-PSM employees are thus an asset for the hospital manager. High-PSM employees report higher support than low-PSM employees, regardless of whether they have high or low political efficacy and are more or less in a position to do something about it.

Table 5.8 shows a number of ordinary-least-squares regressions examining employee support for the austerity reform policy and the strategic service-oriented policy. The expectation that PSM affects support and that it varies between different types of policies are tested in Models 1 and 5. Considering the causal nature of this relationship, relevant control variables are included. Models 2–4 and 6–8 further examine the relationships between support, PSM, internal political efficacy, and employees' degree of participation in management tasks (distributed leadership). This is relevant from the perspective of a manager who wants to know what type of employees they are confronted with in the aggregate; no control variables are included in these models.

**Table 5.8** Determinants of Supportiveness for Organizational Change Policies

| | *Austerity Reform Support* | | | | *Strategic Policy Support* | | | |
|---|---|---|---|---|---|---|---|---|
| | *Model 1* | *Model 2* | *Model 3* | *Model 4* | *Model 5* | *Model 6* | *Model 7* | *Model 8* |
| *Variable* | *Explanatory Perspective* | *Manager Perspective* | | | *Explanatory Perspective* | *Manager Perspective* | | |
| PSM | 0.025 | 0.009 | –0.01 | –0.0372 | 0.147*** | 0.155*** | –0.013 | –0.003 |
| | (0.031) | (0.031) | (0.065) | (0.095) | (0.037) | (0.036) | (0.075) | (0.110) |
| Political efficacy | | 0.014 | –0.122 | –0.174 | | –0.150*** | –0.372** | –0.353 |
| | | (0.022) | (0.105) | (0.170) | | (0.026) | (0.122) | (0.197) |
| DL | | 0.038 | 0.042 | –0.035 | | 0.058* | –0.062 | –0.034 |
| | | (0.023) | (0.111) | (0.226) | | (0.026) | (0.129) | (0.261) |
| PSM × political efficacy | | | 0.001 | 0.002 | | | 0.003* | 0.003 |
| | | | (0.001) | (0.002) | | | (0.002) | (0.003) |
| PSM × DL | | | –0.001 | 0.0001 | | | 0.002 | 0.002 |
| | | | (0.002) | (0.003) | | | (0.002) | (0.004) |
| DL × political efficacy | | | 0.002 | 0.003 | | | –0.0004 | –0.001 |
| | | | (0.001) | (0.005) | | | (0.001) | (0.006) |
| PSM × political efficacy × DL | | | | –0.00003) | | | | 0.00001 |
| | | | | (0.0001) | | | | (0.0001) |
| Gender | 1.562 | | | | 2.602 | | | |
| | (1.866) | | | | (2.219) | | | |
| Age | –0.188*** | | | | –0.113 | | | |
| | (0.056) | | | | (0.067) | | | |

**Table 5.8** *(continued)*

| | *Austerity Reform Support* | | | | *Strategic Policy Support* | | | |
|---|---|---|---|---|---|---|---|---|
| | *Model 1* | *Model 2* | *Model 3* | *Model 4* | *Model 5* | *Model 6* | *Model 7* | *Model 8* |
| *Variable* | *Explanatory Perspective* | *Manager Perspective* | | | *Explanatory Perspective* | *Manager Perspective* | | |
| Tenure (in years) | 0.023 | | | | 0.092 | | | |
| | (0.074) | | | | (0.088) | | | |
| Merger | −1.812 | | | | −0.687 | | | |
| | (1.406) | | | | (1.672) | | | |
| Occupation dummies | – | | | | – | | | |
| Intercept | 62.37*** | 44.70*** | 47.76*** | 49.71*** | 72.22*** | 60.50*** | 72.02*** | 71.31*** |
| | (6.002) | (2.291) | (4.662) | (6.813) | (7.136) | (2.655) | (5.397) | (7.888) |
| $N$ | 1,263 | 1,263 | 1,263 | 1,263 | 1,263 | 1,263 | 1,263 | 1,263 |
| $R^2$ | 0.048 | 0.003 | 0.006 | 0.006 | 0.033 | 0.038 | 0.043 | 0.043 |

*Note:* $^{*}p < 0.05$, $^{**}p < 0.01$, $^{***}p < 0.001$. The results in models 2–4 and 6–8 are robust with controls for gender, age, tenure, occupation, affected by the merger, and hospital ward. cf. tables A and B in the appendix.

Model 1 indicates that there is no significant relationship between PSM and the support for the austerity reform. PSM is thus not a good predictor of employee attitudes toward this type of policy. Instead, older hospital staff and those most affected by the reform appear to be the most critical. Conversely, Model 5 shows a significant, positive impact of PSM concerning the support for the strategic service-oriented performance policy of Hospitalsenhed Midt. PSM thus explains some of the variation in support for the strategic service-oriented reform policy (though the overall model explains very little), which is in line with our expectations. Furthermore, the different effects of PSM in the two models also fit the expectation that PSM would have a more positive effect on support for strategic service-oriented performance policies than for austerity reforms.

From a managerial perspective, the possible systematic relationship between support, PSM, internal political efficacy, and employee participation in management is important because it indicates which configuration of employee types the manager is facing. For instance, if they are all positively related, the manager would face many strong loyalists; but if support is negatively related to PSM, efficacy, and distributed leadership, the manager will face many strong saboteurs.

Model 2 shows that neither PSM, internal political efficacy, nor distributed leadership is significantly correlated with support for performance-increasing austerity reforms. The pattern identified in table 5.6 is, therefore, not a certain empirical pattern. Hence, managers implementing austerity reforms cannot rely on PSM, efficacy, or distributed leadership to predict support, or vice versa. Model 6 shows that PSM is significantly positively correlated with higher support for the strategic service-oriented performance policy, as is employee participation in management tasks (distributed leadership). Conversely, internal political self-efficacy is significantly negatively correlated with support for the strategic service-oriented reform policy. This corresponds to the indications from the simple distribution in table 5.7. Managers should bear in mind, however, that high-PSM employees are likely to support the policy, but employees with a high capacity to affect its implementation tend to oppose it. The key question becomes how these factors interact; Model 7 shows a significant interaction term between PSM and internal political self-efficacy.

Figure 5.1 shows that PSM and internal political efficacy interact in a manner whereby they reduce the correlation of each factor with support. If employees have high internal political efficacy, which correlates negatively with support, PSM has a stronger positive effect on support. Although different types of employees are all present among the hospital staff, there is no systematic pattern of combinations among PSM, internal political self-efficacy, participation

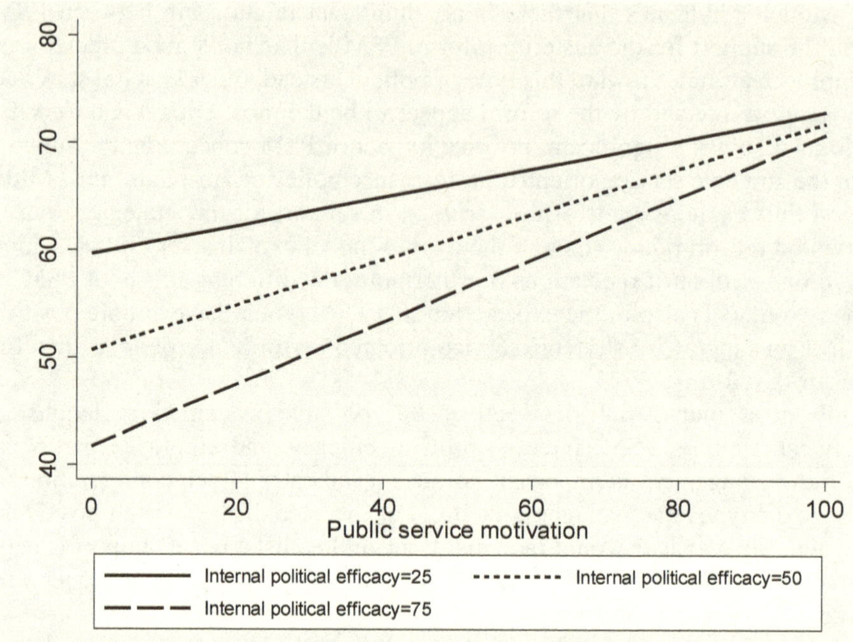


**Figure 5.1** The Interactive Effect of Public Service Motivation and Internal Political Efficacy

in management tasks, and support giving rise to saboteur employees rather than loyal employees.

## IMPLICATIONS

One main finding of the study is that the purposefulness of employee PSM for managing performance in public organizations depends on the policy context; PSM appears to lead to higher support for some types of performance policies rather than others. More specifically, PSM has no impact on the support for austerity reform policies, whereas it increases support for strategic performance policies directed at service improvement. The expectation that PSM has a positive impact on support for performance policies depends on whether the policy enhances or clashes with PSM values.

Another main finding of this study is that there is a systematic relationship between PSM, internal political efficacy, and support for performance policies with regard to strategic service-oriented change policy; but there is no systematic relationship with regard to austerity reform policies independent of whether the employees are in a position to affect the policies or not. With the austerity reform policy, we did find that two-thirds of the employees have high PSM and are critical of the austerity reform. Furthermore, one-quarter of these employees have high political efficacy and are thus potentially strong saboteurs, although few of them actually participate extensively in the management of their hospital units. Still, there are twice as many of these potentially strong saboteurs as there are strong loyalists who will support the manager. This suggests that, in some instances, high-PSM employees can be an impediment to performance improvements in public organizations.

However, the strategic service-oriented performance policy reform provided the opposite picture. About 70 percent of the employees have high PSM levels and express high support for the strategic service-oriented performance policy. Of these, about 12 percent are strong loyalists; there are almost twice as many strong loyalists as strong saboteurs, though only 4 percent can be counted as very strong loyalists who are also in a position to advance the policy. Furthermore, PSM and distributed leadership are also positively correlated with the level of support for the strategic service-oriented performance policy, whereas the opposite is the case for internal political self-efficacy. Taken together, internal political self-efficacy moderates the association between PSM and the support for the strategic service-oriented performance policy; the association between high PSM and high levels of support becomes stronger with higher levels of internal political self-efficacy. However, we have no reinforcing pattern among PSM, internal political efficacy, and employee participation in management tasks producing either strong loyalists or saboteurs.

These results are important for several reasons. First, they show how PSM is related to support for performance policies and whether the dominant positive view of PSM holds empirically across all contexts. In particular, these results shed light on how PSM is associated with the support for austerity policies and strategic service-oriented performance policies, which in recent years have been (with variations) typical policies characterizing the management contexts of many public organizations.

Even though we find that, when controlling for other factors, there is no systematic relationship to explain support for the austerity reform policy, the hospital's management is nevertheless confronted with the fact that the vast majority of employees are highly motivated to provide public service and are critical of the austerity reform. Many of these employees have high political efficacy, and they outnumber the employees who are more loyal and are characterized by high PSM and high political efficacy. In effect, even though PSM-motivated employees are generally more supportive of strategic service-oriented performance policies, they are of no help to the hospital manager when austerity performance policies are on the agenda—quite to the contrary. To put it bluntly, PSM-motivated employees are supportive when the organization's goals are aligned with PSM values, but this support does not translate into acceptance and support when the organization is facing austerity changes that are in conflict, or may come into conflict, with PSM values.

It is not certain whether we can consider this investigation to be a broader indicator of the relationship between PSM and the support for austerity policies and strategic service-oriented performance policies in the public sector. Our case entailed a survey of approximately 1,300 Danish hospital employees in one of Scandinavia's largest public hospitals. Hospitals are very large, complex organizations, with many different kinds of employees in terms of education, responsibility, pay, professional status, and so forth. In this respect, a large, modern hospital is in many ways a reflection of the public sector in a broader sense. Even though the hospital's reforms are very profound, similar types of reforms are also currently being undertaken in the welfare states of many Western countries.

What could be more problematic, however, is that in this case we are investigating a public hospital in Scandinavia, which is renowned for having an extensive public sector that enjoys popular support. In such a setting, there is a risk that the high social capital (see table 5.2) and political correctness of responding in a positive-PSM manner biases responses (Kim and Kim 2013). However, these sentiments may also reflect a broader pattern in the Western world's public sectors. In general, we have very few respondents with low PSM scores, which makes it challenging to investigate the relationship between PSM and employees' support of their workplace and workplace policies when there is limited variation in PSM. Taking the high PSM scores for granted, it would be worthwhile to replicate the investigation in a broader public-sector setting in Scandinavia and elsewhere.

Nonetheless, our results suggest that PSM correlates with perceptions of public-sector reforms, but not necessarily in the way that previous research has expected (Lee, Cayer, and Lan 2006; Naff and Crum 1999; Paarlberg and Lavigna 2010; Paarlberg 2007; Wright, Christensen, and Isett 2013). Conversely, it might not be surprising that PSM-motivated employees are more supportive when the performance goals of the broader organization are aligned with PSM values, but that this support does not necessarily translate into acceptance and active support when the organization faces austerity changes that are or may be in conflict with PSM values.

This study is a cross-sectional investigation based on one type of organization, a large hospital services provider, which functions in the context of a Scandinavian welfare state that has relatively strong PSM values, both in its public sector and among the public in general. Therefore, further research is needed using a longitudinal design that can validate the findings of this study in other contexts—most notably, vis-à-vis the varying possible effects of PSM on support for different kinds of organizational changes.

## NOTES

1. Internal political efficacy is a phenomenon that has been examined in relation to citizens (Lassen and Serritzlew 2011; Morrell 2003) and to users of public-sector services, (Andersen, Kristensen, and Pedersen 2013) but not in relation to public-sector employees.
2. The model fit statistics are $\chi^2$ = 1374.03 (242), RMSEA = .058, CFI = .92, TLI = .92, and SRMR = .04.

# 6

# The Delegation of Municipal Spending in Honduras

## *Does the Decision Context Matter?*

CLAUDIA N. AVELLANEDA

Widespread interest in managerial decision making has led to a considerable body of scholarship on how leaders make decisions. Some scholars have argued that decision makers take cognitive shortcuts due to bounded rationality (Weyland 2007), resulting in biased and imperfect choices (Gilovich, Griffin, and Kahneman 2002). Others view decision makers as utility maximizers who, through cost/benefit analyses, employ rational, comprehensive processes (Buchanan and Tullock 1962; Seasons 2003). Sociological institutionalists, however, reject this utilitarian view, instead emphasizing managerial actors' symbolic and normative concerns (March et al. 1976). Still others describe a contingent process in which choices depend on policymakers' perceived decision difficulty (Landsbergen, Bozeman, and Bretschneider 1992).

Despite the rich literature, most decision-making studies have focused on contexts within developed countries and regions, and little attention has been given to developing areas. This bias may lead scholars to underestimate the potential role of context in explaining how managers and leaders make decisions. This study adds to the managerial decision literature by emphasizing two contextual factors. First, the study focuses on municipalities of Honduras, a developing country rarely examined in research on managerial decision making. Second, following O'Toole and Meier's context framework (as explained in this book's introduction) and its three dimensions—political, environmental, and internal—this study explores whether the political context in which leaders operate influences Honduran local executives' decision making.

In Latin America, the adoption of political, fiscal, and administrative decentralization has made local governments' chief executives the central decision makers in determining which policies to adopt, which programs to implement, and whom these activities will benefit. According to Fiszbein (1997, 1037), since the adoption of decentralization in the 1980s, Latin American mayors have increased both their role and autonomy, and have thus become "one-man bands." Because most studies of decision making in the public sector have focused on national policymakers, this study offers an opportunity to examine whether the factors affecting decision making at the national level also apply to subnational leaders.

This study specifically focuses on local leaders' decisions to either delegate or retain spending authority. The existing literature has offered a number of explanations for policymakers' delegation of power and/or autonomy. Some scholars credit the presence of political disagreement among policymakers with influencing the delegation of power (Bendor and Meirowitz 2004; Torenvlied 2000; Oosterwaal, Payne, and Torenvlied 2012). Others employ a transaction cost perspective to explain delegation (Epstein and O'Halloran 1994; Huber and Shipan 2002). According to this latter view, policymakers are more likely to delegate power and/or autonomy when policy issues require high levels of information. They are also more likely to delegate if agents have little incentive to deviate from the policymakers' preferences. Scholars have also examined delegation as a means of maintaining apparent consistency in commitments (Rogoff 1985; Bendor, Glazer, and Hammond 2001). According to this view, policymakers use delegation as a means of supporting efforts they previously opposed or questioned. Finally, several studies suggest that delegation is more likely in settings where it is difficult to build a consensus (Golub 1999; Schultz and König 2000).

This study tests the decision context–delegation relationship using data obtained from two sources: administrative records and a field-framed survey experiment with 143 incumbent Honduran mayors as respondents. The study builds on a history of public administration experiments, many of which were undertaken in the late 1980s and early 1990s (Bozeman and Shangraw 1989; Bretschneider and Straussman 1992; Bretschneider, Straussman, and Mullins 1988; Coursey 1992; Landsbergen, Bozeman, and Bretschneider 1992; Landsbergen et al. 1997; Wittmer 1992). In the subsequent decade, however, public administration experiments became more scarce, leading Margetts (2011) to advocate more experiments, in particular field experiments with public officials. Recently, public management scholars have turned renewed attention to experimental research (among others, Brewer and Brewer 2011; Avellaneda 2013; Grimmelikhuijsen and Meijer 2014; Herian et al. 2012).

In addition to testing the effect of political context, which is one of the dimensions of the context framework proposed in this book, this study also examines how issue salience and individual-level factors influence leaders' decisions to delegate. The study's results indicate that, in general, mayors prefer not to delegate spending. However, when they do delegate, they opt to work with regional municipal associations rather than the national association of municipalities. Unlike issue salience, local political context does affect mayoral delegation. Specifically, mayors are more inclined to delegate when their margin of victory is smaller and when their political support from the local council is higher. After presenting the study's six hypotheses and reviewing their theoretical underpinnings, this chapter describes the data collection, operationalization of concepts, and the design of the survey-experimental analysis. Following a discussion of the results, the chapter concludes with study limitations and recommendations for further research.

## EXPLAINING THE DECISION TO DELEGATE

In explaining the decision to delegate, this study mainly focuses on the effect of two particular factors: issue salience and political context. The existing literature on delegation also points out the role of other factors, such as the delegator's qualifications and the reputation of the agency to which authority may be delegated. Given their potential explanatory power, this study also tests the effects of leaders' qualifications and agents' reputations on leaders' decision to delegate.

### The Decision Context: Issue Type/Salience and the Decision to Delegate

The effect of issue salience on decision making has been a topic of great interest among researchers. According to Oppermann (2010, 3), "The concept of issue salience refers to the relative importance and significance that an actor ascribes to a given issue on the political agenda" (also see Soroka 2003, 28–29).[1] Tversky and Kahnemann (1981, 11–13) argue that decision makers direct their cognitive faculties to the issues they find salient, and Lavine and colleagues (1996, 297) find that salient issues are "frequently thought of and discussed with others" and are "closely related to people's tangible self-interests, core values, and social identifications" (see also Boninger et al. 1995; Avellaneda 2013). At the municipal level, the salience of an issue is therefore highly likely to affect a mayor's decision to delegate authority. According to Avellaneda (2013, 634), "Although no mayor would like to delegate spending because doing so leads to autonomy loss, mayors may be willing to relinquish their authority in certain issues, but not others. Specifically, the assumption is that the more salient an issue, the less likely a mayor is to delegate his/her authority."

Avellaneda (2013) discusses education and infrastructure as examples of issues that vary in salience, arguing that infrastructure is a more salient issue for mayors than education. Mayors are more likely to derive political benefits from spending on infrastructure, primarily because education is less visible than infrastructure and, in small localities, is extended to the populace as a whole. Conversely, infrastructure projects are visible and tangible and can be used to benefit a targeted area or neighborhood (Avellaneda 2013). In her field experiment with 120 Latin American mayors, Avellaneda finds that mayors are more likely to delegate spending authority for education than for infrastructure issues. Consequently,

> H1. Mayors are more likely to delegate spending authority on education than on infrastructural issues.

## The Political Context: Uncertainty, Political Support, and Delegation

According to O'Toole and Meier's context framework, political context is expected to have a direct and indirect effect on organizational performance. Political context is also expected to influence delegation, which in turn affects performance. For instance, scholars point to political uncertainty as a key contributor to delegation decisions (Moe 1990, 1997; Moe and Caldwell 1994; Horn and Shepsle 1989; Gilardi 2008). Moe (1990) argues that the uncertainty inherent in elections leads legislators and executives to design and/or hardwire political institutions to influence delegated agencies through ex ante control mechanisms. In this way, political uncertainty may motivate incumbent politicians to enact rules that restrict appointments and promotions (De Figueiredo 2002) as well as future spending capacity (Alesina and Tabellini 1990; Persson and Svensson 1989). Within the municipal context, a mayor's chances of reelection may also affect his or her delegation decisions. In politically competitive local environments, mayors might hesitate to delegate spending authority to avoid the risk of unexpected outcomes. Conversely, when a mayor has been elected with a large margin of victory (i.e., a noncompetitive electoral context), he or she may be more willing to take the risks associated with delegation. Consequently,

> H2a. The larger the margin of his or her electoral victory, the more likely a mayor will be to delegate spending authority.

Likewise, a mayor's political support on the local council (unified government) can also affect his or her decisions about delegation. Administrating in a divided-government context, in which the mayor's party lacks a majority in the municipal council, may encourage the mayor to delegate spending authority in order to bypass an obstructive local legislature. In sum,

> H2b. The greater the mayor's political support in the municipal council, the less likely a mayor will be to delegate spending authority.

## ADDITIONAL FACTORS EXPLAINING DELEGATION

Along with issue salience and political context, the existing literature has suggested other factors as drivers of leaders' decisions to delegate. Given their potential explanatory power, this study also examines the effect of actors' proximity, the reputation of the agency to which authority may be delegated, and a delegator's qualifications.

### Actors' Interrelations

Actors' proximity to and interconnectivity with agencies to which spending authority can potentially be delegated may also influence delegation decisions. The geographic proximity of local and decentralized agencies offers flexibility, faster response times, and greater accountability than agencies that are farther removed from the delegator. This proximity allows for more frequent interactions between delegators and those to whom activities are delegated, enabling greater information exchange. Conversely, mayoral delegation to a national or central agency is likely to involve a more formal process, slower response times, and less accountability due to a less personal relationship and infrequent communication.

International donor agencies have demonstrated a growing interest in working with local and decentralized agencies rather than national and central agencies. Satterthwaite (2002, 180) champions this trend, stating that community initiatives are strengthened and local partnerships are enhanced when international agencies channel resources to local agencies. He states: "It is a big step for any international donor to entrust the funding it manages to local institutions, . . . [because they] can respond rapidly, can fund community organizations directly, and can fund a large and diverse range of initiatives."

Andersson (2004) also underscores the benefits of involving local rather than national organizations in local administration. He argues that although local governments often lack the necessary human and physical resources to perform their functions, their interconnectivity with other local actors and agencies can overcome these deficiencies. This local cooperation has the benefit of producing a more inclusive local governance system instead of a unilateral municipal administration. Andersson gives empirical evidence for this argument by testing the benefits of local interconnectivity for Bolivia's forest governance.

Turning to the Honduran context, the 1993 Honduran Law of Municipalities enables local governments to create associations (*mancomunidades*) of municipalities at the local and regional levels. Through these associations, municipalities share the costs of professional assistance, such as the services of lawyers, engineers, architects, physicians, and lobbyists. Provided the municipality can afford association fees, mayors are free to affiliate their municipalities with as many municipal associations as they wish, and they may opt to withdraw membership from an association at any time. Although these local and regional memberships are optional, all 298 Honduran municipalities are members of the National Association of Municipalities of Honduras (Asociación de Municipios de Honduras, AMHON). Given mayors' proximity to and interconnectivity with their regional rather than national association, the next hypothesis can be stated as:

> H3. Mayors are more likely to delegate to a local or regional municipal association than to a national or central municipal association.

## Reputation and Credibility

Decisions to delegate spending authority can also be a function of a mayor's perceptions of the reputation and credibility of the agency to which he or she could delegate. Spulber and Besanko (1992) explain that in formalized principal–agent relationships, principals can employ different instruments (e.g., appointments, statutes, and oversight) as a way to control their agents' behavior. In settings with no formal control instruments, such as the principal–agent relationship between mayors and delegate agencies, principals can still rely on informal mechanisms, such as agents' reputation, past behavior, and credibility (Moe 1984). Graham, Harvey, and Puri (2011), in their study of capital allocation and the delegation of decision-making authority within firms, find that chief executives are more likely to delegate decision-making authority when they rate the divisional manager's reputation highly. Specifically, high-reputation managers are perceived as more likely to provide truthful information to headquarters.

Building on these observations, the next hypothesis follows the notion that delegation is more likely when the potential delegate agent has developed a reputation for delivering on projects. That is, the mayor's perceptions about the reputation of delegate agents (i.e., associations of municipalities) will affect his or her decision to delegate to them. In the Honduran municipal context, a mayor's perceptions regarding the reputation and credibility of municipal associations will be reflected in his or her municipality's memberships in municipal associations, because Honduran mayors have autonomy to either join or withdraw from any local or regional municipal association. Therefore,

> H4. The greater the number of municipal associations with which a mayor's municipality is affiliated, the more he or she will delegate spending to a municipal association.

## Decision Makers' Qualifications

Experienced and educated leaders may be more reluctant to delegate spending authority, viewing themselves as more qualified to handle the job. Fiske, Kinder, and Larter (1983, 396) contend that though novices only use information consistent with their prior knowledge, experts are better able to comprehend nuance and ambiguity. Likewise, Chaiken (1980, 752) finds that nonexperts use rapid, superficial, "heuristic" processing strategies, whereas experts are more systematic in processing information. Additionally, Thurmaier (1992) finds that experienced practitioners tend to incorporate public cues into their decision making to a greater extent than less experienced analysts. Therefore,

> H5a. Mayors with local public-sector experience are less likely to delegate spending authority.

Similar to experience, education is also expected to lend a leader confidence in his or her authority (Avellaneda 2009a, 2009b). Indeed, as Fiedler (1986, 533) states, "Cognitive resource theory assumes that more intelligent and knowledgeable leaders make better plans and decisions than do those with less ability and knowledge." More educated mayors are expected to be more inclined to rely on their own judgment. Consequently,

H5b. The more educated the mayor, the less likely he or she will be to delegate spending authority.

However, the influence of a manager's qualifications on decision making may be conditioned by issue salience. As Avellaneda (2013) has found in her studies of Latin American mayors, leaders' education and experience influence their decisions on some issues but not others. The notion is that with certain issues, leaders may not decide based on their aptitudes but based on their strategic calculations. Given that spending on infrastructure has the potential to generate personal and political gains in developing-country contexts (Mauro 1995, 1997, 1998), leaders' strategic calculations may make them more inclined to delegate spending on other issues but not on infrastructure. For example, Avellaneda (2013) finds that highly educated mayors are more likely to delegate spending authority on education (a nonsalient issue) than less educated mayors, but they are not more likely to delegate authority on infrastructure (a salient issue). As such, the following moderating hypotheses are proposed:

H6a. The more educated the mayor, the less likely he or she will be to delegate spending authority for infrastructure issues, but the more likely he or she will be to delegate spending authority for educational issues.

H6b. The more public experience the mayor has, the less likely he or she will be to delegate spending authority for infrastructure issues, but the more likely he or she will be to delegate spending for educational issues.

## CASE SELECTION: HONDURAN MAYORS

This study relies on data from a survey experiment of 143 Honduran mayors. Honduras comprises eighteen administrative departments, each headed by a presidentially appointed governor. Within these eighteen departments are a total of 298 municipalities (*municipios*). A municipality in Honduras may include more than one city within its boundaries and is therefore comparable to county-level jurisdictions in the United States. Municipalities may also include villages (*aldeas*) and hamlets (*caseríos*), which are scattered concentrations of populations outside urban areas. Elected corporations govern municipalities. These corporations consist of a mayor (*alcalde*), who is the chief executive; a vice mayor, who belongs to the political party of the elected mayor; and a municipal council, which varies in size depending on the population of the municipality.[2] Municipalities with annual revenue of more than 1 million *lempiras* also have an auditor named by the municipal corporation.

The 1990 Law of Municipalities outlines procedures for departmental and municipal administration. According to this law, municipalities have autonomy in local matters, including administration and decision making, organizing and managing public services, collecting and investing revenues, and managing natural resources. The law also states that municipalities are responsible for organizing public administration and services, developing and implementing a municipal budget, appointing public employees and naming needed public commissions, planning urban development, and consulting the public through plebiscites and open public meetings with representatives of municipal sectors (Association of Municipalities of Honduras 1993).

With Honduras's return to democratic rule in 1982, new provisions in the Constitution called for municipal economic and social development. To this end, in 1990 the Callejas government showed its support for political and administrative decentralization by establishing the Modernization of the State Commission, which transferred functions and resources from the central executive branch to the municipalities. In 1993 new electoral laws allowed split-party voting, enabling voters to cast ballots directly for mayoral candidates rather than indirectly electing mayors based on the percentage of votes cast for their party in the presidential election (Merrill 1995).

Two political parties have dominated Honduran elections: the Honduran National Party (Partido Nacional de Honduras) and the Honduras Liberal Party (Partido Liberal de Honduras). The military was long allied with the Partido Nacional, but since the country's return to civilian democratic rule in the 1980s, three small, centrist political parties have emerged: the Innovation and National Unity Party (Partido Innovación y Unidad), the Christian Democratic Party (Partido Demócrata Cristiano de Honduras), and the relatively new Unified Democratic Party (Partido Unificación Democrática) (Taylor-Robinson 2006, 2009).

Table 6.1 depicts the public management context matrix for Honduran municipalities. Honduras has a unitary governmental system with no shared powers. Unlike the United States, it has a centralized rather than a federal system, with one level of government whose decision-making process is adversarial and involves no formal performance appraisal system. The environmental context varies across municipalities in complexity, turbulence, and social capital; their measures of munificence, however, are consistently poor. With respect to internal administrative context, Honduran municipalities vary in their centralization and hierarchy but generally exhibit multiple and conflicting goals and are staffed with nonprofessional public servants.

**Table 6.1** The Public Management Context Matrix: Honduran Municipalities

| *Context* | *Honduran Municipalities* |
|---|---|
| *Political context—Concentration of Power* | |
| Separation of powers | Unitary |
| Federalism | One level of government |
| Process | Adversarial |
| Performance appraisal | No formal system |
| *Environmental Context* | |
| Complexity | Varies across municipalities |
| Turbulence | Varies across municipalities |
| Munificence | Very poor |
| Social capital | Varies across municipalities |
| *Internal Context* | |
| Goals | Multiple and conflicting |
| Centralization and hierarchy | Varies across municipalities |
| Professionalization | Not professional |

## SURVEY-EXPERIMENTAL ANALYSIS AND DESIGN

For this survey-experimental study of 143 Honduran mayors, the investigator conducted the survey and experiment in Spanish during the Honduran National Convention of Mayors, which was held at the Quinta Real Convention Center in the city of La Ceiba, Atlantida, from April 25 to 27, 2012. In addition to obtaining approval from the University Institutional Review Board, the investigator obtained permission to attend the conference from the president of AMHON, and she received an invitation to attend all conference events, including meals, panels, workshops, and the closing ceremony featuring the incumbent president of Honduras. About 240 of the country's 298 mayors attended the conference; no discernible differences were detected between attendees and nonattendees in terms of their municipalities' socioeconomic profiles, population size, or geographic location.

During the three-day conference, the investigator approached mayors after meals, during summit breaks, in the convention lobby, and in the exhibition hall. To guarantee random selection among the participating mayors, the investigator approached them when they were in a group. She explained to each mayor the nature and objectives of the study and asked for his or her cooperation. After agreeing to participate, each mayor received both the experiment and a posttreatment survey of twenty-five questions that collected, among other details, data about their education and public-sector experience.

Because the experiment has a between-group factorial design with a 1 × 3 matrix that results in three possible municipal conditions or scenarios, each selected mayor was randomly assigned to one of these three scenarios. To guarantee an even assignment of the municipal condition across mayors, the investigator organized the municipal scenarios into three printed stacks, each containing eighty cards for one of the possible scenarios. She then cycled from one scenario to the next after each consecutive mayor was interviewed to evenly distribute the three experimental conditions among the subjects. She succeeded in approaching 150 of the 240 attendees, 7 of whom declined to participate due to time constraints. The remaining 143 mayors were fully receptive to the request to participate in the survey experiment. Due to the cyclical scenario distribution process, 47 mayors were placed in each of the two experimental conditions and 48 were placed in the control group.

## Introducing the Issue: The Municipal Problem

Following assignment to one of the three municipal scenarios, each mayor was asked to imagine that he or she was the executive of a hypothetical municipality.[3] In one-third of the sample (47), the municipality was experiencing a hypothetical problem related to education. Specifically, the scenario stated that 60 percent of the municipal population had no access to education. In another third of the sample (47), the municipal problem was related to infrastructure, and scenario stated that 60 percent of the population had no access to sewage, electricity, or running water. The hypothesized problems closely reflect the realities of Latin American municipalities, which still struggle to meet their constituents' basic needs. In the third and final portion of the sample (48 mayors), no particular municipal problem was specified. The mayors assigned to this scenario serve as the control group to elucidate whether mayors are willing to delegate spending in general. Figure 6.1 presents the English translation of the three scenarios. Each mayor was told that his or her municipality had received a donation of 1 million lempiras ($52,631) from an international donor agency. This amount approximates actual municipal donations by the 180 nongovernmental organizations that function in Honduras. In the two scenarios that specified the hypothetical problem, the money was to be earmarked to address that issue, whereas the control group received no instructions on where to direct the funds.

## Delegation Options

Mayors were presented with three choices for spending the donated money. The first option was to retain complete autonomy over 100 percent of the donated money to address the hypothetical problem (or, for the control group,

<table>
<tr><th colspan="2">Issue Introduction</th></tr>
<tr><th>EDUCATION SECTOR</th><th>INFRASTRUCTURE SECTOR</th></tr>
<tr><td>Mr./Mrs. Mayor, accept my sincere thanks for cooperating with this study.<br><br>For the purpose of this project, assume you are the mayor of a municipality in which 60% of its population has no access to education. Although the municipality has other needs, access to education is obviously the vital priority.</td><td>Mr./Mrs. Mayor, accept my sincere thanks for cooperating with this study.<br><br>For the purpose of this project, assume you are the mayor of a municipality, in which 60% of its population has access neither to electricity, nor sewage, nor running water. Although the municipality has other needs, lack of access to basic needs (water, sewage, and electricity) is obviously the vital priority.</td></tr>
<tr><td>Assume you receive 1 million lempiras (about $50,000) from an international donor agency to solve the vital priority in your municipality (that is, no access to education). However, the international donor agency asks you to choose from the following three alternatives to spend the donating money:<br><br>1) You will be allowed to spend the money as you wish, meaning you will have full autonomy over these 1 million lempiras to deal with your municipal priority (access to education).<br><br>2) You can use 500,000 lempiras as you want and the other 500,000 lempiras will be delegated to Association of Municipalities of Honduras (AMHON) for it to fix your municipal vital priority (access to education) with the help of its technical assistance.<br><br>3) You can use 500,000 lempiras as you want and the other 500,000 lempiras will be delegated to the most important regional association of municipalities your municipality belongs to, for it to implement programs and projects targeting your municipal vital priority (access to education).<br><br>Circle the choice above that you would prefer to deal with your municipal problem.</td><td>Assume you receive 1 million lempiras (about $50,000) from an international donor agency to solve the vital priority in your municipality (that is, lack of access to water, sewage, and electricity). However, the international donor agency asks you to choose from the following three alternatives to spend the donating money:<br><br>1) You will be allowed to spend the money as you wish, meaning you will have full autonomy over these 1 million lempiras to deal with your municipal priority (access to water, sewage, and electricity).<br><br>2) You can use 500,000 lempiras as you want and the other 500,000 lempiras will be delegated to AMHON (Association of Municipalities of Honduras) for it to fix your municipal vital priority (access to water, sewage, and electricity) with the help of its technical assistance<br><br>3) You can use 500,000 lempiras as you want and the other 500,000 lempiras will be delegated to the most important regional association of municipalities your municipality belongs to, for it to implement programs and projects targeting your municipal vital priority (access to water, sewage, and electricity).<br><br>Circle the choice above that you would prefer to deal with your municipal problem.</td></tr>
</table>

**Figure 6.1** Survey-Experiment Scenarios—Honduran Mayors

| **Control Group (without a municipal problem )** |
|---|
| Mr./Mrs. Mayor, accept my sincere thanks for cooperating with this study. |
| Assume you receive **1 million lempiras (about $50,000)** from an **international donor agency.** However, the international donor agency asks you to choose from the following three alternatives to spend the donating money:<br>1) You will be allowed to spend the money as you wish, meaning you will have full autonomy over these 1 million lempiras.<br>2) You can use 500,000 lempiras as you wish, and the other 500,000 lempiras will be delegated to AMHON for it to invest in your municipality with the help of its technical assistance.<br>3) You can use 500,000 lempiras as you wish, and the other 500,000 lempiras will be delegated to the most important regional association of municipalities your municipality belongs to, for it to implement programs and projects in your municipality.<br>Circle the choice above that you would prefer to spend your donating money. |

**Figure 6.1** (*continued*)

to invest 100 percent of the funds as the mayor wishes). The second option was to have autonomy over 50 percent of the donated money and to delegate spending on the other 50 percent to AMHON. The third option mayors were given was to retain autonomy over 50 percent of the donated money and to delegate spending of the other 50 percent to "the most important regional association of municipalities" to which his or her municipality belongs. In sum, mayors' three spending alternatives were (1) autonomy over 100 percent of the donated money, (2) autonomy over 50 percent of the donated money and delegation of the other 50 percent to AMHON, and (3) autonomy over 50 percent of the donated money and delegation of the other 50 percent to a key regional association of municipalities.

## Manipulation Checks

The inclusion of a control group that presented mayors with a delegation decision without specifying any specific issue present in the municipality allows for a measure of mayors' willingness to delegate spending authority regardless of issue salience. In addition, two manipulation checks assessed the internal validity of the experiment (i.e., whether and how well the variables and treatments capture the theoretical constructs). The first check assessed whether mayors identified a pressing problem, and the second check determined whether mayors linked a pressing municipal problem with an appropriate solution. The investigator asked each mayor in the posttreatment survey to identify the most pressing problem in his or her actual municipality. Mayors were also asked to identify the municipal sector or policy area to which they would direct additional support if they were to receive extra funding. These two survey questions approximate the hypothetical scenario presented in the experiment. Seventy-nine percent of the participating mayors targeted the hypothetical extra funding to their pressing municipal problem.[4]

In order to test the remaining propositions, two nonmanipulable variables collected from the survey contribute to the analysis: mayors' education, and public-sector experience. Mayors' education is operationalized with a dummy variable, which is coded 1 when the mayor's level of education is above high school and is otherwise coded 0. Mayoral experience is also a dummy variable, which is coded 1 when the mayor reported any kind of public-sector experience preceding his or her current term in office. To test the political context hypotheses (H2a and H2b), data on mayors' margin of victory as well as data on the percentage of council members aligned with the mayors' political party were obtained from the Tribunal Supremo Electoral de Honduras. Finally, three control variables appear in the model: percentage of rural population, number of a mayor's reelection periods, and mayor's party ideology—each of which was obtained from the survey.

## RESULTS

The investigator undertook efforts to randomly assign manipulations among the mayors who attended the conference. However, because mayors' attendance could itself have been affected by the municipality's financial health, the mayors' political status, the municipality's proximity to the city holding the conference, and other such measures, the selection of subjects falls short of true randomization. However, to demonstrate that the subjects across the three experimental conditions are comparable, the investigator conducted statistical tests for equal means and homogeneous variances across groups. The Levene test (Levene 1960) checked across groups for differences among observable conditions, such as mayors' education and experience using STATA's command *levene*.[5] Results from Levene's *T*-tests show that mayors are homogenous across the three experimental conditions in terms of their education and professional experience.[6] In other words, in this experiment, the treatment (scenario) to which each mayor is assigned is independent of his or her background attributes, indicating robustness of randomization among the mayors attending the national convention.[7]

Between-group analysis of variance (ANOVA) tests the effect of the manipulated treatment, issue salience, on mayoral decisions to delegate (see table 6.3 below). ANOVA tests show that issue salience, by itself, had no significant effect on mayoral decisions to delegate spending authority. Although the proportion of mayors who delegated authority across the three different municipal scenarios varied (education $M = 0.295$, infrastructure $M = 0.340$, and control $M = 0.363$), their difference is not statistically significant (prob $> F$: 0.9760). Therefore, hypothesis H1 is not supported, meaning that issue salience has no effect on mayors' decisions to delegate spending authority.

In general, the study's results show that mayors preferred not to delegate, because 99 of 143 mayors (69.2 percent) opted to spend the donated money by themselves (see table 6.2) and only 44 mayors (30.8 percent) decided to delegate any spending authority. However, of these 44 mayors, only 8 decided to delegate to the national association of municipalities, whereas 34 chose to delegate to their preferred local or regional association of municipalities. A standard $t$-test compares the share of mayors who decided to delegate to a regional or local association of municipalities ($M = .251$) against the share of mayors who decided to delegate to the national association of municipalities (0.054). The $t$-test reports that their mean values are statistically different ($p < 0.01$), and hypothesis H3 is supported. Thus, the results show that, in general, mayors prefer not to delegate spending. However, when they do delegate, mayors opt for a local instead of a national association of municipalities.

Among other measures, 53 percent of mayors have an education of high school or more, and 38 percent reported previous local public-sector

**Table 6.2** The Mayoral Decision to Delegate, by Type of Municipal Problem

| *Mayoral Choice* | *No Problem* | *Education* | *Infrastructure* | *Totals* |
|---|---|---|---|---|
| Not to delegate spending | 33 | 33 | 33 | 99 (69.2%) |
| Delegate to a national association of municipalities | 1 | 4 | 3 | 8 (5.6%) |
| Delegate to a regional association of municipalities | 15 | 9 | 12 | 36 (25.2%) |
| Totals | 49 (34.3%) | 46 (32.2%) | 48 (35.5%) | 143 |

experience. The proportion of mayors with local public experience who delegated spending (.488) does not vary statistically from the proportion of mayors without prior experience who delegated spending (.501); hypothesis H5a is not supported. Likewise, although the proportion of mayors with a high school education or more who delegated spending (0.395) varies from the proportion of less-educated mayors who delegated spending (0.525), this difference fails to be statistically significant. ANOVA (table 6.3, column 1) also tested the effect of the three continuous variables that operationalize the number of regional and local associations (H4), electoral competitiveness (H2a), and divided government (H2b). The results show that none of these variables has a statistically significant effect on mayoral decisions to delegate spending.

Logit estimations (table 6.3, column 2) test for interactive effects. The results show that only two coefficients are statistically significant at the .05 level: electoral competitiveness (the margin of electoral victory), and council members' political support. Interestingly, these relationships exhibit an unexpected finding, given that the margin of the electoral victory coefficient is negative. Holding all else constant, as the margin of electoral victory increases, the likelihood of mayoral delegation of spending authority decreases, providing empirical support in the opposite direction of hypothesis H2a. In addition, mayors are considerably more inclined to delegate spending as the percentage of council members aligned with their own party increases, again in the opposite direction of hypothesis H2b. The last column of table 6.3 also reports the logit results for the same model after controlling for the municipal factors of the rural population, the mayor's number of reelections, and the mayor's ideology. The logit results do not vary, indicating that results are robust across the three different models.

These results are not without limitations. It is important to note that survey experiments can lend themselves to misleading inferences (Gaines, Kuklinski, and Quirk 2007). First, this experiment assumes that a single exposure to a strong treatment in a survey is equivalent to frequent exposure to a weaker stimulus in the real world (Gaines, Kuklinski, and Quirk 2007, 7). Correcting for this tendency would require longitudinal studies with multiple treatments.[8] Second, by not measuring the duration of effects, it is difficult to determine the relevance of these findings (Gaines, Kuklinski, and Quirk 2007, 5–6). Third, survey experiments can overlook mutual causation, which calls for identification of the causal process through multiple treatments. Finally, given that the experiment was conducted at a conference to which only 240 out of 298 mayors traveled, it presented a limitation in terms of the random selection of subjects. The survey also has the limitation of being self-reported.

**Table 6.3** Estimates for Factors in Mayoral Decisions to Delegate Spending Authority

| | *ANOVA Test* | | | | | |
|---|---|---|---|---|---|---|
| | *Degrees of Freedom* | *Mean Square* | *F-value* | *Probability > F* | *Logit Coefficient / Robust SE* | *Logit Coefficient / Robust SE* |
| *Variable* | 2 | *.005* | *0.02* | *0.976* | | |
| Type of municipal problem (no problem, education, or infrastructure) | | | | | | |
| Education problem | | | | | –0.60 (0.79) | –0.64 (0.79) |
| No problem (control) | | | | | 0.11(0.48) | 0.20(0.50) |
| Local/regional municipal associations | 1 | 0.320 | 1.10 | 0.297 | 0.15 (0.09) | 0.14(0.10) |
| Local electoral competitiveness | 1 | 1.525 | 7.26 | 0.008** | –0.07(0.02)*** | –0.68(0.02)*** |
| Council's political support | 1 | 0.971 | 4.62 | 0.033** | 0.09(0.04)** | 0.09(0.04)** |
| Mayor's education above high school | 1 | 0.172 | 0.82 | 0.366 | –0.57(0.50) | 0.43(0.49) |
| Mayor's local public experience | 1 | 0.514 | 2.45 | 0.120 | 0.40(0.49) | –0.57(0.50) |
| Local public experience * education problem | 2 | 0.093 | 0.45 | 0.640 | 0.75(0.87) | 0.80(0.91) |
| Mayor's education * education problem | 2 | 0.090 | 0.43 | 0.651 | 0.59(0.89) | 0.72(0.93) |
| Controls | | | | | | |
| Rural population | | | | | | –0.01(0.01) |
| Number of reelections | | | | | | 0.01(0.28) |
| Mayor's liberal ideology | | | | | | –0.3(0.43) |

**Table 6.3** *(continued)*

| | *ANOVA Test* | | | | | |
|---|---|---|---|---|---|---|
| | *Degrees of Freedom* | *Mean Square* | *F-value* | *Probability > F* | *Logit Coefficient / Robust SE* | *Logit Coefficient / Robust SE* |
| *Variable* | *2* | *.005* | *0.02* | *0.976* | | |
| Model | 11 | 0.284 | 1.35 | 0.2034 | | |
| Residual | 126 | 0.210 | | | | |
| Constant | | | | | –5.03(2.19)** | –4.18(2.35)* |
| No. of observations | 143 | | | | 143 | 143 |
| $R^2$ / Pseudo-$R^2$ | 0.11 | | | | 0.09 | 0.11 |
| Wald chi$^2$ (12) | | | | | 15.86 | 17.56 |
| Probability > chi$^2$ | | | | | 0.06 | 0.12 |

*$p < .1$; **$p < .05$; ***$p < .01$

## IMPLICATIONS

This study presented an experimental analysis as an innovative methodological approach to the question: What explains mayoral delegation decisions? The study analyzes the role of the decision context (issue salience and political context) and the direct and indirect effects of decision makers' qualifications on decision making. In doing so, this study provides an additional test, through a survey experiment, of the effect of political context—one of the dimensions of O'Toole and Meier's public management context framework—on managerial delegation. Subjects included 143 Honduran mayors who attended the National Convention of Mayors in 2012. The experiment manipulated issue salience (no local problem, education problem, or infrastructure problem), and type of delegate agency (a local or regional association of municipalities vs. a national association of municipalities). ANOVA results show that, in general, mayors prefer not to delegate spending, but when they do delegate, mayors opt for a local instead of a national association of municipalities. The findings also show that issue salience has no effect on mayors' decisions to delegate. These findings have policy implications for international donors and nongovernmental organizations, because they reveal that mayors are more willing to work with local rather than national agencies.

ANOVA and logit results also indicate that mayors' qualifications (education and local public experience) have neither direct nor indirect effects on their decision to delegate. However, according to the ANOVA and logit results, the local political context (competitiveness and political conflict) does appear to have significant effects on mayors' decisions to delegate spending. Mayors are less likely to delegate spending as their margin of electoral victory increases but are more likely to delegate spending as local council members' political support increases. Contrary to expectations, these results suggest that political uncertainty does not prevent mayors from delegating spending authority. This finding may indicate that under political uncertainty, mayors prefer to delegate because in doing so, they can pass along blame to another agency in case of unforeseen outcomes. These findings have direct policy relevance, as they suggest that locally elected leaders' willingness to share spending authority can be a function of the political context in which they operate, thus providing empirical evidence for the proposed public management context framework.

This study was designed to reflect the real-world delegation decisions that municipal leaders face in developing-country settings. With the adoption of decentralization in Latin America, mayors are tasked with enormous responsibility for the well-being of their constituents. How these local leaders determine whether and with whom to share spending authority is a subject of interest for scholars, donor agencies, and central governments alike. This study provides a number of useful insights into which factors affect these decisions, suggesting that though mayors are generally disinclined to delegate spending decisions, they are more willing to share these responsibilities with local rather than national agencies, and are influenced in these decisions by the local political context. The study calls for further research to assess, for example, the moderating role of political context on the mayoral qualifications–delegation relationship. Additional studies should also explore whether the political context has a direct effect on mayors' decisions to delegate spending authority in dealing with other types of issues.

## NOTES

1. Over time, however, the perceived salience of an issue may change considerably (Price 1978, 548).
2. Municipalities with a population of less than 5,000 have four council members, those with a population of between 5,000 and 10,000 have six, and those with a population between 10,000 and 80,000 have eight. Municipalities with a population of more than 80,000, and all department capitals regardless of their population, have ten council members.
3. By characterizing the question as a hypothetical problem, the experiment avoids ethical concerns of deception (Butler and Broockman 2011; Margetts 2011).
4. If the mayors had not targeted the pressing municipal problem, it would have suggested that (1) mayors were not paying attention to the survey or (2) mayors have specific projects in mind (motivated by morals, politics, or self-interest) that do not necessarily align with perceived municipal needs; Mauro (1995, 1997, 1998).
5. Levene's *T*-test tests the null hypothesis that multiple population variances (corresponding to multiple samples) are equal. In the Levene test, equal standard deviation across groups is the null hypothesis (H0). The *F*-test and Bartlett's test can also be used for testing the difference between the variances of two samples. However, both are quite sensitive to departures from normality (Box 1953; Box and Anderson 1955; Levene 1960). In this case, the data set deviates from normality, thus justifying the Levene test.
6. Although the proportion of mayors with university degrees in condition 3 is relatively low (0.4) compared with the mean value in condition 4 (0.8), on other background variables such as citizenship and local experience, there is balance across the experimental conditions.
7. Levene's *T*-test for equal variances in education across issue: $T = 1.17$, prob $> T = 0.3067$; Levene's *T*-test for equal variances in local experience across issue: $T = 1.18$, prob $> T = 0.2598$.
8. One drawback of the lack of dynamics over time in this study is the absence of measures of the impact of the legacy of the previous mayor on the behavior of his or her successor.

# 7

# Explaining the Expansion of Brazilian Municipal Revenues

## *Does Political Context or Managerial Background Influence Grant Acquisition?*

RICARDO C. GOMES AND CLAUDIA N. AVELLANEDA

To address ever-increasing public needs, governments must continuously seek to expand revenues. Local governments do so through both internal means—primarily taxes and fees—and external grant-seeking activities. Internal revenue strategies are often hindered by the desire to avoid political risks and by the economic constraints of constituents. As a result, local leaders often opt for external revenue expansion through auxiliary state or national grants. This type of expansion is not uniformly seen across municipalities, which leads to the question: Which factors influence local revenue expansion through state and national grants? Given that grant acquisition might be determined by political factors, this study mainly explores whether the local political context and chief executives' managerial competency influence revenue expansion.

Revenue expansion can be viewed as a measure of a manager's entrepreneurialism, because it reflects the innovative strategies and supplementary activities in which a leader engages, beyond the strict requirements of the job. Because a manager's revenue strategies can be a function of his or her demographic or background characteristics (Hambrick and Mason 1984), as well as his or her political context, this study explores the effect of both local leaders' demographics and political context on revenue expansion. To test these relationships, the study uses data from 812 municipalities of the Brazilian state of Minas Gerais over a six-year period (2005–10), which covers two municipal administrations. Municipal revenue expansion is measured through state and national grants, and leaders' demographics are operationalized as mayors' age, education, and job-related experience. Electoral competitiveness as well as mayor–governor and mayor–president partisan alignment operationalize the municipality's political context.

Brazilian localities are particularly worthy of investigation because they are multiservice providers. There are no city managers in Brazil; directly elected mayors perform not only political but also administrative municipal functions and are constitutionally granted full local autonomy. Because every locality is responsible for providing social, economic, developmental, and health services, mayors face daily challenges in making the most efficient use of scarce resources. In accord with the propositions presented in the introduction to this book, managerial capacities are therefore expected to be intertwined with the political context—a fusion that has complicated research efforts to identify the determinants of these distinct types of aptitudes (Boyne 2003; Rainey and Steinbauer 1999; Meier and O'Toole 2002).

Our study seeks to contribute to current scholarship in several ways. First, existing management strategy research has focused on the influence of strategy content on organizational performance, but few studies have explored the determinants of specific organizational strategies, such as revenue expansion. As Andrews and colleagues (2009, 732) state, "very little research has been conducted . . . in the contemporary public sector on the links between strategies and other organizational characteristics." Second, this study shifts the research focus from developed settings, such as US and English local governments, to Brazilian local governments to test the influence of both local political context and managerial capacity in explaining performance management in the public sector (O'Toole and Meier 2015). Third, because this study tests the effect of political context on state and national grants, the research design permits us to operationalize political context at the local, state, and federal levels. In other words, the study seeks to capture the intersectional, complex, and turbulent political context that characterizes federalism in Brazil.

Taking into account the context framework proposed in the introduction, our study seeks to test the effect of context on the revenue expansion of Brazilian municipalities. Table 7.1 presents a matrix for explaining the political, environmental, and internal context of Brazilian local and federal government. Brazilian municipalities are the third level of government within a federal state, with legal separation of powers across the three levels of government. The political context of Brazilian local governments tends to be adversarial and competitive, for their chief executives are usually elected through very competitive elections with many parties participating in local elections. Hence, one recent mayoral election (October 2012) included twenty-nine political parties (TSE 2014). At the municipal level, there are no formal performance appraisals. Performance appraisal, though a subject of considerable interest at the federal and state levels, is still in a nascent stage at the local level. Some state capitals have made progress in assessing mayoral performance, but the practice has not reached small municipalities.

In general, the environmental context of Brazilian municipalities tends to be characterized as complex and turbulent, because mayors need to interact with different kinds of agencies in order to both deliver public services and obtain their revenues. Moreover, Brazilian municipalities' environment is highly political and economically turbulent. For example, the current political and economic crisis in Brazil—with a president facing a very low public opinion rating and an economy with a very devalued currency—has considerably affected the central government's transfers to municipalities. Unfortunately, in this study we are unable to test the effect that these agencies (e.g., number, type, and power) have on the managerial–performance relationship.

Although most Brazilian municipalities share a common dearth of financial resources, leaving many localities consistently underfunded, Brazilian municipalities are also characterized as exhibiting varying levels of munificence. Across the five regions in Brazil (North, Northeast, Central-West, South, and Southeast), there is a high level of disparity in terms of munificence, with the Southeast region being the richest and the Northeast the poorest; this study focuses on the municipalities of the state of Minas Gerais, which is part of the richest region. Consequently, this study does not test the effect of munificence on the managerial–performance relationship. Finally, Brazilian municipalities also exhibit variant levels of social capital, with some communities enjoying strong interpersonal networks and membership organizations while others lack such connections.

With respect to the dimensions of internal context in the proposed framework, Brazilian municipalities also vary considerably, in having clear and defined administrative goals, a centralized managerial style, and professionalization. For instance, mayors are expected to come to office with a concrete program of governance, outlining clear and doable goals for their administration. However, while some mayors govern to pursue multiple and ambiguous goals, others fail to follow the originally outlined goals. In addition, directly elected mayors administer local governments, and, although legislative bodies oversee their administrations, mayors are the municipal decision makers. Finally, Brazilian municipalities exhibit a diverse level of professionalization at both the mayoral and administrative staff levels. Although some mayors

**Table 7.1** The Public Management Context Matrix: Brazilian Municipalities

| *Context* | *Brazilian Municipalities* | *Brazilian Federal Government* |
|---|---|---|
| *Political context—Concentration of Power* | | |
| Separation of powers | Unitary | Unitary |
| Federalism | A level within the federation | Multiple levels |
| Process | Adversarial | Adversarial |
| Performance appraisal | No formal system | No formal system |
| *Environmental Context* | | |
| Complexity | Varies across municipalities | Varies across states |
| Turbulence | Varies across municipalities | Varies across states |
| Munificence | Poor | Varies along time |
| Social capital | Varies across municipalities | Varies across functional areas and states |
| *Internal Context* | | |
| Goals | Varies across municipalities | Multiple and conflicting |
| Centralization and hierarchy | Varies across municipalities | Decentralized |
| Professionalization | Varies across municipalities | Professional |

hire professional staff members, others hire employees who have provided political support. In this study, however, we only test the effect of mayoral professionalization on municipal performance when it is assessed in terms of revenue expansion.

The results of this study reveal that the factors affecting the receipt of state grants differ from those influencing the receipt of federal grants. After controlling for other municipal indicators, the results offer partial support for the expected effect of political context on revenue expansion. Our results suggest that less electorally competitive municipalities tend to obtain more state grants and show that younger mayors are more successful in securing these grants. Contrary to our expectations, mayoral education and job-related experience are negatively correlated with state grants and have no apparent effect on federal grants.

The first section of this chapter draws on upper echelons theory to develop hypotheses for the relationship between mayors' competency and municipal revenue strategy. We then examine the literature addressing electoral competition and partisanship to derive our hypotheses related to the political context. Case selection, units of analysis, data, and measures are subsequently outlined. We then present the multivariate statistical results from the panel data and discuss their implications for how contextual factors (political and professionalization) affect both performance and management–performance relationships.

# MANAGERIAL COMPETENCE AS INTERNAL PROFESSIONALIZATION

Few research studies have attempted to explain the expansion of revenue in local governments in developing economies (but see Avellaneda 2012; Kim and Oh 2014; and Sebaa, Wallace, and Cornelius 2009). According to Stevens and McGowan (1983, 527), "There is a need for public administration, organization, and management theory to address, systematically, important aspects of public managerial strategies in cases in which the potential impact of these strategies has significant human and long-term economic implications." Revenue expansion exemplifies these types of strategies because it creates new opportunities for local activity and investment.

The preponderant evidence indicates that revenue expansion through external grants is among mayors' and managers' most pursued strategies. Stevens and McGowan's (1983) study of ninety local governments in Pennsylvania supports this view, identifying five key local strategy patterns and highlighting external revenue seeking as the most important among them.[1] Existing studies addressing the determinants of revenue expansion align with research on intergovernmental grants, but they often focus on political explanations and neglect the potential roles of both managers' competency and the environmental context in explaining the expansion of governmental revenue. This study contributes to the existing literature by proposing an explanatory model of municipal revenue expansion that includes managerial, institutional, political, and contextual variables.

## Managerial Competence

Although there is still a lack of consensus on the definition and determinants of managerial competence, three definitions are widely accepted. Armstrong and Stephens (2008) describe managerial competence as "any individual characteristic that can be measured or counted reliably and that can demonstrate significant distinction between effective and ineffective performance," and "all personal traits related to the work, knowledge, skills, and values [that] encourage people to [do] their job well." For Hroník (2007), managerial competence is a "bunch of knowledge, skills, experience" that support the achievement of organizational objectives. Similarly, Krontorád and Trčka (2005) define competence as "a combination of knowledge, skills, abilities, and behaviors that an employee uses in carrying out [his or her] work." In sum, these definitions characterize knowledge, experience, skills, and other individual characteristics as the foundations of managerial competence.

The literature on public management also suggests that individual managers' characteristics partially explain organizational actions (Lynn 1981; Meier and O'Toole 2002; Boyne 2004; Avellaneda 2009a). This view is reflected in Hambrick and Mason (1984, 193), who argue that "organizational outcomes are viewed as reflections of the values and cognitive bases of powerful actors in the organization." Upper echelons theory (UET) assumes that individuals act under bounded rationality (March and Simon 1958), with the core premise that executives' behavior and perspectives are functions of their values, experiences, and personalities (Hambrick and Mason 1984; Hambrick 2007; Finkelstein and Hambrick 1997). This theory also suggests that executives' demographic characteristics such as age, education, and sectorial backgrounds can function as proxies for their cognitive frames (Hambrick and Mason 1984). Although UET focuses on the characteristics of the top management team (TMT), Hambrick (2007, 334) clarifies that UET does not require a group of executives and that, in fact, "a number of significant contributions have examined CEOs or other individual leaders." As a result, the background characteristics of individual executives as well as top management teams have been examined as determinants of organizational growth (Boeker 1997), finances (Matsunaga and Yeung 2008), accounting (Bamber, Jiang, and Wang 2010), and bankruptcy (D'Aveni 1990), as well as local government performance in Israel (Carmeli 2004, 2006), Colombia (Avellaneda 2009a, 2009b, 2012), Dubai (Sebaa, Wallace, and Cornelius 2009), and the United States (Damanpour and Schneider 2009).[2]

## Managers' Individual Characteristics and Revenue Expansion

The literature on the private sector suggests that a manager's age tends to be associated with less organizational growth (Child 1974; Hart and Mellors 1970; Weinzimmer 1997). The rationale highlights the tendency among younger managers to take more risks, leading them to diversify outputs, policies, programs, and revenues (Wiersema and Bantel 1992), which contributes to organizational growth (Damanpour and Schneider 2006). Conversely, some of the public-sector literature associates young managers with inexperience, resulting in declining and/or unpredictable performance (Kearney, Feldman, and Scavo 2000). Other research in the public sector has found that city managers' ages are not systematically associated with strategy innovation (Damanpour and Schneider 2009). These inconsistent findings across the public and private sectors may suggest that managerial age–performance relationships depend on the nature of the task. However, because revenue expansion in the public sector parallels revenue expansion in the private sector, this study adopts the framework put forth by scholars in the private sector:

H1. Younger managers will be more likely to expand organizational revenue.

Next, education is commonly associated with technological and administrative innovation (Kimberly and Evanisko 1981; Bantel and Jackson 1989; Damanpour and Schneider 2006, 2009). As Hambrick and Mason (1984, 203) argue, "Professionally trained managers may view situations differently from those without a college degree."[3] Wiersema and Bantel (1992) find that managers with higher educational levels are more likely to undergo changes in organizational strategy. Damanpour and Schneider (2009), in their study of 725 US city managers, also found support for the education–innovation association. Likewise, Avellaneda's (2009b) study of Colombian mayors also finds support for an association between mayoral education and municipal performance:

H2. The higher a manager's level of educational achievement, the more successful he or she is likely to be in expanding organizational revenue.

According to Ericsson, Krampe, and Tesch-Römer (1993, 365–66), expertise refers to "domain-specific skills and knowledge, which are important to attainment of expert performance" and "is acquired slowly over a very long time as a result of practice." They also argue that "experts are faster and more accurate, . . . and their memory for representative stimuli from their domain is vastly superior to that of lesser experts, especially for briefly presented stimuli." Empirical research linking expertise and expert performance (Chi, Glaser, and Farr 2014; Ericsson and Smith 1991) has shown that experts' superior performance is acquired through long experience, and that the effect of practice on performance is large (Ericsson, Krampe, and Tesch-Römer 1993, 365–68):

H3. Managers with job-related experience tend to be more successful in expanding municipal revenue.

## Political Context and Organizational Performance

In addition to managerial competence, the political context in which managers perform is also expected to influence their organizations' performance. In accord with the introduction, any theory of context and public management must consider how public organizations are expected to respond to political demands. Whether political power is concentrated or dispersed is one of the key contextual variables that can be logically linked to public organizations' performance.

Electorally competitive contexts are one example of dispersed political power. In these electorally competitive or conflictual environments, managers seek to gain support from as much of the population as possible. In doing so, they may pursue more aggressive approaches to expanding organizational revenue in order to deliver more services. This model aligns with the electoral competitiveness hypothesis, which suggests that when elections are tight, incumbents have an incentive to provide more services in order to gain support from many segments of the population (Key 1949). Conversely, as Sharpe and Newton (1984, 180) observe, "Where there is little or no competition, parties in power rest on their laurels."

Although the party competition hypothesis has received some support (Holbrook and Van Dunk 1993), other quantitative studies of US state politics (Dye 1966) and Latin American municipal politics (Avellaneda 2009a, 2009b) conclude that party competition has little or no impact on service delivery. Nevertheless, the logical plausibility of improved managerial performance in electorally competitive settings calls for an additional test of the hypothesis:

> H4. Managers performing in politically competitive contexts are more likely to be successful in expanding municipal revenue.

Next, the impact of partisan alignment on state and federal transfers has received considerable attention. There are two possible hypotheses for the relationship between co-partisan and intergovernmental grants. One considers the positive political effect that grant acquisition may have on jurisdictions with a high number of swing voters (Lindbeck and Weibull 1987; Dixit and Londregan 1998). The alternative hypothesis suggests that, due to risk aversion, grants tend to be allocated to politically aligned jurisdictions (Cox and McCubbins 1986).

Although some scholars have underscored both the difficulty of separating these two hypotheses (Rodden and Wilkinson 2004) and the endogeneity problem inherent in grants, the evidence supports both views. For instance, in examining 255 Swedish municipalities from 1981 to 1995, Johansson (2003) finds that intergovernmental transfers are used to win votes. Likewise, Guinand, Botero, and Raga's (2008) study of Colombian municipalities from 2004 to 2006 reports that budgetary allocations for road infrastructure projects were used to win votes in localities whose party affiliation did not align with that of the president. Dahlberg and Johansson (2002) also provide evidence, though weak, in favor of the swing voters hypothesis, whereas Brollo and Nannicini (2012) find that Brazilian municipalities in which the mayor is affiliated with the coalition of the president received larger grant transfers in the final two years of the mayoral term. Solé-Ollé and Sorribas-Navarro (2008) find that in Spanish municipalities, grants given to co-partisans led to some political support, while grants given to opposition parties did not bring more votes:

H5. Partisan alignment increases the likelihood of revenue expansion.

## DATA AND METHODS

We test our hypotheses using data from 812 municipalities in the Brazilian state of Minas Gerais. Brazilian municipalities are equivalent in scope and structure to US counties and enjoy extensive, constitutionally granted fiscal and political autonomy, including the authority to design, fund, and implement policies and programs. Brazil, like most Latin American countries, has its own unique form of local government leadership: a strong, elected mayor. This structure stands in contrast to local government systems in the United States (council–manager and mayor–council) and the United Kingdom (four forms of local political leadership, including an elected mayor with a cabinet, an elected mayor with a council manager, a cabinet with a leader, and a modified committee system). As the position of city manager does not exist in Brazil, Brazilian mayors perform both political and administrative functions. Indeed, Latin American mayors are "in charge of most activities that require a certain degree of qualification" (Fiszbein 1997, 1037).

Unlike US city managers, who perform only administrative functions and are professional public administrators with extensive training in public policy (Feiock and Stream 1998), Brazilian mayors enter office with varying degrees of professional training and previous experience. Mayors are elected for four-year terms and may serve two consecutive terms, after which they must wait one term before running again. The Brazilian Constitution of 1988 stipulates a legislative body that oversees a directly elected mayor. This municipal council is elected concurrently with the mayor for a four-year period and consists of no fewer than nine and no more than twenty-one members in municipalities with populations smaller than 1 million; this number can reach up to fifty-five in cities with more than 5 million inhabitants.

In contrast to the United States, most Brazilian municipal spending is financed through state and federal transfers. Unlike these earmarked transfers, however, municipalities' own revenues—collected from royalties, service provisions, property and commerce taxes, and sales of their own assets and/or service provisions—can be spent in any sector. Municipalities may also submit grant proposals to state and national agencies requesting funding to cofinance projects or programs. These proposals are judged on their quality, justification, and clarity. Despite the availability of these cofinancing awards, very few mayors pursue these funds. This disinclination may be due to a lack of motivation, a lack of information, a lack of administrative support, competing managerial priorities, and/or a perception that these proposals are rarely successful. The exceptional nature of this type of grant seeking makes this measure a worthwhile indicator of innovative revenue expansion strategy.

The unit of analysis in this study is a municipality-year. Data availability limited the study to a six-year period (2005–10), covering the four years of the 2005–8 mayoral administration and the first two years of the 2009–12 administration. Mayoral inaugurations normally occur on January 1, unless municipal elections are rescheduled from the nationally designated date for extraordinary reasons. Because the beginning of the mayoral administration coincides with the beginning of the calendar year, it is possible to associate annual municipal indicators with a specific mayoral administration.

The Brazilian state of Minas Gerais has 853 municipalities with populations ranging from 884 to 2,350,000 inhabitants, a mean value of 18,744, and a standard deviation of 40,693. A large number of these municipalities, like those in the other twenty-three Brazilian states, are small, with populations below 20,000. Data availability limited the study to 812 municipalities in Minas Gerais. Data were obtained from three Brazilian federal agencies: the Brazilian Institute of Statistics and Geography (Instituto Brasileiro de Geografia e Estatística, IBGE), the Finbra system of the National Treasury (Secretaria do Tesouro Nacional), and the Superior Electoral Court (Tribunal Superior Eleitoral, TSE).

## Variable Definitions and Operationalization

It is important to clarify that the mechanisms affecting the amount of grant funds received may be very different from the factors affecting a mayor's motivation to apply for grants. Because data on grant applications are not available, however, our hypotheses are framed in terms of grants obtained. Two dependent variables capture grant acquisition in terms of the funds received from state and from national grants. Both types of revenue are distinct from mandatory central transfers, so they represent additional revenue obtained through efforts beyond the strict requirements of the job. Moreover, by disaggregating state and federal grants, this study allows us to determine whether factors influencing state grants vary from those explaining federal grant acquisition.

Every year, each federal ministry's website lists calls for proposals for cofinanced projects under its respective control. According to Luiz Carlos D'Antonino, the secretary of the Treasury in the municipality of Viçosa, the primary sources of federal grants are the ministries of cities, of health, and of education. D'Antonino says the federal government offers resources for the construction of new facilities. He adds that the state of Minas Gerais offers grants to buy municipal equipment, including ambulances, vehicles, and medical and educational equipment. D'Antonino also states that resources were made available to attend the 2014 World Cup Finals (held in Brazil).[4]

In Brazil, all financial transfers not required by law are regarded as voluntary transfers or grants. Brazil's Decree No. 6170 in 2007 (Brazil 2007), states that voluntary transfers can take the form of agreements, transfer contracts, and/or partnership agreements. Agreements, which can be made between the federal and state or local governments, between state and local governments, or between private organizations and state or local governments, are collaborative tools that may involve the development of projects, activities, and services; the purchasing of equipment; or the outsourcing of social services. Federal contributions to bilateral agreements are added to the federal budget. Transfer contracts are formal instruments similar to agreements, but the financing process instead involves a federal grant that is transferred to an intermediary organization, which in turn transfers the funds to the beneficiary state or local government. Partnership agreements take still another form of financial transfer, with funds moving from one federal institution to another. For example, public universities in Brazil receive research funding from federal ministries through partnership agreements.

The minimum value for an agreement between the federal government and a municipality is R$100,000 (approximately $50,000). Agreements are created for specific projects and require the following information: the objectives of the proposed project (e.g., a new building or a service), a technical description of the proposed project, a justification of the project's technical feasibility, an environmental impact report for the project, a cost estimation, and a description of the methods to be employed as well as a timetable for completion.

In order to be eligible for these grants, a municipality must have an excellent financial record, which is achieved by operating in strict accordance with federal and state financial regulations. According to Erik Guedes, secretary of the Treasury of the city of Juatuba, "A bad state or federal review of a municipality's accounting reports blacklists the municipality and makes it ineligible for applying for both agreements and transfer contracts."[5] Guedes also described the time-consuming nature of pursuing grants, stating that "accessing grants from federal and state government is a mining task, as the municipality, through its mayor, needs to consult the [Agreement and Transfer Contract Management System, Sistema de Convênios] every day, since new grant opportunities are posted almost hourly." He added, "This source of information has become so important that some mayors have created and staffed a specific procuring unit (or department), so they can (1) consult the system (bank of agreements), and (2) prepare projects and contact regional and federal representatives." The mayor of Juatuba created one such procuring unit, Guedes says, which has led to the municipality having a federal and state grant success rate of 70 to 80 percent.[6]

Ana Nabuco, secretary of planning in Belo Horizonte's City Hall, also highlighted the importance of mayoral innovation with respect to assigning staff to grant acquisition. Nabuco posited, "This is the right way of getting a good grasp of the process of increasing money from voluntary transfers."[7] When asked about the importance of a mayor's party affiliation in obtaining voluntary transfers, Nabuco responded, "Party affiliation is not an issue in ensuring grants because, in general, the mayor's goals include the public good, to do well, and to focus on the task at hand, that is, bringing grant monies." Nabuco did suggest that some national legislators advocate for additional state and federal monies for specific municipalities and subnational units in order to gain their political support. These modifications or additions (amendments) take place during the budget creation process. With respect to this budgeting process, Nabuco said that political contacts and connections are important.

The values for state, national, and total grants are reported in thousands of Brazilian real by IBGE. We transform these values into per capita amounts to make measures comparable across municipalities. Table 7.2 lists the

**Table 7.2** Descriptive Statistics for Brazilian Municipalities

| *Variable* | *Mean* | *Standard Deviation* | *Minimum* | *Maximum* |
|---|---|---|---|---|
| 1. State grants / cap | 308.71 | 315.81 | 30.43 | 5,899.87 |
| 2. Federal grants / cap | 1,108.94 | 2,005.73 | 6.58 | 57,580.93 |
| 3. Mayor's age | 48.81 | 10.06 | 23 | 85 |
| 4. Mayor's education | 5.03 | 1.97 | 1 | 7 |
| 5. Reelected mayor | 0.19 | 0.39 | 0 | 1 |
| 6. Governor–mayor party | 0.45 | 0.5 | 0 | 1 |
| 7. Competitive elections (margin of victory) | 17.86 | 19.37 | 0.01 | 100[a] |
| 8. President–mayor party | 0.13 | 0.33 | 0 | 1 |
| 9. Left ideology | 0.19 | 0.39 | 0 | 1 |
| 10. Mayor's councilmen support | 26.55 | 14.19 | 0 | 100 |
| 11. Population | 18,934.23 | 41,224.98 | 815 | 60,4013 |
| 12. Gross domestic product | 8,477.55 | 10,333.7 | 1,428.88 | 239,773.6 |
| 13. Royalties | 319,835.2 | 2.14E + 06 | 0 | 4.99E + 07 |

[a]There was a single candidate.

descriptive statistics for all variables. The study covers the four years of the 2005–8 mayoral administration and the first two years of the 2009–12 mayoral administration, for a total six-year period. However, because the estimation model includes the lag of the dependent variables, observations for 2005 are lost.

## Mayoral Competency as Individual Characteristics

In this study, *age* is a continuous variable. Values were obtained from the TSE, which gathers this information when mayoral candidates register their candidacy. *Level of Educational Achievement* is a categorical variable measuring a prospective mayor's education and ranging from 1 to 7. Brazil has no educational requirements for mayoral candidates. The categories are as follows: (1) can barely read or write their own name (2.81 percent in our sample), (2) incomplete primary education (17.09 percent), (3) completed primary education (8.55 percent), (4) incomplete high school degree (3.79 percent), (5) high school degree (25.40 percent), (6) incomplete undergraduate degree (3.79), and (7) formal undergraduate degree (38.58 percent). Data on mayoral education were obtained from TSE.

*Job-Related Experience* is a dummy variable for mayors who were elected in previous administrations, as they are expected to have acquired job-related expertise and awareness of potential grant sources and grant application processes. The variable is coded "1" for mayors who have served more than one term, whether consecutively or nonconsecutively.

*Partisan Alignment* measures party alignment between both the mayor and state officials and the mayor and federal leadership. For state-level convergence, this dummy variable is coded "1" when the mayor and the governor belong to the same political party ("0" otherwise). To measure party alignment at the national level, a dichotomous variable is coded "1" when the mayor and president are affiliated with the same political party ("0" otherwise). Although cofinanced federal grants can come from different institutions whose directors' partisanship is not publicly known, party alignment with the president may still benefit mayors, as many directors of these central entities are appointed by the president. Moreover, because party alignment at the federal level may influence mayors' inclination to apply for grants at the state level, and alignment at the state level might influence applications at the national level, each estimation model—state grants, federal grants, and total grants—includes both types of party alignment.

Neither presidential nor gubernatorial elections are concurrent with mayoral elections.[8] The study covers two presidential terms (2003–6 and 2007–10) in which the center-left Workers' Party, headed by Ignacio Lula, held the presidency. Likewise, the study includes two gubernatorial terms (also 2003–6 and 2007–10). In both gubernatorial periods, the Brazilian Social Democratic Party (Partido da Social Democracia Brasileira), with a center ideology, held power in Minas Gerais.[9]

## Control Variables

To avoid misattributing municipality effects to mayors' demographic characteristics and to avoid omitted variable bias, the study controls for government ideology, mayor–council political alignment, gross domestic product (GDP) per capita, municipal total revenues, and municipal revenues from royalty transfers. Mayoral ideology is included as a control variable to account for the government ideology thesis, which holds that parties are not only vote seekers but also office and policy seekers (Petry 1982). Although conservatives prefer low spending and low taxes, liberals prefer high spending and high taxes. Consequently, liberals are expected to seek more revenue in order to have more resources to spend (e.g., Alt and Lowry 1994).

Historically, Brazil has maintained a multiparty system. Moreover, in the last two decades, dissidents from the traditional parties have created several smaller groups, such that twenty-nine parties were represented in the mayoral elections in 2012 (TSE 2014). The proliferation of parties makes it difficult to delineate two clear ideological camps to test the government ideology thesis. This study takes the approach of comparing leftist mayors, who we expect to be associated with a more liberal position, against all other mayors. We create a dichotomous variable that received the value of "1" when a mayor's party is considered leftist, adopting Carreirão's (2006) left–right classification of political parties.[10]

We also control for partisan alignment between the mayor and the municipal council, whose members are also elected at the local level. We include this variable to address the possibility that mayors operating in politically divided governments (when more than 51 percent of the council members are not aligned with the mayor's party) may face difficulty in obtaining the council's support for their projects. Under these circumstances, mayors may be more aggressive in seeking federal or state grants, as these funds may not require the council's oversight. We operationalize this as a continuous variable reporting the percentage of council members that are politically aligned with the mayor. These values were obtained from TSE.

We also control for the socioeconomic level of each municipality, measured as GDP per capita. These data were collected from IBGE. Finally, we control for municipal revenues from royalty transfers as the presence of sufficient funds from these sources may discourage mayors from seeking to

**Table 7.3** Correlation Matrix for Brazilian Municipalities

| | *1* | 2 | 3 | 4 | 5 | 6 | 7 | 8 | 9 | *10* | *11* | 12 | *13* |
|---|---|---|---|---|---|---|---|---|---|---|---|---|---|
| 1. State grants / cap | 1 | | | | | | | | | | | | |
| 2. Federal grants / cap | 0.09 | 1 | | | | | | | | | | | |
| 3. Mayor's age | –0.02 | –0.02 | 1 | | | | | | | | | | |
| 4. Mayor's education | 0.03 | –0.1 | –0.17 | 1 | | | | | | | | | |
| 5. Reelected mayor | 0.02 | 0.02 | 0.01 | –0.02 | 1 | | | | | | | | |
| 6. Governor–mayor party | –0.01 | 0.00 | –0.04 | 0.08 | 0.01 | 1 | | | | | | | |
| 7. Competitive elections | 0.01 | 0.05 | –0.08 | 0.03 | 0.13 | 0.02 | 1 | | | | | | |
| 8. President–mayor party | –0.01 | –0.05 | –0.07 | 0.1 | –0.01 | 0.35 | 0.00 | 1 | | | | | |
| 9. Left ideology | 0.00 | –0.05 | –0.1 | 0.09 | 0.01 | 0.01 | –0.03 | 0.31 | 1 | | | | |
| 10. Mayor's councilmen support | 0.01 | 0.06 | –0.06 | –0.06 | 0.05 | 0.01 | 0.15 | 0.02 | –0.12 | 1 | | | |
| 11. Population | 0.03 | –0.14 | 0.1 | 0.15 | –0.03 | 0.02 | –0.04 | 0.06 | 0.04 | –0.15 | 1 | | |
| 12. Gross domestic product | 0.68 | 0.00 | 0.03 | 0.09 | –0.01 | 0.01 | –0.02 | 0.02 | 0.03 | –0.08 | 0.14 | 1 | |
| 13. Royalties | 0.3 | –0.02 | 0.01 | 0.08 | 0.01 | 0.00 | 0.01 | 0.03 | 0.04 | –0.06 | 0.12 | 0.25 | 1 |

expand municipal revenues. These values are reported in Brazilian real and were obtained through the Finbra system, which has been developed and maintained by the Federal Treasury. Correlations for all variables (table 7.3) report no high-value pairwise correlations.

## FINDINGS

Tables 7.4 and 7.5 provide the estimations for two dependent variables: state grants per capita and federal grants per capita. For each model, the variance inflation factors suggest that multicollinearity is not an issue. Models utilize random-effects estimations with White–Huber standard errors to correct for heteroskedasticity.

Table 7.4 reports the estimations for state grants per capita. Two of the coefficients on mayors' individual characteristics (age and education) report statistical significance. As expected, the coefficient on mayors' age is negative and statistically significant at the 0.05 level. Specifically, holding all else constant, as a mayor's age increases by one year, the amount of state grants in a municipality tends to decrease by R0.28 per capita. Therefore, H1 receives empirical support. Contrary to our expectations, the sign on the coefficient of education, although statistically significant, is negative. All else being equal, as mayor's education increases by one unit, the amount of state grants in a municipality tends to decrease by R3.21 per capita. Therefore, H2 fails to receive empirical support.

With respect to the political contextual variables, the coefficients on competitive elections (operationalized as the margin of victory) are positive and statistically significant at the 0.05 and 0.1 levels, respectively. For each percentage-point increase in the margin of victory between the winner and the runner-up, the amount of state grants in a municipality tends to increase by R0.1 per capita. Given that the relationship is contrary to expectations, H4 fails to receive empirical support. The other political contextual variables—mayor–president and mayor–governor partisan alignment—fail to achieve statistical significance.

Table 7.4 also reports that multiple control variables are meaningful. Municipalities collect fewer state grants in the first year of a mayoral administration than in the fourth (last) year of the same administration (the baseline category), suggesting some gains from experience in a term. Additionally, municipalities with higher income (GDP) tend to earn more grants.

Table 7.5 reports the estimations for federal grants per capita. The coefficient on mayor's age is positive and statistically significant at the 0.1 level, but the relationship is not consistent across the two models. For municipalities

**Table 7.4** State Grants in Brazilian Municipalities, 2005–10

| *Variable* | *State Grants / Cap* |
|---|---|
| Mayor's age | –0.284** |
| | (0.128) |
| Mayor's education | –3.212*** |
| | (0.994) |
| Ex-mayor | 3.097 |
| | (4.565) |
| Governor–mayor party | 0.485 |
| | (3.468) |
| Competitive elections | 0.101* |
| | (0.0559) |
| President–mayor party | –2.099 |
| | (7.829) |
| Left ideology | 6.053 |
| | (7.876) |
| Mayor's councilmen support | 0.0508 |
| | (0.141) |
| Gross domestic product (log) | 31.68*** |
| | (9.807) |
| Royalties (log) | 4.368 |
| | (3.965) |
| Distance to state capital (log) | –5.076* |
| | (2.726) |
| First administration year | –85.45*** |
| | (6.186) |
| Second administration year | –5.501 |
| | (3.791) |
| Third administration year | –11.04*** |
| | (3.573) |
| Lag state grants / cap | 1.015*** |
| | (0.0443) |
| Constant | –228.7** |
| | (91.16) |
| Observations | 3,736 |
| Number of municipalities | 812 |
| $R^2$ within | 0.43 |
| $R^2$ between | 0.87 |
| $R^2$ overall | 0.82 |

*Note:* Robust standard errors in parentheses. *** $p < 0.01$, ** $p < 0.05$, * $p < 0.1$.

**Table 7.5** Federal Grants in Brazilian Municipalities, 2005–10

| *Variable* | *Federal Grant / Cap* |
|---|---|
| Mayor's age | 0.755* |
| | (0.436) |
| Mayor's education | 1.019 |
| | (1.587) |
| Ex-mayor | –15.50** |
| | (6.645) |
| Governor–mayor party | 13.69 |
| | (16.78) |
| Competitive elections | –0.148 |
| | (0.154) |
| President–mayor party | 3.364 |
| | (7.306) |
| Left ideology | 9.354 |
| | (8.232) |
| Mayor's councilmen support | 0.418* |
| | (0.253) |
| Gross domestic product (log) | –19.77*** |
| | (6.296) |
| Royalties (log) | 9.849** |
| | (3.990) |
| Distance to state capital (log) | –5.970 |
| | (4.348) |
| First administration year | –286.2*** |
| | (18.07) |
| Second administration year | –155.1*** |
| | (9.323) |
| Third administration year | –96.83*** |
| | (9.794) |
| Lag federal grants / cap | 1.143*** |
| | (0.0186) |
| Constant | 156.5** |
| | (63.23) |
| Observations | 3,736 |
| Number of municipalities | 812 |
| $R^2$ within | 0.86 |
| $R^2$ between | 0.89 |
| $R^2$ overall | 0.88 |

*Note:* Robust standard errors in parentheses. *** $p < 0.01$, ** $p < 0.05$, * $p < 0.1$.

where mayors have been in office in the previous administration, the amount of state grants tends to decrease by R15.50 per capita, compared with those municipalities whose mayors are in office for the first time.

Interestingly, neither political variable is statistically significant. The results do, however, show that six control variables affect grants. Municipalities whose mayors have higher partisan support in the city council tend to earn more federal grants. Municipalities receiving higher royalties are also not prevented from acquiring more federal grants. Further, municipalities with higher income (GDP) tend to earn fewer federal grants.

## IMPLICATIONS

This study explores whether a municipality's political context and mayoral competency influence municipal revenue expansion through state and federal grants, testing two dimensions of the public management contextual matrix proposed in this book. The study focuses on 812 Brazilian municipalities from 2005 to 2010, covering two mayoral administrations: the four years of the 2005–8 administration and the first two years of the 2009–12 administration. Brazilian municipalities are appropriate settings to examine the drivers of revenue expansion because mayors are responsible for both political and administrative responsibilities. Moreover, because Brazil has few constitutional requirements for mayoral candidacy, mayors' individual characteristics vary considerably. We assess political context in terms of electorally competitive environments and both mayor–governor and mayor–president partisan alignment. Mayors' competencies (professionalization), as associated values, are operationalized through age, education level, and job-related experience (Hambrick and Mason 1984; Hambrick 2007).

This study has explored the mechanisms that explain municipal revenue expansion through two types of supplementary revenues—state grants and federal grants—assuming that the political context across these two levels of government may vary in important ways. Our findings show that younger mayors may be more proactive in exploring alternative channels for enlarging municipal coffers. Contrary to our expectations, mayoral education and job-related experience are negatively correlated with municipal revenue expansion. The negative correlation between job-related experience (e.g., ex-mayor) and revenue expansion may be explained by mayors' inability to run for a third term, thus discouraging them from spending time and resources on obtaining additional revenue. This finding suggests that, given the nature of grant acquisition, political and network factors have a greater role than other mayoral characteristics. Moreover, this finding indirectly suggests that the complexity and turbulence of the municipal environment matter, as mayors have to work with numerous stakeholder groups.

These results are also consistent with Avellaneda's (2012, 2016) studies of Colombian and Salvadorian municipalities, in which mayoral characteristics (e.g., education and experience) fail to explain the expansion of revenues through state and national grants. Nevertheless, these findings contradict studies in the public sector that find a positive relationship between city managers' background characteristics and their decision to innovate in the United States (Damanpour and Schneider 2009), their strategy type in Dubai's local governments (Sebba et al. 2009), and their collecting efficiency ratio in Israeli municipalities (Carmeli 2006). Still, these results do appear to align with scholarship arguing that the influence of individual top managers on organizational actions is more limited in some contexts than others and may be contingent on the nature of the organizational outcome that is assessed (Lieberson and O'Connor 1972; Salanick and Pfeffer 1977). Future research should explore the revenue expansion effects of other dimensions of the proposed context framework, including complexity, turbulence, social capital, and munificence.

Finally, the results provide mixed support for the role of political context in securing grants. Electoral competition appears to matter, whereas partisan alignment does not. The latter finding is contrary to our expectations; one possible explanation might be that in less politically competitive contexts, there is no crucial need to convince swing voters, and mayors can dedicate more time to finding alternative ways to expand municipal revenues. The findings also reveal that the electoral cycle matters for grant acquisition. In general, municipalities tend to earn more annual grant funding in the last (fourth) year of the mayoral administration than in the administration's first three years.

## NOTES

1. The other four strategy patterns are trade-offs between autonomous versus central financing, internal revenue seeking, additional state aid and authority seeking, and having the state pay for high-cost items.
2. Critics of UET suggest that the influence of individual top managers is limited (Lieberson and O'Connor 1972; Salanick and Pfeffer 1977), and that executive selection and socialization processes produce homogeneity in organizational choices and actions (Datz 2000).
3. Some argue that neither type nor degree of education has a substantial effect on managerial competence, as these factors only serve as a filtering device for matching up individuals with jobs they are suited to perform (Pfeffer 1981).
4. Telephone interview in December 2013; translated from Portuguese.
5. Telephone interview in December 2013; translated from Portuguese.

6. Telephone interview in November 2013; translated from Portuguese.
7. Telephone interview in December 2013; translated from Portuguese.
8. For the period covered in this study, presidential elections took place in 2002, 2006, and 2010.
9. According to the Brazilian Constitution, governors are elected directly to a four-year term, with a limit of two terms.
10. According to Carreirão (2006), the political parties DEM, PR, PP, PFL, PRN, PDC, PL, PTB, PSC, PSP, PRP, PSL, PSD, and PRONA represent the right wing. PMDB and PSDB are regarded as central; but due to their conservative orientation, we considered them part of the rightist category. The PHS, PPS, PRB, PRTB, PSD, PSDC, PT DO B, PTC, and PTN are considered centrist parties. PT (President Lula's party), PDT, PPS, PCdoB, PSB, PV, PSTU, PCO, and PMN are regarded as left-wing parties.

# Conclusion

## *The Future Role of Context: The International Research Agenda*

AMANDA RUTHERFORD, LAURENCE J. O'TOOLE JR., AND KENNETH J. MEIER

Effective management of public organizations is a universal concern. The receptivity of governments around the world to New Public Management reforms (Pollitt and Bouckaert 2000), for instance, indicates that this issue is salient at the highest levels of governance on several continents.[1] Reforms, however, are generally plagued by what one might term "Taylor's disease," or the idea that there is one best way to manage and that a one-size-fits-all approach is applicable to all circumstances and settings.[2] The quest for the one best way to manage, however, has been so consistently disappointing for such a long period that one expects to hear the theme from *Man of La Mancha* playing in the background. An alternative view of management is that it is highly contingent (for classic expositions, see Burns and Stalker 1961; Lawrence and Lorsch 1967; and Thompson 1967), and that what works depends critically on the context in which management operates.

The objective of this book is to go beyond the basic "it all depends" generalization of some context approaches (Sherman 1966) to specify more precisely how context mitigates the relationship between management and performance. The book's introduction started the process by presenting a systematic framework for incorporating context into studies of public management. The espoused theory considers political, environmental, and organizational contexts and presents a series of testable hypotheses for studies of public management. Although the theory moves far away from the idea that there is one best way to manage, it still seeks to pursue the development and testing of a general theory of public management, a theory that begins with a clear, albeit inevitably partial, specification of context. Chapters 1 through 7 then provide a set of empirical studies using a wide range of public organizations in several different settings. This concluding chapter reviews the findings of the empirical chapters in light of the overall theory to determine what we have learned. It uses these findings to set the agenda for future studies of public management.

## RECAPPING THE THEORY

The theory of context used in this book is unapologetically a theory of *public* management; indeed, it is premised on an earlier theoretical argument about how the relationship between management and performance is likely to vary between public and private settings (Meier and O'Toole 2011). It begins with a discussion of the centralization of political power. If public management differs from private management, then the characteristics of an organization's political context is the logical place to begin a theory of public management. The centralization of political power implies bringing in the authority of the state to resolve conflicts and set clear public policy goals that are supported by adequate resources to implement programs. If the political system does not perform such tasks, managers themselves need to perform them—a circumstance that, in turn, can be expected to make their jobs more difficult. A unitary political system that does not use federalism as an organizing principle and has a corporatist political process that also establishes a clear performance appraisal system provides the most conducive context for effective public management. The separation of powers, federal systems, adversarial political processes, and the absence of a performance appraisal system all can either create additional political challenges that public managers must overcome or, in the worst case scenario, even make it impossible to define what the job of a public manager entails.

The second level of context is organizational and draws heavily from the literature on the open systems theories of organizations (Thompson 1967). Organizations' environments vary in complexity, turbulence, and munificence (Dess and Beard 1984), as well as in social capital, a specific element of munificence that can directly affect program implementation. Public management is likely to be easier and more effective in environments that are simple and placid but are also characterized by ample resources, including (supportive) social capital. Management actions that work in such conducive environments are less likely to be as successful, to the extent that environments are complex, change rapidly, lack resources, or operate in communities that lack social capital.

The third level of context is internal to the organization and deals with goals, centralization, and professionalization. Clear and consistent goals are thought to enhance management effectiveness by simplifying the tasks that managers need to coordinate and perform (Chun and Rainey 2005). Centralization and decentralization are frequently used as organization strategies, but their impact depends on the locus of skill levels in the organization and how important it is to implement programs consistently. Professionalization can enhance the impact of management on performance, but it is also thought to change or require that the style of management be more decentralized and participatory to be effective with highly skilled and educated professionals who may prize discretion (Raelin 1989).

## THE RANGE OF STUDIES

Given the large number of variables in the contextual theory of public management and the even wider range of activities that management can perform (e.g., networking, developing human resources, learning from experience, clarifying goals, providing feedback to employees, creating incentives, and adjusting to employee values), no single set of studies can be definitive. Even classifying this book's seven empirical chapters by the dimensions of the context typology proves to be somewhat difficult, because many of the dimensions stipulated in the theory vary across units *within* the actual individual studies themselves. In some cases, the chapter authors have been able to incorporate the contextual variable into the study and use an interaction effect to test the theory at the organizational level—much as the theoretical argument stipulates. Torenvlied and Akkerman's study of Dutch primary education in chapter 4, for example, takes advantage of the different organizational environments of denominational schools relative to nondenominational schools, because denominational schools have environments that are less complex and less turbulent but more munificent with greater social capital. Wimpy, Jackson, and Meier's study of health care in Africa in chapter 1 is able to operationalize administrative capacity (a form of professionalization) and show how it directly affects performance as well as mitigates the impact of path dependence. In other cases, the individual organizations vary too much for the authors to classify them into groups; this is especially the case for the

Honduran and Brazilian local governments described, respectively, by Avellaneda in chapter 6 and by Gomes and Avellaneda in chapter 7.

Given such variance, the empirical studies included here do not sum to a simple conclusion. They present management-and-performance results for many settings, with quite different contexts, while testing or emphasizing different dimensions of context in different locations. As emphasized below, many types of possible contextual variation are also not represented in this volume. There is no comparison, for instance, of public organizational settings with and without established performance appraisal systems, nor is there an explicit comparison of corporatist and adversarial political systems (both types are represented in the studies, with the Danish and Dutch studies operating in the former, and several others in versions of the latter). Indeed, the theoretical argument offers more dimensions of contextual variation than there are cases to examine, thus making it impossible in principle to precisely specify a set of validated conclusions overall. Nevertheless, the empirical studies draw from a range of data sources and methodological approaches, and the authors offer many theoretical and empirical insights for addressing questions of management, context, and performance. Accordingly, we tease out some of these by sketching a set of lessons to be drawn from this set of investigations.

## Lesson 1: Management Matters Directly for Performance

As has been demonstrated in numerous other studies, these analyses provide ample evidence that management matters. For instance, in chapter 2 Andrews shows that organizational strategies of English local governments, a feature largely shaped by management, help to determine performance (defined as the Comprehensive Performance Assessment rating from the Audit Commission). Similarly, albeit with respect to a different facet of management, Torenvlied and Akkerman show that networking by managers matters for the performance of Dutch primary education. In chapter 3 Stieg and Rutherford provide evidence that some features of the top management of US universities—that is, university presidents—are related to various performance metrics. Limitations across these studies are readily identifiable, of course. None of the studies in this book estimates all or even most of the ways in which management shapes performance, and none incorporates the influence of multiple levels of management within public organizations. Some of this research, further, generates null findings regarding certain aspects of management (e.g., Gomes and Avellaneda find that mayoral competency in Brazil—as measured by age, educational attainment, and level of experience—is unrelated to local grant acquisition). Nevertheless, the complete set of analyses presented in this book adds much support to the mounting evidence that public management is necessarily linked to organizational performance.

## Lesson 2: Context Is More Varied Than the Theory Presents

The authors of the cases used in this book were not required to shoehorn their research into the contextual framework as a precondition for inclusion in the volume, but rather were asked post hoc to place their study within the framework. A reading of the individual chapters clearly indicates that the context of public management contains elements that were not expressly included in the model. In other words, the theory presented by O'Toole and Meier in the book's introduction, though large in scope, is not fully comprehensive. Both Gomes and Avellaneda's study of local management in Brazil and Avellaneda's experimental study of local managers' spending decisions in Honduras incorporate aspects of the political context that might be termed turbulence or uncertainty. Electoral competitiveness, political ideology, and political support from the legislative body or other political officials are all influential in either the decisions made by local officials (in Honduras) or the effectiveness of local chief executives (in Brazil). Although the public officials studied are mayors and thus are likely to be very sensitive to political forces, appointed officials also need to be sensitive to the forces of political change (Wood and Waterman 1994). There is no a priori reason, therefore, to dismiss these electoral forces as irrelevant to the activities of most public managers. Similarly, we have enough data on political influences on bureaucracies in more developed countries to not discount or limit these findings as unique to the developing world (Meier and Bohte 2007).

The electoral and political uncertainty and thus the policy uncertainty created by political forces at the same time tap into the underlying dimensions of the political environment presented in the theory. In the same manner that the electoral uncertainty in the two Latin American cases affects mayors, a number of factors—the separation of powers, federalism, corporatism / adversarial politics, and performance appraisal systems—all contribute to the relative degree of uncertainty faced by public managers. These factors could well exacerbate the role of electoral uncertainty, in that more centralized systems facing electoral uncertainty are likely to create frequent change and complicate the role of public managers. Decentralized systems, conversely, create uncertainty about what types of policy and management are acceptable, but they also have the advantage of being able to politically change at the local level, where the change should be less disruptive (in the sense that change affects fewer programs and people). This relatively stable environment might be preferred over one that is more certain but highly turbulent politically.

In chapter 5, Jacobsen, Kjeldsen, and Pallesen's study of public service motivation in Danish hospitals illustrates another dimension of context: policy. Developing public service motivation is generally seen as a positive thing, in that it serves as an incentive for modestly paid public servants to invest heavily in organizational performance. The policy context, however, can change the predicted relationship between public service motivation and performance. When a policy requires fewer services or a reduction in access, public service motivation becomes a hindrance to the implementation of public programs—a notion that, in somewhat different terms (organizational "zealots"), was sketched long ago by Downs (1967). The role of public service motivation and whether managers should attempt to cultivate it are contingent on how programs are designed.[3] Public service motivation is only one possible value that might interact with the policy context. The literature on street-level bureaucracy provides a variety of other examples whereby bureaucratic values displace or resist policy objectives, thus moderating the efforts of management to encourage implementation (Brehm and Gates 1997; May and Winter 2009).

## Lesson 3: Context Can Have Direct Effects

The theory of context has been presented to illuminate how context might influence the relationship between managerial action and organizational performance. Stressing this element means less emphasis on the traditional impact of context—the direct link to organizational performance. Nevertheless, the initial framing of the theoretical argument also calls for contextual features' direct effects on performance, as well as the interaction with management that can moderate the management–performance relationship. Regarding the direct effects of context, it can be noted that the studies in this volume clearly demonstrate such a relationship with performance. The Brazil and Honduran studies, as noted above, show that political context both affects the decisions managers make (Honduras) and also influences the effectiveness of chief executives in raising revenue (Brazil). Task difficulty is a key influence in a variety of other studies. The number of disadvantaged students is negatively linked to Dutch education outcomes; similarly, the percentage of black, Latino, and part-time students can constrain the salient indicators of performance for US colleges and universities. Ethnic diversity is negatively linked to local government performance in the England, whereas ethnic fractionalization, poverty, rurality, and generally low levels of development have major influences on health outcomes in Africa.

## Lesson 4: Context Can Be Embedded within Context

The theory considered in the introduction presented context and its impact as a series of independent influences on the link between management and performance. Even though this theory is interactive in nature, at its core, the effects of context on the management–performance relationship were presented as linear and additive. This oversimplification made the theoretical presentation easier, but the studies in this book demonstrate that context includes many intersections. Torenvlied and Akkerman show that the percentage of female teachers is negatively linked to performance in the Netherlands, a finding that directly contradicts the positive relationship found in the United States (Keiser et al. 2012). The interaction of one contextual element (gender) with other dimensions of context (likely historical patterns of job segregation) is virtually unexplored and needs further research. Only with more studies in a wider variety of contexts will the implications of intersectionality in context become clearer.

The notion of intersectionality in contextual characteristics implies, in turn, that at least some embedded features of context-within-context can be considered and estimated via multilevel modeling. There is no inherent reason why context must be considered at only one level, and thus both organizational-level contextual variation and also variation at the level of, for instance, national or subnational political systems could be treated simultaneously. None of the studies presented in this book provide such an analysis, but in principle this approach is feasible and likely to yield intriguing results.

## Lesson 5: Context Turns Some Variables into Constants

Comparing the study of health policy in Africa with education in the Netherlands or the United States provides insights on the meaning of organizational context in a field that seeks to be more international in orientation. Wealth—measured as per capita income, or levels of unemployment, or number of disadvantaged students—appears to affect performance in all contexts, even though what might be thought of as "wealth" in Sub-Saharan Africa is much different from what would be considered wealth in the United States. At the same time, contextual variation can completely disappear. Such contextual factors that indicate task difficulty in Africa—access to improved water, a lack of domestic armed conflict, access to the internet—become constants or nearly so in the Netherlands or the United States, such that they are not even measured.

Similarly, if the relationship between management and performance is subject to diminishing marginal returns, changing the context can place the relationship at different points on the marginal returns line. Access to clean water is an excellent example. Within Sub-Saharan Africa, access to clean water is limited, and waterborne diseases become a major health problem to be solved. Health gains made by improving water quality can be substantial in this context. Within a developed country, the marginal returns from investments in water quality on waterborne diseases are close to being exhausted. Public management issues are likely to shift in such circumstances to problems that are more difficult to address, like health issues involving toxins or industry-linked pollutants.

### Lesson 6: The Level of Development Is an Additional Aspect of Environmental Context

The situation described above about different points on the marginal returns line can be connected to a larger matter. As explained in the introduction, the vast majority of studies about public management and performance have been conducted in North American and European settings, where the level of economic development is quite high in relative terms. The studies in this book, however, range much more broadly on this dimension. Management in Northern Europe and the United States is included, but so are studies drawn from Latin America and Sub-Saharan Africa. To further extend consideration of the environmental context, in theoretical terms, an incorporation of the level or degree of (economic) development can supplement the theoretical arguments provided in the introduction. Here we can provide several additional theoretical notions.

Public managerial contexts differ greatly in the level or extent of development, especially economic development. This is particularly true, of course, when considering how public management operates in countries that differ vastly in educational levels, social stability, and economic advancement. Management should operate best when provided with relatively stable settings, competent and depoliticized civil service systems, and a well-developed infrastructure for generating performance. Accordingly, an additional hypothesis can be offered based on the fact that more management (via more highly trained and better-educated managers, and more opportunities to manage) has a larger effect than less management:

> H25. The total contribution of management—internal and external—to performance will be greater in more developed contexts.

In one sense, of course, we could consider the level of development as a broad way of interpreting the concept of environmental munificence. However, because "munificence" is usually employed to characterize the settings of organizations in advanced market economies (and therefore the range of the munificence variable is usually relatively modest), we can treat developmental contexts as a broader and more wide-ranging set of considerations.

In addition, it is helpful to consider not only the general level of development of a context but also the competitive advantage of certain aspects of management in such settings. Management training might be a variable that means something different as the development context changes. In a developing economy, a rudimentary knowledge of the causal linkages in policy might be all that is necessary. Simple and inexpensive incentives are likely to be effective in poor countries where subsistence living is the norm, but the incentives for dentists to participate in national health programs in the United Kingdom appear much more complex (Chalkley et al. 2010).

Obviously, we have much more to learn about how the level of development in a context is likely to affect the relationship between management and performance, and we await a much larger array of systematic management studies in a wide variety of developmental circumstances. This topic too, therefore, could benefit from more thorough theoretical and also empirical scholarship.

Although the level of management capacity and the total impact of management are likely to be greater in more developed contexts, we should expect management to be subject to diminishing marginal returns. As an illustration, education clearly contributes to a manager's ability, either by exposing the individual to management theory or by contributing to his or her ability to analyze problems. As such talents become widely available, however, the relative contribution to one organization is unlikely to stand out. This suggests that the same level of education or the same level of managerial effort in a developing context might actually have a larger marginal impact. Similarly, policy instruments such as clean water and mosquito nets are highly relevant in health policy administration in Africa but are unlikely to matter in more developed contexts. Thus:

> H26. The marginal impact of a given level of managerial effort or quality will have a greater relative impact for an organization in a developing context than it will in a developed context.

## Lesson 7: The Basic Interactive Hypothesis Is Supported

The theoretical argument opening this volume suggests that there are good reasons to expect not only that management might influence performance directly, and not only might context affect performance directly, but also that management and context may have interactive effects, thus influencing how much management can affect performance. Such a moderating effect might enhance, diminish, or even reverse the sign of how management shapes performance.

Several empirical analyses included in this volume offer evidence validating this expected moderating effect. In considering English local governments, Andrews shows that a prospecting managerial strategy can mitigate the negative impact of task complexity, and that defending and reacting strategies can increase the negative impact of task difficulty. Wimpy, Jackson, and Meier demonstrate that administrative capacity interacts with path dependence (in this case, historically existing bureaucratic capacity) to generate even larger positive effects on health outcomes. And Torenvlied and Akkerman show similar results, in that administrative capacity (administrative intensity) can enhance the impact of a team involvement approach but undercut the benefits of human capital quality. The experimental evidence presented by Avellaneda indicates that the Honduran political context affects how mayors shape decisions about whether to delegate spending authority. Stieg and Rutherford find that public versus private ownership has modest influences on the relationship between various managerial traits and outcomes in higher education. As Jakobsen, Kjeldsen, and Pallesen show, an aspect of internal context in a Danish hospital—the presence of employees who are highly motivated to provide public service—facilitates some aspects of management reform and impedes others. Torenvlied and Akkerman present results that indicate that a school's sector (i.e., denominational vs. nondenominational) fundamentally changes the influence that managerial networking has on performance, which leads nodes to become important, as well as how much each node matters. Collectively, the empirical studies offer many good reasons for researchers to explore in greater detail the various ways and circumstances in which features of context shape the management–performance relationship.

Each of the interactions reported in this book's set of studies relies on having contextual variation within the study itself, so that it can be incorporated directly into the modeling process. To the extent that such designs are possible, they contribute to the overall theory of context, management, and performance. At the same time, the contextual differences within these studies are highly constrained, especially if the study takes place within a single country. Cross-national assessments such as the one done here for Sub-Saharan Africa, which allow for large differences in context, face another limitation, in that measures of management are typically absent or are difficult to develop. Progress in such areas will require numerous studies that contain the specifics necessary to fit the study within the context matrix, and studies that are similar enough so that results can still be compared.

To assess the range of studies relative to the contextual theory, table C.1 merges the various chapter tables into a single table to indicate the range of contextual variation covered, in one way or another, in this book. Yet even though the current volume is explicitly crafted to move empirical studies of public management and performance beyond the normal US and UK databases to generate greater variety in context, the cells of table C.1 are not equally populated. Studies of unitary political systems clearly outnumber studies of separation-of-powers systems; in fact, only Stieg and Rutherford's study of higher education in the United States includes a political context characterized by the separation of powers. Similarly, only two studies are set in corporatist political systems—Jacobsen, Kjeldsen, and Pallesen's study of Danish hospitals and Torenvlied and Akkerman's examination of Dutch primary education. In a third example, aside from Wimpy, Jackson, and Meier's study of Sub-Saharan African health outcomes, none of the chapters deals unambiguously with contexts of low levels of social capital (the investigations set in Brazil and Honduras indicate varied levels of social capital).

**Table C.1** Studies of the Public Management Context

| **The Political Context—Concentration of Power** | | |
|---|---|---|
| Separation of powers | *Unitary*<br>Holland<br>Honduras<br>Brazil<br>Denmark<br>Africa<br>England | *Shared*<br>United States |
| Federalism | *One level of government*<br>Holland<br>Brazil<br>Denmark<br>United States | *Multiple levels*<br>England<br>Honduras<br>Africa |
| Process | *Corporatist*<br>Holland<br>Denmark | *Adversarial*<br>Brazil<br>Honduras<br>Africa<br>England<br>United States |
| Performance appraisal | *Established*<br>Holland<br>United States<br>England<br>Denmark | *No formal system*<br>Honduras<br>Brazil<br>Africa |

**Table C.1** (*continued*)

| **The Environmental Context** | | |
|---|---|---|
| Complexity | *Complex*<br>Holland<br>Denmark<br>England<br>United States | *Simple*<br>Africa |
| Turbulence | *Turbulent*<br>Holland<br>Denmark<br>Africa<br>England<br>United States | *Placid*<br>None |
| Munificence | *Rich*<br>Holland<br>Denmark<br>England | *Poor*<br>Honduras<br>Brazil<br>United States<br>Africa |
| Social capital | *Present*<br>Holland<br>Denmark<br>England<br>United States | *Absent*<br>Africa |
| **The Internal Context** | | |
| Goals | *Clear and Consistent*<br>Holland | *Multiple and conflicting*<br>England<br>Honduras<br>Denmark<br>United States<br>Africa |
| Centralization | *Centralized, hierarchical*<br>England<br>Denmark<br>Africa | *Decentralized*<br>United States<br>Holland |
| Professionalization | *Professional*<br>Holland<br>Denmark<br>England<br>United States | *Not professional*<br>Africa<br>Honduras |

*Note:* The authors were unable to classify Brazil and Honduras on all dimensions.

The studies in this book also reflect the contexts and problems that public management scholars find most interesting. Although there was a serious effort to break away from the focus on studies in North America and Northern Europe, public management scholars also tend to focus on areas that pose significant challenges for public managers, such as highly turbulent and challenging environments. Only the study of Sub-Saharan Africa categorized the management environment as placid and not complex. At the same time, we think that valuable information has been gained from the study of health policy in Africa and that similar contexts also merit study. In short, though the research included in this book considerably expands the contextual variation typically present in the field's study of public management and performance, much more exploration of many dimensions of context needs to be done.

A reminder here is also in order: As mentioned in passing in the introductory theoretical discussion, context may well have additional effects that have not been explored here and that have not been systematically developed in the theoretical arguments sketched thus far. We can speculate that context might affect such relationships as the role of organization structure, incentives, culture, and other variables, and how they relate to each other as well as to performance. We have ignored these possibilities so as to render a coherent theoretical treatment of management, context, and performance, but such work may be part of the field's future directions.

For the present, and with the focus on the issues raised in this book, considerable additional research is warranted. Note, for instance, that more than twenty hypotheses have been developed here about the moderating effects of context on the public management–performance link. The authors of the studies included here report a range of findings that are largely supportive of the lessons sketched in this chapter, and yet not a single one of the hypotheses is now close to being either confirmed or rebutted. Making substantial additional progress will definitely require sustained attention from many scholars over a considerable period of time. It is likely that some of the theoretical ideas sketched here will eventually be found to be wrong, or at least incomplete. Essentially, the agenda involving context as moderator has barely been launched at this point. In considering the requisites for substantial additional progress, therefore, eight additional points about furthering the agenda for the field are worthy of emphasis.

## NOTES FOR THE FUTURE

In addition to the application of time and scholarly attention, how are we likely to make significant advances in our understanding of context's conditional effects on management and performance? Eight steps can be suggested.

Most of these are not new or particularly obscure, but they are worth identifying briefly here, because major improvements in a theory of context require considerable research advancement of several kinds.

*First, systematic cross-national comparative research on public management and performance is essential.* There have been false starts in the development of a research literature on comparative administration, and this field of specialty stands in need of much further development. The impediments to solid work on which others can build are multiple and significant, including on such issues as comparative measurement (e.g., see Bekke, Perry, and Toonen 1996 and Jilke, Meuleman, and Van de Walle 2015). But without such cross-national work, especially outside the usual US and UK settings, the range of contextual variation regarding political context in particular, along with some aspects of environmental and internal context, will remain quite limited. Other work that includes cases across national settings but also integrates them into a common contextual framework—such as the research presented in this volume—can also help. But truly comparative scholarship must be part of the picture as well.

*Second, it is important that the field not be largely limited to convenience samples in comparative cross-national research.* There are many understandable reasons why convenience can come to dominate comparative scholarship. The priorities of funding agencies, the location of resources essential to good comparative research, the availability of reliable data, and the distribution of highly trained research partners all contribute to the inevitable pattern of oversampling from highly developed contexts, especially in North America and Western Europe. But if we are to learn systematically how dimensions of context condition the relationship between management and performance, researchers need to be selecting cases for their considerable variation along selected dimensions of context. The relative gains from rare cases or from cases that pose challenges to existing theories far exceed the gains from repeatedly re-tilling a field.

*Third, in a related point, it may be particularly useful to coordinate comparative research involving indigenous scholars from national settings that have been studied much less.* For reasons of language, culture, and access, among many others, involving and closely integrating the combined efforts of such scholars may be the best way to explore and compare many countries in the developing world, in particular.

*Fourth, as part of comparative cross-national studies of management and performance, it will be especially important to seek measures of performance—outputs and outcomes of public programs and public agencies—that are reasonably comparable.* The frequently chosen route of relying on perceptual measures of performance should be avoided, especially when the measures of management are also drawn from the same respondents. Such approaches have been shown to produce biased results (Meier and O'Toole 2013a, 2013b; Favero and Bullock 2015).

*Fifth, although comparative cross-national research is particularly important, much can also be learned by undertaking systematic studies of several aspects of contextual variation within national settings.* Public agencies pursuing rather similar goals within the same country can vary considerably in such dimensions as complexity, turbulence, munificence, social capital, centralization, and professionalization. And though the ranges are likely to be more truncated than would be the case worldwide, there may be corresponding advantages. For instance, other important variables may be physically (e.g., political context) or statistically controllable, and the potentially moderating effect of the contextual dimension of interest may be able to be isolated. A priority can be made, therefore, of examining sets of cases—especially, but not exclusively, large-*N* sets–where such contextual variation can be rigorously analyzed.

*Sixth, studies over time that explore the management–performance relationship when context shifts might be particularly revealing.* Some aspects of context are likely to be very stable over extended periods of time, but others may shift considerably in a relatively rapid manner. Public management has very few longitudinal data sets, and those that do exist span relatively short periods. We expect that managers will learn over time and, therefore, that some management actions might become more effective while others might fall into disuse.

*Seventh, as suggested above, multilevel analyses of how context moderates the management–performance relationship could be valuable.* Such investigations might be able to take into account managerial influences from more than one level—note that in the current volume, there are several instances in which managerial efforts from levels other than the one centrally in focus are necessarily ignored for lack of data—as well as different aspects of context operating at these multiple levels. At this stage, it is not clear to what extent underspecification of the management situation might understate or modify performance effects; more ambitious studies can help answer this question.

*Eighth, and finally, it is apropos to repeat an often-mentioned refrain: Bigger, better data sets will be necessary for a more complete explication of how context conditions the relationship between public management and performance.* Especially valuable will be data sets that include specific measures of context, as well as multiple aspects of performance and appropriate controls. Data sets that contain this information for an extended period are to be preferred. Given that almost no archival data sets include good measures of management, it is likely that these will need to be supplemented by further data-gathering efforts to tap public management, primarily by surveys of managers themselves or their employees. Most of the progress that has been made in estimating the impact of management on performance has taken advantage of a few data sets with this set of characteristics, including the addition of management to archival data and the development of several measures of management. Pointing out the limitations of current data sets is certainly appropriate, but what is most needed is a serious effort to build better data sets, which should be regularly expanded where feasible and made available generally to interested researchers.

## CONCLUSION

There are many challenges in advancing this line of research, but the potential gains from pursuing the hypotheses offered here in longitudinal, comparative data sets promise to substantially influence the study of public organizations. The chapters in this book have provided a small step forward in this endeavor, but much more effort is required from scholars of public administration to build a generalizable theory that incorporates context into the management–performance relationship. We have suggested many ways in which this research may be advanced, as applied to fewer than two dozen hypotheses. Yet context is likely to be a powerful intervening factor in many other relationships outside of the management–performance link, and scholars should not be hesitant to explore these avenues of inquiry. In fact, we encourage researchers to pursue these more ambitious goals rather than remain focused on the low-hanging fruit that may come from revisiting existing data or verified causal linkages.

Our goal in this book is to broaden the approach to important questions about how and when management matters in the broadest sense. At worst, this book will be of interest to readers but will not be extended further. At best, these studies can initiate an innovative line of scholarship in which we compare and contrast data across public services, across subnational jurisdictions, and across developed and undeveloped countries.

### NOTES

1. The New Public Management itself has not been offered as a tight, logically coherent approach, and its adoption and implementation in different countries have actually been highly varied (Barzelay 2001). There are plenty of other examples of overhyped and popularized management "reforms," including such venerable instances as pay for performance (hyped by political leaders) and following the injunctions of so-called best practices research (Overman and Boyd 1994).

2. The one-best-way philosophy of management dates back at least to Frederick Taylor (1911), in his *Principles of Scientific Management*.
3. A parallel example involves the implementation of welfare reform in the United States after the passage of the Personal Responsibility and Welfare Reform Act. Welfare programs transitioned from providing support to focusing on job training and limiting time on welfare. Welfare agencies, often via contracts, replaced social workers with nonprofessionals on rigid production schedules (Soss, Fording, and Schram 2011; Watkins-Hayes 2011). Public service motivation in this case would have limited the ability to implement this change in welfare policy.

# References

Adam, Frane. 2008. "Mapping Social Capital across Europe: Findings, Trends and Methodological Shortcomings of Cross-National Surveys." *Social Science Information* 47, no. 2: 159–86.

Agbor, Julius A. 2011. *How Does Colonial Origin Matter for Economic Performance in Sub-Saharan Africa?* Working paper. Helsinki: World Institute for Development Economics Research.

Akkerman, Agnes, and René Torenvlied. 2011. "Managing the Agency Environment: Effects of Network Ambition on Agency Performance." *Public Management Review* 13, no. 1: 159–74.

Alary, Michel, Leonard Mukenge-Tshibaka, France Bernier, Nassirou Geraldo, Catherine M. Lowndes, Honore Meda, Cyriaque A. B. Gnintoungb'e, Severin Anagonou, and Jean R. Joly. 2002. "Decline in the Prevalence of HIV and Sexually Transmitted Diseases among Female Sex Workers in Cotonou, Benin, 1993–1999." *AIDS* 16, no. 3: 463–70.

Aldrich, Howard E. 1979. *Organizations and Environments*. Upper Saddle River, NJ: Prentice Hall.

Alesina, Alberto, Arnaud Devleeschauwer, William Easterly, Sergio Kurlat, and Romain Wacziarg. 2003. "Fractionalization." *Journal of Economic Growth* 8, no. 2: 155–94.

Alesina, Alberto, and Guido Tabellini. 1990. "A Positive Theory of Fiscal Deficits and Government Debt." *Review of Economic Studies* 57, no. 3: 403–14.

Alonso, Pablo, and Gregory B. Lewis. 2001. "Public Service Motivation and Job Performance: Evidence from the Federal Sector." *American Review of Public Administration* 31, no. 4: 363–80.

Alt, James E., and Robert C. Lowry. 1994. "Divided Government, Fiscal Institutions and Budget Deficits: Evidence from the States." *American Political Science Review* 88, no. 4: 811–28.

American School and University. 2015. "Largest School Districts in Texas." http://asumag.com/top-10s/largest-school-districts-texas.

Andersen, Lotte Bøgh, Nicolai Kristensen, and Lene Holm Pedersen. 2013. "Models of Public Service Provision: When Will Knights and Knaves Be Responsive to Pawns and Queens?" *International Journal of Public Administration* 36, no. 2: 126–36.

Andersen, Lotte Bøgh, and Søren Serritzlew. 2012. "Does Public Service Motivation Affect the Behavior of Professionals?" *International Journal of Public Administration* 35, no. 1: 19–29.

Andersen, Simon Calmar, and Søren C. Winter. 2011. *Ledelse, Læring og Trivsel i Folkeskolerne.* Copenhagen: SFI–Det Nationale Forskningscenter for Velfærd.

Andersson, Krister P. 2004. "Who Talks with Whom? The Role of Repeated Interactions in Decentralized Forest Governance." *World Development* 32, no. 2: 233–49.

Andrews, Rhys. 2008. "Perceived Environmental Uncertainty in Public Organizations: An Empirical Exploration." *Public Performance & Management Review* 32, no. 1: 21–46.

———. 2009. "Organizational Task Environments and Performance: An Empirical Analysis." *International Public Management Journal* 12, no. 1: 1–23.

———. 2010. "Organizational Social Capital, Structure and Performance." *Human Relations* 63, no. 5: 583–608.

Andrews, Rhys, and George A. Boyne. 2010. "Capacity, Leadership, and Organizational Performance: Testing the Black Box Model of Public Management." *Public Administration Review* 70, no. 3: 443–54.

Andrews, Rhys, George A. Boyne, Jennifer Law, and Richard M. Walker. 2005. "External Constraints on Local Service Standards: The Case of Comprehensive Performance Assessment in English Local Government." *Public Administration* 83, no. 3: 639–56.

———. 2009. "Centralization, Organizational Strategy, and Public Service Performance." *Journal of Public Administration Research and Theory* 19, no. 1: 57–80.

———. 2012. *Strategic Management and Public Service Performance*. London: Palgrave Macmillan.

Andrews, Rhys, George A. Boyne, Kenneth J. Meier, Laurence J. O'Toole Jr., and Richard M. Walker. 2005. "Representative Bureaucracy, Organizational Strategy, and Public Service Performance: An Empirical Analysis of English Local Government." *Journal of Public Administration Research and Theory* 15, no. 4: 489–504.

———. 2010. "Wakeup Call: Strategic Management, Network Alarms, and Performance." *Public Administration Review* 70, no. 5: 731–41.

———. 2013. "Managing Migration? EU Enlargement, Local Government Capacity and Performance in England." *Public Administration* 91, no. 1: 174–93.

Andrews, Rhys, George A. Boyne, and Richard M. Walker. 2006. "Strategy Content and Organizational Performance: An Empirical Analysis." *Public Administration Review* 66, no. 1: 52–63.

———. 2011. "Dimensions of Publicness and Organizational Performance: A Review of the Evidence." *Journal of Public Administration Research and Theory* 21, supp. 3: i301–19.

Antonsen, Marianne, and Torben B. Jørgensen. 1997. "The 'Publicness' of Public Organizations." *Public Administration* 75, no. 2: 337–57.

Armstrong, Michael, and Tina Stephens. 2008. *Management and Leadership*. Prague: Grada Publishing.

Armstrong, Scott, and Terry S. Overton. 1977. "Estimating Non-Response Bias in Mail Surveys." *Journal of Marketing* 14, no. 3: 396–402.

Ashworth, Rachel, George A. Boyne, and Tom Entwistle, eds. 2010. *Public Service Improvement: Theories and Evidence*. Oxford: Oxford University Press.

Association of Municipalities of Honduras. 1993. "Ley de Municipalidades." http://amhon.hn/files/pdfs/Ley%20De%20Municipalidades%20y%20Su%20Reglamento.pdf.

Audit Commission. 2002. *Comprehensive Performance Assessment.* London: Audit Commission.

Avellenada, Claudia N. 2009a. "Mayoral Quality and Local Public Finance." *Public Administration Review* 69, no. 3: 469–86.

———. 2009b. "Municipal Performance: Does Mayoral Quality Matter?" *Journal of Public Administration Research and Theory* 19, no. 2: 285–312.

———. 2012. "Municipal Revenue Strategy in a Latin American Setting: Does the Public Manager's Background Matter?" *Public Management Review* 14, no. 8: 1061–86.

———. 2013. "Mayoral Decision-Making: Issue Salience, Decision Context, and Choice Constraint? An Experimental Study with 120 Latin American Mayors." *Journal of Public Administration Research and Theory* 23, no. 3: 631–62.

———. 2016. "Government Performance and Chief Executives' Intangible Assets: Motives, Networking, and/or Capacity?" *Public Management Review* 18, no. 6: 918–47.

Bamber, Linda Smith, John Jiang, and Isabel Yanyan Wang. 2010. "What's My Style? The Influence of Top Managers on Voluntary Corporate Financial Disclosure." *The Accounting Review* 85, no. 4: 1131–62.

Bamberger, Peter. 2008. "From the Editors: Beyond Contextualization—Using Context Theories to Narrow the Micro-Macro Gap in Management Research." *Academy of Management Journal* 51, no. 5: 839–46.

Bandura, Albert. 1986. *Social Foundations of Thought and Action: A Social Cognitive Theory.* Upper Saddle River, NJ: Prentice Hall.

Bantel, Karen A., and Susan E Jackson. 1989. "Top Management and Innovations in Banking: Does the Composition of the Top Team Make a Difference?" *Strategic Management Journal* 10, no. S1: 107–24.

Barnard, Chester. 1938. *The Functions of the Executive.* Cambridge, MA: Harvard University Press.

Barro, Robert J. 1999. "Determinants of Democracy." *Journal of Political Economy* 107, no. S6: S158–83.

Barzelay, Michael. 2001. *The New Public Management, Volume 3: Improving Research and Policy Dialogue.* Berkeley: University of California Press.

Beam, George. 2001. *Quality Public Management: What It Is and How It Can be Improved and Advanced.* Chicago: Rowman & Littlefield.

Beck, Nathaniel, and Jonathan N. Katz. 1995. "What to Do (and Not to Do) with Time-Series Cross-Section Data." *American Political Science Review* 89, no. 3: 634–47.

Bekerom, Petra, E. A. Van Den, René Torenvlied, and Agnes Akkerman. 2014. "Managing All Quarters of the Compass: How School Principals Moderate the Impact of Environmental Turbulence on School Performance." Working paper, Leiden University.

Bekke, Hans A. G. M., James L. Perry, and Theo A. J. Toonen. 1996. "Introduction: Conceptualizing Civil Service Systems." In *Civil Service Systems in Comparative Perspective,* edited by Hans A. G. M. Bekke, James L. Perry, and Theo A. J. Toonen. Bloomington: Indiana University Press.

Bendor, Jonathan, Amihai Glazer, and Thomas Hammond. 2001. "Theories of Delegation." *Annual Review of Political Science* 4, no. 1: 235–69.

Bendor, Jonathan, and Adam Meirowitz. 2004. "Spatial Models of Delegation." *American Political Science Review* 98, no. 2: 293–309.

Benson, Todd, and Meera Shekar. 2006. "Trends and Issues in Child Undernutrition." In *Disease and Mortality in Sub-Saharan Africa*, edited by Dean T. Jamison, Richard G. Feachem, Malegapuru W. Makgoba, Eduard R. Bos, Florence K. Baingana, Karen J. Hofman, and Khama O. Rogo. Washington, DC: World Bank.

Berlew, David E., and Douglas T. Hall. 1966. "The Socialization of Managers: Effects of Expectations on Performance." *Administrative Science Quarterly* 11, no. 2: 207–23.

Besley, Timothy, and Maitreesh Ghatak. 2001. "Government Versus Private Ownership of Public Goods." *Quarterly Journal of Economics* 116: 1343–72.

Betts, Julian R., and Laurel L. McFarland. 1995. "Safe Port in a Storm: the Impact of Labor Market Conditions on Community College Enrollments." *Journal of Human Resources* 30, no. 4: 741–65.

Bevan, Gwyn, and Christopher Hood. 2006. "What's Measured Is What Matters: Targets and Gaming in the English Public Healthcare System." *Public Administration* 84, no. 3: 517–38.

Blatter, Joachim, and Markus Haverland. 2014. *Designing Case Studies: Explanatory Approaches in Small-*N *Research.* Basingstoke: Palgrave Macmillan.

Boaden, Noel T., and Robert R. Alford. 1969. "Sources of Diversity in English Local Government Decisions." *Public Administration* 47, no. 2: 203–24.

Boeker, Warren. 1997. "Strategic Change: The Influence of Managerial Characteristics and Organizational Growth." *Academy of Management Journal* 40, no. 1: 152–70.

Bohn, James G. 2010. "Development and Exploratory Validation of an Organizational Efficacy Scale." *Human Resource Development Quarterly* 21, no. 3: 227–51.

Boninger, David S., Jon A. Krosnick, Matthew K. Berent, and Leandre R. Fabrigar. 1995. "The Causes and Consequences of Attitude Importance." In *Attitude Strength: Antecedents and Consequences*, edited by Richard E. Petty and Jon A. Krosnick. Hillsdale, NJ: Erlbaum.

Bordia, Prashant, Elizabeth Hobman, Elizabeth Jones, Cindy Gallois, and Victor J. Callan. 2004. "Uncertainty during Organizational Change: Types, Consequences, and Management Strategies." *Journal of Business and Psychology* 18, no. 4: 507–32.

Bowerman, Bruce L., and Richard T. O'Connell. 1990. *Linear Statistical Models: An Applied Approach*, 2nd ed. Boston: PWS-Kent.

Bowman, Ann O'M., and Neal D. Woods. 2007. "Strength in Numbers: Why States Join Interstate Compacts." *State Politics and Policy Quarterly* 7, no. 4: 347–68.

Box, George E. P. 1953. "Non-Normality and Tests on Variance." *Biometrika* 40: 318–35.

Box, George E. P., and Sigurd L. Anderson. 1955. "Permutation Theory in the Derivation of Robust Criteria and the Study of Departures from Assumptions." *Journal of the Royal Statistical Society* 17, no. 1: 1–34.

Box, Richard C. 1999. "Running Government Like a Business: Implications for Public Administration Theory and Practice." *American Review of Public Administration* 29, no. 1: 19–43.

Boyd, Brian K., and Steve Gove. 2006. "Managerial Constraint: The Intersection between Organizational Task Environment and Discretion." *Research Methodology in Strategy and Management* 3: 57–95.

Boyle, Michael H., Yvonne Racine, Katholiki Georgiades, Dana Snelling, Sungjin Hong, Walter Omariba, Patricia Hurley, and Purnima Rao-Melacini. 2006. "The Influence of Economic Development Level, Household Wealth and Maternal Education on Child Health in the Developing World." *Social Science & Medicine* 63, no. 8: 2242–54.

Boyne, George A. 1996. "The Intellectual Crisis in British Public Administration: Is Public Management the Problem or the Solution?" *Public Administration* 74, no. 4: 679–94.

———. 2002. "Public and Private Management: What's the Difference?" *Journal of Management Studies* 39, no. 1: 97–122.

———. 2003. "Sources of Public Service Improvement: A Critical Review and Research Agenda." *Journal of Public Administration Research and Theory* 13, no. 3: 367–94.

———. 2004. "Explaining Public Service Performance: Does Management Matter?" *Public Policy and Administration* 19, no. 4: 100–117.

Boyne, George A., and Kenneth J. Meier. 2009. "Environmental Turbulence, Organizational Stability, and Public Service Performance." *Administration and Society* 40, no. 8: 799–824.

———. 2013. "Burdened by Bureaucracy? Determinants of Administrative Intensity in Public Organisations." *International Public Management Journal* 16, no. 2: 307–27.

Boyne, George A., Kenneth J. Meier, Laurence J. O'Toole Jr., and Richard M. Walker. 2005. "Where Next? Research Directions on Organizational Performance in Public Organizations." *Journal of Public Administration Research and Theory* 15, no. 4: 633–39.

———, eds. 2006. *Public Service Performance: Perspectives on Measurement and Management.* Cambridge: Cambridge University Press.

Boyne, George A., and Richard. M. Walker. 2004. "Strategy Content and Public Service Organizations." *Journal of Public Administration Research and Theory* 14, no. 2: 231–52.

Bozeman, Barry. 1987. *All Organizations Are Public: Bridging Public and Private Organizational Theories.* San Francisco: Jossey-Bass.

Bozeman, Barry, and Steve Loveless. 1987. "Sector Context and Performance: A Comparison of Industrial and Government Research Units." *Administration & Society* 19, no. 2: 197–235.

Bozeman, Barry, and R. F. Shangraw Jr. 1989. "Computers and Commitment to a Public Management Decision: An Experiment." *Knowledge in Society* 2, no. 3: 42–56.

Brazil, Government of. 2007. *Decreto 6170*. Brasília: Imprensa Nacional.

Brehm, John, and Scott Gates. 1997. *Working, Shirking, and Sabotage: Bureaucratic Response to a Democratic Public*. Ann Arbor: University of Michigan Press.

Bretschneider, Stuart, and Jeffery Straussman. 1992. "Statistical Laws of Confidence versus Behavioural Response: How Individuals Respond to Public Management Decisions under Uncertainty." *Journal of Public Administration Research and Theory* 2, no. 3: 333–45.

Bretschneider, Stuart, Jeffrey J. Straussman, and Daniel Mullins. 1988. "Do Revenue Forecasts Influence Budget Setting? A Small Group Experiment." *Policy Sciences* 21, no. 4: 305–25.

Brewer, Gene A. 2005. "In the Eye of the Storm: Frontline Supervisors and Federal Agency Performance." *Journal of Public Administration Research and Theory* 15, no. 4: 505–27.

———. 2008. "Employee and Organizational Performance." In *Motivation in Public Management: The Call of Public Service*, edited by James L. Perry and Annie Hondeghem. Oxford: Oxford University Press.

Brewer, Gene A., and Gene A. Brewer Jr. 2011. "Parsing Public/Private Differences in Work Motivation and Performance: An Experimental Study." *Journal of Public Administration Review and Theory* 21, no. 3: 347–62.

Brewer, Gene A., and Sally C. Selden. 1998. "Whistle Blowers in the Federal Civil Service: New Evidence of the Public Service Ethic." *Journal of Public Administration Research and Theory* 8, no. 3: 413–39.

———. 2000. "Why Elephants Gallop: Assessing and Predicting Organizational Performance in Federal Agencies." *Journal of Public Administration Research and Theory* 10, no. 4: 685–711.

Brickley, James A. 2003. "Empirical Research on CEO Turnover and Firm-Performance: A Discussion." *Journal of Accounting and Economics* 36, no. 1: 227–33.

Bright, Leonard. 2008. "Does Public Service Motivation Really Make a Difference on the Job Satisfaction and Turnover Intentions of Public Employees?" *American Review of Public Administration* 38, no. 2: 149–66.

Brollo, Fernanda, and Tommaso Nannicini. 2012. "Tying Your Enemy's Hands in Close Races: The Politics of Federal Transfers in Brazil." *American Political Science Review* 106, no. 4: 742–61.

Bryson, John M., Fran S. Berry, and Kaifeng Yang. 2010. "The State of Public Strategic Management Research: A Selective Literature Review and Set of Directions." *American Review of Public Administration* 40, no. 5: 495–521.

Buchanan, Bruce. 1975. "Red Tape and the Service Ethic: Some Unexpected Differences between Public and Private Managers." *Administration & Society* 6, no. 4: 423–44.

Buchanan, James M., and Gordon Tullock. 1962. *The Calculus of Consent*. Ann Arbor: University of Michigan Press.

Burns, Tom E., and George Macpherson Stalker. 1961. *The Management of Innovation.* London: Tavistock.

Butler, Daniel M., and David E. Broockman. 2011. "Do Politicians Racially Discriminate against Constituents? A Field Experiment on State Legislators." *American Journal of Political Science* 55, no. 3: 463–77.

Cable, Daniel M., and Charles K. Parsons. 2001. "Socialization Tactics and Person-Organization Fit." *Personnel Psychology* 54, no. 1: 1–23.

Cannon, Alan R., and Caron H. St. John. 2007. "Measuring Environmental Complexity: A Theoretical and Empirical Assessment." *Organizational Research Methods* 10, no. 2: 296–321.

Carmeli, Abraham. 2004. "Strategic Human Capital and the Performance of Public Sector Organizations." *Scandinavian Journal of Management* 20, no. 4: 375–92.

———. 2006. "The Managerial Skills of the Top Management Team and the Performance of Municipal Organisations." *Local Government Studies* 32, no. 2: 153–76.

Carreirão, Yan de Souza. 2006. "Ideologia e Partidos Políticos: Um Estudo Sobre Coligações em Santa Catarina." *Opinião Pública* 12, no. 1: 136–63.

Center on International Education Benchmarking. 2009. "Netherlands: System and School Organization." National Center on Education and the Economy, Washington, DC. www.ncee.org/programs-affiliates/center-on-international-education-benchmarking/top-performing-countries/netherlands-overview/netherlands-system-and-school-organization/.

Chabal, Patrick, and Jean-Pascal Daloz. 1999. *Africa Works: Disorder as Political Instrument.* Bloomington: Indiana University Press.

Chaiken, Shelly. 1980. "Heuristic versus Systematic Information Processing and the Use of Source versus Message Cues in Persuasion." *Journal of Personality and Social Psychology* 39, no. 5: 752–66.

Chalkley, Martin, Colin Tilley, Linda Young, Debbie Bonetti, and Jan Clarkson. 2010. "Incentives for Dentists in Public Service: Evidence from a Natural Experiment." *Journal of Public Administration Research and Theory* 20, supp. 2: i207–23.

Chi, Michelene T. H., Robert Glaser, and Marshall J. Farr. 2014. *The Nature of Expertise.* New York: Psychology Press.

Child, John. 1974. "Managerial and Organizational Factors Associated with Company Performance, Part I." *Journal of Management Studies* 11, no. 3: 175–89.

Chun, Young Han, and Hal G. Rainey. 2005. "Goal Ambiguity and Organizational Performance in US Federal Agencies." *Journal of Public Administration Research and Theory* 15, no. 4: 529–57.

Cito. 2009. "Terugblik en Resultaten 2009" (Reflection and Results 2009). Cito, Arnhem, the Netherlands.

———. 2010. "Terugblik en Resultaten 2010" (Reflection and Results 2010). Cito, Arnhem, the Netherlands.

Clague, Christopher, Suzanee Gleason, and Stephen Knack. 2001. "Determinants of Lasting Democracy in Poor Countries: Culture, Development, and Institutions." *Annals of the American Academy of Political and Social Science* 573, no. 1: 16–41.

Common Core of Data. 2016. "Total Number of School Districts: 2013–2014." http://eddataexpress.ed.gov/data-element-explorer.cfm/tab/data/deid/3275/.

Conant, Jeffrey S., Michael P. Mokwa, and P. Rajan Varadarajan. 1990. "Strategic Types, Distinctive Marketing Competencies and Organizational Performance: A Multiple Measures Based Study." *Strategic Management Journal* 11, no. 5: 365–83.

Cooper-Thomas, Helena D., Annelies Van Vianen, and Neil Anderson. 2004. "Changes in Person-Organization Fit: The Impact of Socialization Tactics on Perceived and Actual P-O Fit." *European Journal of Work and Organizational Psychology* 13, no. 1: 52–78.

Coursey, David H. 1992. "Information Credibility and Choosing Policy Alternatives: An Experimental Test of Cognitive Response Theory." *Journal of Public Administration Research and Theory* 2, no. 3: 315–31.

Cox, Gary W., and Mathew D. McCubbins. 1986. "Electoral Politics as a Redistributive Game." *Journal of Politics* 48, no. 2: 370–89.

Creese, Andrew, Katherine Floyd, Anita Alban, and Lorna Guinness. 2002. "Cost-Effectiveness of HIV/AIDS Interventions in Africa: A Systematic Review of the Evidence." *The Lancet* 359, no. 9318: 1635–42.

Crowder, Michael. 1964. "Indirect Rule: French and British Style." *Africa* 34, no. 3: 197–205.

Cyert, Richard M., and James G. March. 1963. *A Behavioral Theory of the Firm.* Englewood Cliffs, NJ: Prentice Hall.

Daft, Richard L., Juhani Sormunen, and Don Parks. 1988. "Chief Executive Scanning, Environmental Characteristics and Company Performance: An Empirical Study." *Strategic Management Journal* 9, no. 2: 123–39.

Dahl, Robert, and Charles Lindblom. 1953. *Politics, Economics, and Welfare.* Chicago: University of Chicago Press.

Dahlberg, Matz, and Eva Johansson. 2002. "On the Vote-Purchasing Behavior of Incumbent Governments." *American Political Science Review* 96, no. 1: 27–40.

Daily, Catherine M. 1995. "The Relationship between Board Composition and Leadership Structure and Bankruptcy Reorganization Outcomes." *Journal of Management* 21, no. 6: 1041–56.

Damanpour, Fariborz, and Marguerite Schneider. 2006. "Phases of the Adoption of Innovation in Organizations: Effects of Environment, Organization and Top Managers." *British Journal of Management* 17, no. 3: 215–36.

———. 2009. "Characteristics of Innovation and Innovation Adoption in Public Organizations: Assessing the Role of Managers." *Journal of Public Administration Research and Theory* 19, no. 3: 495–522.

Datz, Todd. 2000. "Equity? Workplace Diversity: The Percentage of African Americans in Senior Management Positions Doesn't Reflect Their Representation in Society." *CIO* 13, no. 7: 74–87.

D'Aveni, Richard A. 1990. "Top Managerial Prestige and Organizational Bankruptcy." *Organization Science* 1, no. 2: 121–42.

Davis, Belinda Creel, Michelle Livermore, and Younghee Lim. 2011. "The Extended Reach of Minority Political Power: The Interaction of Descriptive Representation, Managerial Networking, and Race." *Journal of Politics* 73, no. 2: 494–507.

Davis, David R., and Joel N. Kuritsky. 2002. "Violent Conflict and Its Impact on Health Indicators in Sub-Saharan Africa, 1980 to 1997." Paper prepared for Annual Meeting of International Studies Association, New Orleans.

DeCanio, Samuel. 2013. "Democracy, the Market, and the Logic of Social Choice." *American Journal of Political Science* 58, no. 3: 637–52.

De Figueiredo, Rui J. P. 2002. "Electoral Competition, Political Uncertainty, and Policy Insulation." *American Political Science Review* 96, no. 2: 321–33.

Delaney, Jennifer A., and William R. Doyle. 2011. "State Spending on Higher Education: Testing the Balance Wheel over Time." *Journal of Education Finance* 36, no. 4: 343–68.

Denhardt, Robert B., and Jay D. White. 1982. "Beyond Explanation: A Methodological Note." *Administration & Society* 14, no. 2: 163–69.

DeSarbo, Wayne S., Anthony C. Di Benedetto, Michael Song, and Indrajit Sinha. 2005. "Revisiting the Miles and Snow Strategic Framework: Uncovering Interrelationships between Strategic Types, Capabilities, Environmental Uncertainty, and Firm Performance." *Strategic Management Journal* 26, no. 1: 47–74.

Dess, Gregory G., and Donald W. Beard. 1984. "Dimensions of Organizational Task Environment." *Administrative Science Quarterly* 29, no. 1: 52–73.

De Vijlder, Frans J. 2000. *Dutch Education: A Closed or an Open System? Or: The Art of Maintaining an Open System Responsive to Its Changing Environment.* The Hague: Dutch Ministry of Education, Culture, and Science.

DiMaggio, Paul, and Walter W. Powell. 1983. "The Iron Cage Revisited: Collective Rationality and Institutional Isomorphism in Organizational Fields." *American Sociological Review* 48, no. 2: 147–60.

Dixit, Avinash, and John Londregan. 1998. "Ideology, Tactics, and Efficiency in Redistributive Politics." *Quarterly Journal of Economics* 113, no. 2: 497–529.

Donahue, Amy K., Willow S. Jacobson, Mark D. Robbins, Ellen V. Rubin, and Sally C. Selden. 2004. "Management and Performance Outcomes in State Government." In *The Art of Governance: Analyzing Management and Administration*, edited by Patricia W. Ingraham and Laurence E. Lynn Jr. Washington, DC: Georgetown University Press.

Donaldson, Lex. 2001. *The Contingency Theory of Organizations.* Thousand Oaks, CA: Sage.

Douglas, M., and John V. Lombardi. 2006. "Public and Private: What's the Difference." *Inside Higher Ed.* www.insidehighered.com/views/2006/03/06/lombardi.

Downe, James, and Steve Martin. 2007. "Regulation inside Government: Processes and Impacts of Inspection of Local Public Services." *Policy & Politics* 35, no. 2: 215–32.

Downs, Anthony. 1967. *Inside Bureaucracy*. Prospect Heights, IL: Waveland Press.

Duderstadt, James J., and Farris W. Womack. 2011. *The Future of the Public University in America: Beyond the Crossroads*. Baltimore: Johns Hopkins University Press.

Duncan, Robert. 1972. "Characteristics of Organizational Environments and Perceived Uncertainty." *Administrative Science Quarterly* 17, no. 3: 313–27.

Dutch Education Council. 2009. "The State of Affairs in Dutch Education 2009." The Hague: Dutch Education Council.

Dutch Ministry of Education, Culture, and Science. 2014. *Core Indicators 2009–2013: Education, Culture, and Science*. The Hague: Ministry of Education, Culture, and Science.

Dutton, Jane M., Liam Fahey, and Vijay K. Narayanan. 1983. "Toward Understanding Strategic Issue Diagnosis." *Strategic Management Journal* 4, no. 40: 307–23.

Dye, Thomas R. 1966. *Politics, Economics, and The Public: Policy Outcomes in the American States.* Chicago: Rand McNally.

Earley, P. Christopher, and Terri R. Lituchy. 1991. "Delineating Goal and Efficacy Effects: A Test of Three Models." *Journal of Applied Psychology* 76, no. 1: 81–98.

Ellis, Bret Easton. 1998. *Glamorama.* New York: Alfred A. Knopf.

Emery, F. E., and Eric Trist. 1965. "The Causal Texture of Organizational Environments." *Human Relations* 18, no. 1: 21–32.

Epstein, David, and Sharyn O'Halloran. 1994. "Administrative Procedures, Information, and Agency Discretion." *American Journal of Political Science* 38, no. 3: 697–722.

Ericsson, K. Anders, Ralf T. Krampe, and Clemens Tesch-Römer. 1993. "The Role of Deliberate Practice in the Acquisition of Expert Performance." *Psychological Review* 100, no. 3: 363–406.

Ericsson, K. Anders, and Jacqui Smith, eds. 1991. *Toward a General Theory of Expertise: Prospects and Limits.* Cambridge: Cambridge University Press.

Esping-Andersen, Gøsta. 1990. *The Three Worlds of Welfare Capitalism.* Princeton, NJ: Princeton University Press.

Esteve, Marc, George A. Boyne, Vicenta Sierra, and Tamyko Ysa. 2013. "Organizational Collaboration in the Public Sector: Do Chief Executives Make a Difference?" *Journal of Public Administration Research and Theory* 23, no. 4: 927–52.

Favero, Nathan, and Justin B. Bullock. 2015. "How (Not) to Solve the Problem: An Evaluation of Scholarly Responses to Common Source Bias." *Journal of Public Administration Research and Theory* 25, no. 1: 285–308.

Fearon, James D., and David D. Laitin. 2003. "Ethnicity, Insurgency, and Civil War." *American Political Science Review* 97, no. 1: 75–90.

Feiock, Richard C., and Christopher Stream. 1998. "Explaining the Tenure of Local Government Managers." *Journal of Public Administration Research and Theory* 8, no. 1: 117–30.

Fernandez, Sergio. 2005. "Developing and Testing an Integrative Framework of Public-Sector Leadership: Evidence from the Public Education Arena." *Journal of Public Administration Research and Theory* 15, no. 2: 197–217.

Fernandez, Sergio, and Hal G. Rainey. 2006. "Managing Successful Organizational Change in the Public Sector." *Public Administration Review* 66, no. 2: 168–76.

Fiedler, Fred E. 1986. "The Contribution of Cognitive Resources and Leader Behavior to Organizational Performance." *Journal of Applied Social Psychology* 16, no. 6: 532–48.

Finkelstein, Sydney, and Donald C Hambrick. 1990. "Top-Management-Team Tenure and Organizational Outcomes: The Moderating Role of Managerial Discretion." *Administrative Science Quarterly* 35, no. 3: 484–503.

———. 1997. "Review: Strategic Leadership: Top Executives and Their Effects on Organizations." *Australian Journal of Management* 22, no. 3: 802–5.

Fiske, Susan T., Donald R. Kinder, and W. Michael Larter. 1983. "The Novice and the Expert: Knowledge-Based Strategies in Political Cognition." *Journal of Experimental Social Psychology* 19, no. 4: 381–400.

Fiszbein, Ariel. 1997. "The Emergence of Local Capacity: Lessons from Colombia." *World Development* 25, no. 7: 1029–43.

Floyd, Katherine, David Wilkinson, and Charles Gilks. 1997. "Comparison of Cost Effectiveness of Directly Observed Treatment (DOT) and Conventionally Delivered Treatment for Tuberculosis: Experience from Rural South Africa." *BMJ* 315, no. 7120: 1407–11.

Forbes, Melissa and Larry E. Lynn Jr. 2005. "How Does Public Management Affect Government Performance? Findings from International Research." *Journal of Public Administration Research and Theory* 15, no. 4: 559–84.

Franssen, Joost, Marco Pastors, and Erwin Van Rooijen. 2010. *Schoolleiders Ontketend.* The Hague: B&A Group.

Furtado, Eugene, and Vijay Karan. 1990. "Causes, Consequences, and Shareholder Wealth Effects of Management Turnover: A Review of the Empirical Evidence." *Financial Management* 19, no. 2: 60–75.

Gailmard, Sean. 2010. "Politics, Principal–Agent Problems, and Public Service Motivation." *International Public Management Journal* 13, no. 1: 35–45.

Gaines, Brian J., James H. Kuklinski, and Paul J. Quirk. 2007. "The Logic of the Survey Experiment Revisited." *Political Analysis* 15, no. 1: 1–20.

Gaisie, S. K. 1979. "Mortality, Socio-economic Differentials and Modernization in Africa." In *Population Dynamics: Fertility and Mortality in Africa.* Monrovia: United Nations Economic Commission for Africa.

Gander, James P. 1999. "Administrative Intensity and Institutional Control in Higher Education." *Research in Higher Education* 40, no. 3: 309–22.

Ghobarah, Hazem, Paul Huth, and Bruce Russett. 2004. "Comparative Public Health: The Political Economy of Human Misery and Well-Being." *International Studies Quarterly* 48, no. 1: 73–94.

Gilardi, Fabrizio. 2008. *Delegation in the Regulatory State: Independent Regulatory Agencies in Western Europe.* Cheltenham, UK: Edward Elgar.

Gilovich, Thomas, Dale Griffin, and Daniel Kahneman. 2002. *Heuristics and Biases: The Psychology of Intuitive Judgment.* Cambridge: Cambridge University Press.

Goerdel, Holly T. 2006. "Taking Initiative: Proactive Management and Organizational Performance in Networked Environments." *Journal of Public Administration Research and Theory* 16, no. 3: 351–67.

Golub, Jonathan. 1999. "In the Shadow of the Vote? Decision Making in the European Community." *International Organization* 53, no. 4: 737–68.

Goodsell, Charles T. 2003. *The Case for Bureaucracy: A Public Administration Polemic*. Washington, DC: CQ Press.

Graham, John R., Campbell R. Harvey, and Manju Puri. 2011. *Capital Allocation and Delegation of Decision-Making Authority within Firms*. NBER Working Paper 17370. Cambridge, MA: National Bureau of Economic Research.

Greve, Henrich R. 2003. *Organizational Learning from Performance Feedback: A Behavioural Perspective on Innovation and Change*. Cambridge: Cambridge University Press.

Grier, Robin M. 1999. "Colonial Legacies and Economic Growth." *Public Choice* 98, nos. 3–4: 317–35.

Grimmelikhuijsen, Stephan G., and Albert J. Meijer. 2014. "The Effects of Transparency on the Perceived Trustworthiness of a Government Organization: Evidence from an Online Experiment." *Journal of Public Administration Research and Theory* 24, no. 1: 137–57.

Grosskopf, Shawna, and Suthathip Yaisawamg. 1990. "Economies of Scope in the Provision of Local Public Services." *National Tax Journal* 43, no. 1: 61–74.

Guinand, Luis Bernardo Mejía, Felipe Botero, and Juan Carlos Rodríguez Raga. 2008. "Pavimentando on Votos?" *Colombia Internacional* 68, no. 1: 14–42.

Gupta, Sanjeev, and Marijn Verhoeven. 2001. "The Efficiency of Government Expenditure: Experiences from Africa." *Journal of Policy Modeling* 23, no. 4: 433–67.

Hambrick, Donald C. 2007. "Upper Echelons Theory: An Update." *Academy of Management Review* 32, no. 2: 334–43.

Hambrick, Donald C., and Phyllis A. Mason. 1984. "Upper Echelons: The Organization as a Reflection of Its Top Managers." *Academy of Management Review* 9, no. 2: 193–206.

Hannan, Michael T., and John Freeman. 1984. "Structural Inertia and Organizational Change." *American Sociological Review* 49, no. 2: 149–64.

Haque, M. Shamsul. 2001. "The Diminishing Publicness of Public Service under the Current Mode of Governance." *Public Administration Review* 61, no. 1: 65–82.

Harris, Alma. 2008. "Distributed Leadership: According to the Evidence." *Journal of Educational Administration* 46, no. 2: 172–88.

Hart, Peter, and John Mellors. 1970. "Management Youth and Company Growth: A Correlation?" *Management Decision* 4, no. 1: 50–53.

Heinrich, Carolyn J., and Larry E. Lynn. 2000. *Governance and Performance: New Perspectives*. Washington, DC: Georgetown University Press.

Herbst, Jeffrey. 2000. *State and Power in Africa: Comparative Lessons in Authority and Control*. Princeton, NJ: Princeton University Press.

Herian, Michael N., Joseph A. Hamm, Alan J. Tomkins, and Lisa M. Pytlik Zillig. 2012. "Public Participation, Procedural Fairness, and Evaluations of Local Governance: The Moderating Role of Uncertainty." *Journal of Public Administration Research and Theory* 22, no. 4: 815–40.

Hero, Rodney E. 2007. *Racial Diversity and Social Capital: Equality and Community in America*. Cambridge: Cambridge University Press.

Hicklin, Alisa, Laurence J. O'Toole Jr., and Kenneth J. Meier. 2008. "Serpents in the Sand: Managerial Networking and Nonlinear Influences on Organizational Performance." *Journal of Public Administration Research and Theory* 18, no. 2: 253–73.

Hill, Gregory C. 2005. "The Effects of Managerial Succession on Organizational Performance." *Journal of Public Administration Research and Theory* 15, no. 4: 585–97.

Hill, Kenneth, and Agbessi Amouzou. 2006. "Trends in Child Mortality, 1960–2000." In *Disease and Mortality in Sub-Saharan Africa*, edited by Dean T. Jamison, Richard G. Feachem, Malegapuru W. Makgoba, Eduard R. Bos, Florence K. Baingana, Karen J. Hofman, and Khama O. Rogo. Washington, DC: World Bank.

Hodge, Graeme. A. 2000. *Privatization: An International Review of Performance.* Boulder, CO: Westview Press.

Holbrook, Thomas M., and Emily Van Dunk. 1993. "Electoral Competition in the American States." *American Political Science Review* 87, no. 4: 955–62.

Hondeghem, Annie, and James L. Perry. 2009. "EGPA Symposium on Public Service Motivation and Performance: Introduction." *International Review of Administrative Sciences* 75, no. 1: 5–9.

Hood, Christopher, and Martin Lodge. 2006. *The Politics of Public Service Bargains.* Oxford: Oxford University Press.

Horn, Murray J., and Kenneth A. Shepsle. 1989. "Commentary on Administrative Arrangements and the Political Control of Agencies: Administrative Process and Organizational Form as Legislative Responses to Agency Costs." *Virginia Law Review* 75, no. 2: 499–508.

Hroník, František. 2007. *Rozvoj a Vzdělávání Pracovníků.* Prague: Grada.

Huber, John D., and Nolan McCarty. 2004. "Bureaucratic Capacity, Delegation, and Political Reform." *American Political Science Review* 98, no. 3: 481–94.

Huber, John D., and Charles C. Shipan. 2002. *Deliberate Discretion? The Institutional Foundations of Bureaucratic Autonomy.* Cambridge: Cambridge University Press.

Hvidman, Ulrik, and Simon Calmar Andersen. 2014. "Impact of Performance Management in Public and Private Organizations." *Journal of Public Administration Research and Theory* 24, no. 1: 35–58.

Ingraham, Patricia W. 2007. *In Pursuit of Performance: Management Systems in State and Local Government.* Baltimore: Johns Hopkins University Press.

Ingraham, Patricia W., Philip G. Joyce, and Amy Kneedler Donahue. 2003. *Government Performance: Why Management Matters.* Baltimore: Johns Hopkins University Press.

Iqbal, Zaryab. 2006. "Health and Human Security: The Public Health Impact of Violent Conflict." *International Studies Quarterly* 50, no. 3: 631–49.

Isett, Kimberly R., Sherry A. M. Glied, Michael S. Sparer, Lawrence D. Brown. 2013. "When Change Becomes Transformation." *Public Management Review* 15, no. 1: 1–17.

Isett, Kimberly R., Joseph P. Morrissey, and Sharon Topping. 2006. "Systems Ideologies and Street-Level Bureaucrats: Policy Change and Perceptions of Quality in a Behavioral Health Care System." *Public Administration Review* 66, no. 2: 217–27.

Jain, Anrudh K. 1985. "Determinants of Regional Variations in Rural Drinking Water in India." *Population Studies* 39, no. 3: 407–24.

Jilke, Sebastian, Bart Meuleman, and Steven Van de Walle. 2015. "We Need to Compare, but How? Measurement Equivalence in Comparative Public Administration." *Public Administration Review* 75, no. 1: 36–48.

Johansen, Morgen S. 2012. "The Direct and Interactive Effects of Middle and Upper Managerial Quality on Organizational Performance." *Administration & Society* 44, no. 4: 383–411.

Johansen, Morgen S., and Ling Zhu. 2014. "Market Competition, Political Constraint, and Managerial Practice in Profit, Non-Profit, and Private American Hospitals." *Journal of Public Administration Research and Theory* 24, no. 1: 185–207.

Johansson, Eva. 2003. "Intergovernmental Grants as a Tactical Instrument: Empirical Evidence from Swedish Municipalities." *Journal of Public Economics* 87, no. 5: 883–915.

John, Peter. 2014. "The Great Survivor: The Persistence and Resilience of English Local Government." *Local Government Studies* 40, no. 5: 687–704.

John, Peter, and Colin Copus. 2011. "The United Kingdom: Is There Really an Anglo Model?" In *The Oxford Handbook of Local and Regional Democracy in Europe*, edited by Frank Hendriks, Anders Lidstrom, and John Loughlin. Oxford: Oxford University Press.

Johns, Gary. 2006. "The Essential Impact of Context on Organizational Behavior." *Academy of Management Review* 31, no. 2: 396–408.

Johnson, Renée, and David J. Randall. 2013. "Measuring Bureaucratic Capacity in State Government: The Case for Section 1115 Medicaid Waivers." Paper prepared for Annual Meeting of American Political Science Association, Chicago.

Johnson, Ronald W., and Arie Y. Lewin. 1984. "Management and Accountability Models of Public Sector Performance." In *Public Sector Performance: A Conceptual Turning Point*, edited by Trudi C. Miller. Baltimore: Johns Hopkins University Press.

Jreisat, Jamil E. 2002. *Comparative Public Administration and Policy*. Boulder, CO: Westview Press.

Juenke, Eric. G. 2005. "Management Tenure and Network Time: How Experience Affects Bureaucratic Dynamics." *Journal of Public Administration Research and Theory* 15, no. 1: 113–31.

Kearney, Richard C., Barry M. Feldman, and Carmine P. F. Scavo. 2000. "Reinventing Government: City Manager Attitudes and Actions." *Public Administration Review* 60, no. 6: 535–48.

Kearns, Ade, and Ray Forrest. 2000. "Social Cohesion and Multilevel Urban Governance." *Urban Studies* 37, nos. 5–6: 995–1017.

Keiser, Lael R., Vicky M. Wilkins, Kenneth J. Meier, and Catherine A. Holland. 2012. "Lipstick and Logarithms: Gender, Institutional Context, and Representative Bureaucracy." *American Political Science Review* 96, no. 3: 553–64.

Kelman, Steven. 2005. *Unleashing Change: A Study of Organizational Renewal in Government.* Washington, DC: Brookings Institution Press.

Key, V. O. 1949. *Southern Politics in State and Nation.* New York: Alfred A. Knopf.

Kim, Jungbu, and Seong Soo Oh. 2014. "Local Managerial Strategies for External versus Own Source Fiscal Resources: Do Administrators' Previous Career and Education Matter?" *American Review of Public Administration* 46, no. 1.

Kim, Sangmook, Wouter Vandenabeele, Bradley E. Wright, Lotte Bogh Andersen, Francesco Paolo Cerase, Robert K. Christensen, Céline Desmarais, Maria Koumenta, Peter Leisink, Bangcheng Liu, Jolanta Palidauskaite, Lene Holm Pedersen, James L. Perry, Adrian Ritz, Jeanette Taylor, and Paola De Vivo. 2013. "Investigating the Structure and Meaning of Public Service Motivation across Populations: Developing an International Instrument and Addressing Issues of Measurement Invariance." *Journal of Public Administration Research and Theory* 23, no. 1: 79–102.

Kim, Seung Hyun, and Sangmook Kim. 2013. "National Culture and Social Desirability Bias in Measuring Public Service Motivation." *Administration & Society* 260, no. 12: 3161–64.

Kimberly, John R., and Michael J Evanisko. 1981. "Organizational Innovation: The Influence of Individual, Organizational, and Contextual Factors on Hospital Adoption of Technological and Administrative Innovations." *Academy of Management Journal* 24, no. 4: 689–713.

King, Gary. 1995. "Replication, Replication." *PS: Politics and Political Science* 28: 444–52.

Kingsley, John Donald. 1967. "Bureaucracy and Political Development, with Particular Reference to Nigeria." In *Bureaucracy and Political Development*, edited by Joseph La Palombara. Princeton, NJ: Princeton University Press.

Kjeldsen, Anne Mette. 2012. *Dynamics of Public Service Motivation.* Aarhus, Denmark: Forlaget Politica.

Kjeldsen, Anne Mette, and Lotte Bogh Andersen. 2013. "How Pro-Social Motivation Affects Job Satisfaction: An International Analysis of Countries with Different Welfare State Regimes." *Scandinavian Political Studies* 36, no. 2: 153–76.

Klasen, Stephan. 2008. "Poverty, Undernutrition, and Child Mortality: Some Inter-Regional Puzzles and Their Implications for Research and Policy." *Journal of Economic Inequality* 6, no. 1: 89–115.

Koch, Michael T. 2012. "Targeted Aid, Stability and Growth in Post Conflict States." Paper prepared for Annual Meeting of Midwest Political Science Association, Chicago.

Konisky, David M., and Christopher Reenock. 2013. "Case Selection in Public Management Research: Problems and Solutions." *Journal of Public Administration Research and Theory* 23, no. 2: 361–93.

Krontorád, František, and Milan Trčka. 2005. *Manažérske Standardy ve Veřejné Správě: Národní Informační Středisko pro Podporujakosti.* Prague: Národní Informační Střediskopro Podporu Jakosti.

Krueger, Skip, and Robert W. Walker. 2010. "Management Practices and State Bond Ratings." *Public Budgeting and Finance* 30, no. 4: 47–70.

Kudamatsu, Masayuki. 2012. "Has Democratization Reduced Infant Mortality in Sub-Saharan Africa? Evidence from Micro Data." *Journal of the European Economics Association* 10, no. 6: 1294–317.

Kwofie, Kwame Mayer. 1976. "A Spatio-Temporal Analysis of Cholera Diffusion in Western Africa." *Economic Geography* 52, no. 2: 127–35.

Landsbergen, David, Barry Bozeman, and Stuart Bretschneider. 1992. "Internal Rationality and the Effects of Perceived Decision Difficulty: Results of a Public Management Decision-Making Experiment." *Journal of Public Administration Research and Theory* 2, no. 3: 247–64.

Landsbergen, David, David H. Coursey, Stephen Loveless, and R. F. Shangraw Jr. 1997. "Decision Quality, Confidence, and Commitment with Expert Systems: An Experimental Study." *Journal of Public Administration Research and Theory* 7, no. 1: 131–57.

La Porta, Rafael, Florencio Lopez-de Silanes, Andrei Shleifer, and Robert Vishny. 1999. "The Quality of Government." *Journal of Law, Economics and Organization* 15, no. 1: 222–79.

Lassen, David Dreyer, and Soren Serritzlew. 2011. "Jurisdiction Size and Local Democracy: Evidence on Internal Political Efficacy from Large-Scale Municipal Reform." *American Political Science Review* 105, no. 2: 238–58.

Lavine, Howard, John L. Sullivan, Eugene Borgida, and Cynthia J. Thomsen. 1996. "The Relationship of National and Personal Issue Salience to Attitude Accessibility on Foreign and Domestic Policy Issues." *Political Psychology* 17, no. 2: 293–316.

Lawrence, Paul R., and Jay W. Lorsch. 1967. "Differentiation and Integration in Complex Organizations." *Administrative Science Quarterly* 12, no. 1: 1–47.

Le Grand, Julian. 2010. "Knights and Knaves Return: Public Service Motivation and the Delivery of Public Services." *International Public Management Journal* 13, no. 1: 56–71.

Lee, Alexander, and Kenneth A. Schultz. 2011. "Comparing British and French Colonial Legacies: A Discontinuity Analysis of Cameroon." Paper prepared for Annual Meeting of American Political Science Association, Seattle.

Lee, Haksoo, N. Joseph Cayer, and G. Zhiyong Lan. 2006. "Changing Federal Government Employee Attitudes since the Civil Service Reform Act of 1978." *Review of Public Personnel Administration* 26, no. 1: 21–51.

Leisink, Peter, and Bram Steijn. 2009. "Public Service Motivation and Job Performance of Public Sector Employees in the Netherlands." *International Review of Administrative Sciences* 75, no. 1: 35–52.

Levene, Howard. 1960. "Robust Tests for Equality of Variances." In *Contributions to Probability and Statistic*, edited by Ingram Olkin, Sudhish G. Ghurye, Wassily Hoeffding, William G. Madow, and Henry B. Mann. Stanford, CA: Stanford University Press.

Lieberson, Stanley, and James F. O'Connor. 1972. "Leadership and Organizational Performance: A Study of Large Corporations." *American Sociological Review* 37, no. 2: 117–30.

Lijphart, Arend. 1999. *Patterns of Democracy.* New Haven, CT: Yale University Press.

Lindbeck, Assar, and Jörgen W. Weibull. 1987. "Balanced-Budget Redistribution as the Outcome of Political Competition." *Public Choice* 52, no. 3: 273–97.

Lipset, Seymour Martin, Kyoung-Ryung Seong, and John Charles Torres. 1993. "A Comparative-Analysis of the Social Requisites of Democracy." *International Social Science Journal* 45, no. 2: 154–75.

Lodge, Martin, and Christopher Hood. 2012. "Into an Age of Multiple Austerities? Public Management and Public Service Bargains across OECD Countries." *Governance* 25, no. 1: 79–101.

London, Howard B. 1993. "Transformations: Cultural Challenges Faced by First-Generation Students." *New Directions for Community Colleges* 80: 5–11.

Long, Norton E. 1949. "Power and Administration." *Public Administration Review* 9, no. 4: 257–64.

———. 1952. "Bureaucracy and Constitutionalism." *American Political Science Review* 46, no. 3: 808–18.

Louis, Meryl Reis. 1980. "Surprise and Sense Making: What Newcomers Experience in Entering Unfamiliar Organizational Settings." *Administrative Science Quarterly* 25, no. 2: 226–51.

Lowndes, Vivien and Leila Thorp. 2011. "Interpreting 'Community Cohesion': Modes, Means and Mixes." *Policy & Politics* 39, no. 4: 513–32.

Lowry, Robert C. 2009. "Reauthorization of the Federal Higher Education Act and Accountability for Student Learning: The Dog That Didn't Bark." *Publius: The Journal of Federalism* 39, no. 3: 506–26.

Lynn, Laurence E. 1981. *Managing the Public's Business: The Job of the Government Executive*. New York: Basic Books.

Lynn, Laurence E., Carolyn J. Heinrich, and Carolyn J. Hill. 2001. *Improving Governance: A New Logic for Empirical Research*. Washington, DC: Georgetown University Press.

Maesschalck, Jeroen, Zeger Van der Wal, and Leo Huberts. 2008. "Public Service Motivation and Ethical Conduct." In *Motivation in Public Management: The Call of Public Service*, edited by James L. Perry and Annie Hondeghem. Oxford: Oxford University Press.

March, James G. 1991. "Exploration and Exploitation in Organizational Learning." *Organization Science* 2, no. 1: 71–87.

March, James G., Johan P. Olsen, Soren Christensen, and Michael D. Cohen. 1976. *Ambiguity and Choice in Organizations*. Bergen, Norway: Universitetsforlaget.

March, James G., and Herbert A. Simon. 1958. *Organizations*. New York: Wiley.

Margetts, Helen Z. 2011. "Experiments for Public Management Research." *Public Management Review* 13, no. 2: 189–208.

Marshall, Monty G., Keith Jaggers, and Ted Robert Gurr. 2012. *Polity IV Project: Dataset Users' Manual*. College Park: University of Maryland, Center for Systemic Peace, Polity IV Project.

Matsunaga, Steven R., and P. Eric Yeung. 2008. "Evidence on the Impact of a CEO's Financial Experience on the Quality of the Firm's Financial Reports and

Disclosures." Paper prepared for Annual Meeting of American Accounting Association Financial Accounting and Reporting Section, Phoenix.

Mauro, Paolo. 1995. "Corruption and Growth." *Quarterly Journal of Economics* 110, no. 3: 681–712.

———. 1997. "The Effects of Corruption on Investment, Growth, and Government Expenditure." In *Corruption and the Global Economy*, edited by Kimberly A. Elliot. Washington, DC: Institute for International Economics.

———. 1998. "Corruption and the Composition of Government Expenditure." *Journal of Public Economics* 69, no. 2: 263–79.

May, Peter J., and Søren C. Winter. 2009. "Politicians, Managers, and Street-Level Bureaucrats: Influences on Policy Implementation." *Journal of Public Administration Research and Theory* 19, no. 3: 453–76.

Mboup, Souleymane, Rosemary Musonda, Frad Mhalu, and Max Essex. 2006. "HIV/AIDS." In *Disease and Mortality in Sub-Saharan Africa*, edited by Dean T. Jamison, Richard G. Feachem, Malegapuru W. Makgoba, Eduard R. Bos, Florence K. Baingana, Karen J. Hofman, and Khama O. Rogo. Washington, DC: World Bank.

McLendon, Michael K., James C. Hearn, and Christine G. Mokher. 2009. "Partisans, Professionals, and Power: The Role of Political Factors in State Higher Education Funding." *Journal of Higher Education* 80, no. 6: 686–713.

Meier, Kenneth. J., Simon Calmar Andersen, Laurence J. O'Toole Jr., Nathan Favero, and Søren Winter. 2015. "Taking Managerial Context Seriously: Public Management and Performance in US and Denmark Public Schools." *International Public Management Journal* 18, no. 1: 130–50.

Meier, Kenneth. J., and John Bohte. 2003. "Not with a Bang, but a Whimper: Explaining Organizational Failures." *Administration & Society* 35, no. 1: 104–21.

———. 2007. *Politics and the Bureaucracy, 5th Edition.* Independence, KY: Cengage Learning.

Meier, Kenneth. J., and Alisa Hicklin. 2008. "Employee Turnover and Organizational Performance: Testing a Hypothesis from Classical Public Administration." *Journal of Public Administration Research and Theory* 18, no. 4: 573–90.

Meier, Kenneth. J., and Tabitha S. M. Morton. 2015. "Representative Bureaucracy in a Cross-National Context: Politics, Identity, Structure and Discretion." In *The Politics of Representative Bureaucracy: Power, Legitimacy, Performance*, edited by Eckhard Schroeter, Patrick von Maravic, and B. Guy Peters. Northampton, MA: Edward Elgar.

Meier, Kenneth. J., and Laurence J. O'Toole Jr. 2002. "Public Management and Organizational Performance: The Effect of Managerial Quality." *Journal of Policy Analysis and Management* 21, no. 4: 629–43.

———. 2003. "Public Management and Educational Performance: The Impact of Managerial Networking." *Public Administration Review* 63, no. 6: 689–99.

———. 2008. "Management Theory and Occam's Razor: How Public Organizations Buffer the Environment." *Administration and Society* 39, no. 8: 931–58.

———. 2009. "The Dog That Didn't Bark: How Public Managers Handle Environmental Shocks." *Public Administration* 87, no. 3: 485–502.

———. 2010. "Beware of Managers Not Bearing Gifts: How Management Capacity Augments the Impact of Managerial Networking." *Public Administration* 88, no. 4: 1025–44.

———. 2011. "Comparing Public and Private Management: Theoretical Expectations." *Journal of Public Administration Research and Theory* 21, supp. 3: 283–301.

———. 2013a. "I Think (I Am Doing Well), Therefore I Am: Assessing the Validity of Administrators' Self-Assessments of Performance." *International Public Management Journal* 16, no. 1: 1–27.

———. 2013b. "Subjective Organizational Performance and Measurement Error: Common Source Bias and Spurious Relationships." *Journal of Public Administration Research and Theory* 23, no. 2: 429–56.

Meier, Kenneth. J., Laurence J. O'Toole Jr., George A. Boyne, and Richard M. Walker. 2007. "Strategic Management and the Performance of Public Organizations: Testing Venerable Ideas against Recent Theories." *Journal of Public Administration Research and Theory* 17, no. 3: 357–77.

Meier, Kenneth. J., Laurence J. O'Toole Jr., George A. Boyne, Richard M. Walker, and Rhys Andrews. 2010. "Alignment and Results: Testing the Interaction Effects of Strategy, Structure, and Environment from Miles and Snow." *Administration & Society* 42, no. 2: 160–92.

Meier, Kenneth. J., Laurence J. O'Toole Jr., and Alisa Hicklin. 2010. "I've Seen Fire and I've Seen Rain: Public Management and Performance after a Natural Disaster." *Administration & Society* 41, no. 8: 979–1003.

Merrill, Tim. 1995. *Honduras: A Country Study.* Washington, DC: US Government Printing Office.

Meyer, Marshall W. 1975. "Leadership and Organizational Structure." *American Journal of Sociology* 81, no. 3: 514–42.

Miles, Raymond E., Charles C. Snow, Alan D. Meyer, and Henry J. Coleman. 1978. "Organizational Strategy, Structure and Process." *Academy of Management Review* 3, no. 3: 546–62.

Miles, William F. S. 1994. *Hausaland Divided: Colonialism and Independence in Nigeria and Niger.* Ithaca, NY: Cornell University Press.

Miller, Danny. 1986. "Configurations of Strategy and Structure: Towards a Synthesis." *Strategic Management Journal* 7, no. 3: 233–49.

———. 1991. "Stale in the Saddle: CEO Tenure and the Match between Organization and Environment." *Management Science* 37, no. 1: 34–52.

Mintrom, Michael and Richard Walley. 2013. "Education Governance in Comparative Perspective." In *Education Governance for the Twenty-First Century: Overcoming the Structural Barriers to School Reform,* edited by Patrick McGuinn and Paul Manna. Washington, DC: Brookings Institution.

Moe, Terry M. 1984. "The New Economics of Organization." *American Journal of Political Science* 28, no. 4: 739–77.

———. 1990. "Political Institutions: The Neglected Side of the Story." *Journal of Law, Economics, and Organization* 6: 213–53.

———. 1997. "The Positive Theory of Public Bureaucracy." In *Perspectives on Public Choice: A Handbook*, edited by Dennis C. Mueller. New York: Cambridge University Press.

Moe, Terry M. and Michael Caldwell. 1994. "The Institutional Foundations of Democratic Government: A Comparison of Presidential and Parliamentary Systems." *Journal of Institutional and Theoretical Economics* 150, no. 1: 171–95.

Molina, Maribel. 2014. "14 Texas High Schools Are among the Biggest in the US." *Houston Chronicle*. www.chron.com/news/houston-texas/article/14-Texas-high-schools-are-among-the-most-populous-5744431.php#photo-6841429.

Monsted, Mette, and Parveen Walji. 1978. *A Demographic Analysis of East Africa: A Sociological Interpretation*. Uppsala: Scandinavian Institute of African Studies.

Moore, Mark H. 1995. *Creating Public Value: Strategic Management in Government*. Cambridge, MA: Harvard University Press.

Morrell, Michael. E. 2003. "Survey and Experimental Evidence for a Reliable and Valid Measure of Internal Political Efficacy." *Public Opinion Quarterly* 67, no. 4: 589–602.

Mosher, Frederick C. 1982. *Democracy and the Public Service*, 2nd ed. New York: Oxford University Press.

Mosley, W. Henry, and Lincoln C. Chen. 1984. "An Analytical Framework for the Study of Child Survival in Developing Countries." *Population and Development Review* 10: 25–45.

Mott, L. Frank. 1982. *Infant Mortality in Kenya: Evidence from the Kenya Fertility Survey*. Voorburg, the Netherlands: International Statistical Institute.

Moynihan, Donald P. 2008. *The Dynamics of Performance Management*. Washington, DC: Georgetown University Press.

———. 2010. "A Workforce of Cynics? The Effects of Contemporary Reforms on Public Service Motivation." *International Public Management Journal* 13, no. 1: 24–34.

Moynihan, Donald P., and Sanjay K. Pandey. 2007. "The Role of Organizations in Fostering Public Service Motivation." *Public Administration Review* 67, no. 1: 40–53.

Murray, Christopher J. L., and Alan D. Lopez. 1997. "Alternative Projections of Mortality and Disability by Cause 1990–2020: Global Burden of Disease Study." *The Lancet* 349, no. 9064: 1498–504.

Naff, Katherine. C., and John Crum. 1999. "Working for America." *Review of Public Personnel Administration* 19, no. 4: 5–16.

Newland, Kathleen. 1982. *Infant Mortality and the Health of Societies*. Worldwatch Paper 47. Washington, DC: Worldwatch Institute.

Nicholson-Crotty, Sean, and Laurence J. O'Toole Jr. 2004. "Public Management and Organizational Performance: The Case of Law Enforcement Agencies." *Journal of Public Administration Research and Theory* 14, no. 1: 1–18.

Nielsen, Poul A. 2014. "Performance Management, Managerial Authority, and Public Service Performance." *Journal of Public Administration Research and Theory* 24, no. 2: 431–58.

Niemi, Richard G., Stephen C. Craig, and Franco Mattei. 1991. "Measuring Internal Political Efficacy in the 1988 National Election Study." *American Political Science Review* 85, no. 4: 1407–13.

Nutt, Paul C. 2006. "Comparing Public and Private Sector Decision-Making Practices." *Journal of Public Administration Research and Theory* 16, no. 2: 289–318.

Oosterwaal, Annemarije, Diane Payne, and René Torenvlied. 2012. "The Effect of Political Disagreement on Discretion: Mechanisms and Conditions." *Administration & Society* 44, no. 7: 800–824.

Oppermann, Kai. 2010. "The Concept of Issue Salience in Foreign Policy Analysis: Delineating the Scope Conditions of Theoretical Approaches in the Field." Paper prepared for Annual Meeting of SGIR Pan-European Conference on International Relations, Stockholm.

Osborn, Richard N., and James G. Hunt. 1974. "Environment and Organizational Effectiveness." *Administrative Science Quarterly* 19, no. 2: 231–46.

O'Toole, Laurence J., Jr. 1997. "Treating Networks Seriously: Practical and Research-Based Agendas in Public Administration." *Public Administration Review* 57, no. 1: 45–52.

O'Toole, Laurence J., Jr., and Kenneth J. Meier. 1999. "Modeling the Impact of Public Management: Implications of Structural Context." *Journal of Public Administration Research and Theory* 9, no. 4: 505–26.

———. 2011. *Public Management: Organizations, Governance, and Performance*. Cambridge: Cambridge University Press.

———. 2015. "Public Management, Context, and Performance: In Quest of a More General Theory." *Journal of Public Administration Research and Theory* 25, no. 1: 237–56.

O'Toole, Laurence J., Jr., and Mogens Jin Pedersen. 2011. "External Cooperation of School Leadership." In *Leadership, Learning, and Well-being in Schools*, edited by Simon C. Andersen and Søren C. Winter. Copenhagen: Danish National Centre for Social Research.

O'Toole, Laurence J., Jr., René Torenvlied, Agnes Akkerman, and Kenneth J. Meier. 2013. "Human Resource Management and Public Organizational Performance: Educational Outcomes in the Netherlands." In *Human Resource Management in the Public Sector*, edited by Ronald Burke, Andrew J. Noblet, and Cary L. Cooper. Northampton, MA: Edward Elgar.

Overman, E. Sam, and Kathy J. Boyd. 1994. "Best Practice Research and Postbureaucratic Reform." *Journal of Public Administration Research and Theory* 4, no. 1: 67–84.

Paarlberg, Laurie E. 2007. "The Impact of Customer Orientation on Government Employee Performance." *International Public Management Journal* 10, no. 2: 201–31.

Paarlberg, Laurie E., and Bob Lavigna. 2010. "Transformational Leadership and Public Service Motivation: Driving Individual and Organizational Performance." *Public Administration Review* 70, no. 5: 710–18.

Page, Hilary J., and A. J. Coale. 1972. "Fertility and Child Mortality South of the Sahara." In *Population Growth and Economic Development in Africa*, edited by Simeon H. Ominde and C. N. Ejiogu. London: Heinemann.

Pandey, Sanjay K. 2010. "Cutback Management and the Paradox of Publicness." *Public Administration Review* 70, no. 4: 564–71.

Pandey, Sanjay K., and Hal G. Rainey. 2006. "Public Managers' Perceptions of Organizational Goal Ambiguity: Analyzing Alternative Models." *International Public Management Journal* 9, no. 2: 85–112.

Pandey, Sanjay K., and Bradley E. Wright. 2006. "Connecting the Dots in Public Management: Political Environment, Organizational Goal Ambiguity, and the Public Manager's Role Ambiguity." *Journal of Public Administration Research and Theory* 16, no. 4: 511–32.

Pawson, Ray, and Nick Tilley. 1997. *Realistic Evaluation*. London: Sage.

Payne, Roy L., and Roger Mansfield. 1973. "Relationships of Perception of Organizational Climate to Organizational Structure, Context and Hierarchical Position." *Administrative Science Quarterly* 18, no. 4: 515–26.

Perry, James L. 1996. "Measuring Public Service Motivation: An Assessment of Construct Reliability and Validity." *Journal of Public Administration Research and Theory* 6, no. 1: 5–22.

Perry, James L., and Annie Hondeghem. 2008. *Motivation in Public Management: The Call of Public Service*. Oxford: Oxford University Press.

Perry, James L., Annie Hondeghem, and Lois R. Wise. 2010. "Revisiting the Motivational Bases of Public Service: Twenty Years of Research and an Agenda for the Future." *Public Administration Review* 70, no. 5: 681–90.

Perry, James L. and Hal G. Rainey. 1988. "The Public–Private Distinction in Organization Theory: A Critique and Research Strategy." *Academy of Management Review* 13, no. 2: 182–201.

Persson, Torsten, and Lars E. O. Svensson. 1989. "Why a Stubborn Conservative Would Run a Deficit: Policy with Time-Inconsistent Preferences." *Quarterly Journal of Economics* 104, no. 2: 325–45.

Petrovsky, Nicolai, Oliver James, and George A. Boyne. 2015. "New Leaders' Managerial Background and the Performance of Public Organizations: The Theory of Publicness Fit." *Journal of Public Administration Research and Theory* 25, no. 1: 217–36.

Petry, François. 1982. "Vote-Maximizing versus Utility-Maximizing Candidates: Comparing Dynamic Models of Bi-Party Competition." *Quality & Quantity* 16, no. 6: 507–26.

Pfeffer, Jeffrey. 1981. *Power in Organizations*. Marsfield, MA: Pitman.

Pfeffer, Jeffrey, and Gerald R. Salancik. 1978. *The External Control of Organizations: A Resource Dependence Approach.* New York: Harper & Row.

Pollitt, Christopher. 2006. "Performance Information for Democracy: The Missing Link?" *Evaluation* 12, no. 1: 38–55.

———. 2008. *Time, Policy, and Management: Governing with the Past.* Oxford: Oxford University Press.

———. 2012. *New Perspectives on Public Services: Place and Technology*. Oxford: Oxford University Press.

Pollitt, Christopher, and Geert Bouckaert. 2000. *Public Management Reform: A Comparative Analysis—New Public Management, Governance, and the Neo-Weberian State*. New York: Oxford University Press.

Popper, Karl R. 1968. *The Logic of Scientific Discovery*. London: Hutchinson.

Posner, Daniel N. 2004a. "Measuring Ethnic Fractionalization in Africa." *American Journal of Political Science* 48, no. 4: 849–63.

———. 2004b. "The Political Salience of Cultural Difference: Why Chewas and Tumbukas Are Allies in Zambia and Adversaries in Malawi." *American Political Science Review* 98, no. 4: 529–45.

———. 2005. *Institutions and Ethnic Politics in Africa*. New York: Cambridge University Press.

Price, David E. 1978. "Policy Making in Congressional Committees: The Impact of 'Environmental' Factors." *American Political Science Review* 72, no. 2: 548–74.

Rabovsky, Thomas M. 2012. "Accountability in Higher Education: Exploring Impacts on State Budgets and Institutional Spending Patterns." *Journal of Public Administration Research and Theory* 22, no. 4: 675–700.

Raelin, Joseph A. 1989. "An Anatomy of Autonomy: Managing Professionals." *Academy of Management Executive* 3, no. 3: 216–28.

Rainey, Hal G. 2009. *Understanding and Managing Public Organizations*, 4th ed. San Francisco: Jossey-Bass.

Rainey, Hal G., Robert W. Backoff, and Charles H. Levine. 1976. "Comparing Public and Private Organizations." *Public Administration Review* 36, no. 2: 233–44.

Rainey, Hal G., and Barry Bozeman. 2000. "Comparing Public and Private Organizations: Empirical Research and the Power of the A Priori." *Journal of Public Administration Research and Theory* 10, no. 2: 447–70.

Rainey, Hal G., Sanjay K. Pandey, and Barry Bozeman. 1995. "Research Note: Public and Private Managers' Perceptions of Red Tape." *Public Administration Review* 55, no. 6: 567–74.

Rainey, Hal G., and Paula Steinbauer. 1999. "Galloping Elephants: Developing Elements of a Theory of Effective Government Organizations." *Journal of Public Administration Research and Theory* 9, no. 1: 1–32.

Rao, Chalapati, Alan D. Lopez, and Yusuf Hemed. 2006. "Causes of Death." In *Disease and Mortality in Sub-Saharan Africa*, edited by Dean T. Jamison, Richard G. Feachem, Malegapuru W. Makgoba, Eduard R. Bos, Florence K. Baingana, Karen J. Hofman, and Khama O. Rogo. Washington, DC: World Bank.

Region Midtjylland. 2011. *Omstilling til Fremtidens Sundhedsvæsen i Region Midtjylland*. Viborg, the Netherlands: Region Midtjylland.

Reidpath, Daniel D., and Pascale Allotey. 2003. "Infant Mortality Rate as an Indicator of Population Health." *Journal of Epidemiology and Community Health* 57, no. 5: 344–46.

Robinson, Jane, and Heather Wharrad. 2000. "Invisible Nursing: Exploring Health Outcomes at a Global Level: Relationships between Infant and Under-5 Mortality

Rates and the Distribution of Health Professionals, GNP per Capita, and Female Literacy." *Journal of Advanced Nursing* 32, no. 1: 28–40.

Roch, Christine H., and David W. Pitts. 2012. "Differing Effects of Representative Bureaucracy in Charter Schools and Traditional Public Schools." *American Review of Public Administration* 42, no. 3: 282–302.

Rodden, Jonathan, and Steven Wilkinson. 2004. "The Shifting Political Economy of Redistribution in the Indian Federation." Paper prepared for Annual Meeting of International Science for New Institutional Economics, Tucson.

Rodriguez, Awilda, and Andrew P. Kelly. 2014. "Access, Affordability, and Success: How Do America's Colleges Fare, and What Could It Mean for the President's Ratings Plan?" American Enterprise Institute, Washington, DC. www.aei.org/publication/access-affordability-and-success-how-do-americas-colleges-fare-and-what-could-it-mean-for-the-presidents-ratings-plan/.

Rogoff, Kenneth. 1985. "The Optimal Degree of Commitment to an Intermediate Monetary Target." *Quarterly Journal of Economics* 100, no. 40: 1169–90.

Rourke, Francis E. 1984. *Bureaucracy, Politics and Public Policy*, 3rd ed. Boston: Little, Brown.

Rutherford, Amanda, and Thomas Rabovsky. 2014. "Evaluating Impacts of Performance Funding Policies on Student Outcomes." *Annals of the American Academy of Political and Social Science* 655: 185–208.

Salanick, Gerald R., and Jeffrey Pfeffer. 1977. "Constraints on Administrator Discretion: The Limited Influence of Mayors on City Budgets." *Urban Affairs Review* 12, no. 4: 475–98.

Santerre, Rexford E., Stephen G. Grubaugh, and Andrew J. Stollar. 1991. "Government Intervention in Health Care Markets and Health Care Outcomes: Some International Evidence." *Cato Journal* 11, no. 1: 1–12.

Satterthwaite, David. 2002. "Local Funds and Their Potential to Allow Donor Agencies to Support Community Development and Poverty Reduction in Urban Areas." *Environment and Urbanization* 14, no. 1: 179–88.

Sayre, Wallace S. 1958. "Premises of Public Administration." *Public Administration Review* 18, no. 2: 102–5.

Schultz, Heiner, and Thomas König. 2000. "Institutional Reform and Decision-Making Efficiency in the European Union." *American Journal of Political Science* 44, no. 4: 653–66.

Scott, Marc, Thomas Bailey, and Greg Kienzl. 2006. "Relative Success? Determinants of College Graduation Rates in Public and Private Colleges in the US." *Research in Higher Education* 47, no. 3: 249–79.

Seasons, Mark L. 2003. "Monitoring and Evaluation in Municipal Planning: Considering the Realities." *Journal of the American Planning Association* 69, no. 4: 430–40.

Sebaa, Ali Ahmed, James Wallace, and Nelarine Cornelius. 2009. "Managerial Characteristics, Strategy and Performance in Local Government." *Measuring Business Excellence* 13, no. 4: 12–21.

Sebba, Judy, Vivienne Griffiths, Barry Luckock, Frances Hunt, Carol Robinson, and Steve Flowers. 2009. *Youth-Led Innovation: Enhancing the Skills and Capacity of the Next Generation of Innovators*. London: Nesta.

Sharpe, Laurence James, and Kenneth Newton. 1984. *Does Politics Matter? The Determinants of Public Policy*. Oxford: Clarendon Press.

Sherman, Harvey. 1966. *It All Depends: A Pragmatic Approach to Organization*. Tuscaloosa: University of Alabama Press.

Simon, Herbert A. 1965. "The Architecture of Complexity." *General Systems* 10: 63–73.

Skelcher, Chris. 2010. "Fishing in Muddy Waters: Principals, Agents, and Democratic Governance in Europe." *Journal of Public Administration Research and Theory* 20, supp. 1: 161–75.

Snow, Charles C., and Lawrence G. Hrebiniak. 1980. "Strategy, Distinctive Competence, and Organizational Performance." *Administrative Science Quarterly* 25, no. 2: 317–36.

Solé-Ollé, Albert, and Pilar Sorribas-Navarro. 2008. "The Effects of Partisan Alignment on the Allocation of Intergovernmental Transfers: Differences-in-Differences Estimates for Spain." *Journal of Public Economics* 92, no. 12: 2302–19.

Soroka, Stuart N. 2003. "Media, Public Opinion, and Foreign Policy." *Harvard International Journal of Press and Politics* 8, no. 1: 27–48.

Soss, Joe, Richard C. Fording, and Sanford F. Schram. 2011. *Disciplining the Poor: Neoliberal Paternalism and the Persistent Power of Race*. Chicago: University of Chicago Press.

Spulber, Daniel F., and David Besanko. 1992. "Delegation, Commitment, and the Regulatory Mandate." *Journal of Law, Economics, & Organization* 8, no. 1: 126–54.

Steen, Trui P. S., and Mark R. Rutgers. 2011. "The Double-Edged Sword." *Public Management Review* 13, no. 3: 343–61.

Stevens, John M., and Robert P. McGowan. 1983. "Managerial Strategies in Municipal Government Organizations." *Academy of Management Journal* 26, no. 3: 527–34.

Stigler, George J. 1958. "The Economies of Scale." *Journal of Law and Economics* 1: 54–71.

Stripling, Jack. 2014. "With U. of Michigan Hire, Another Ivy League Provost Goes Public." *Chronicle of Higher Education*. http://chronicle.com/article/With-U-of-Michigan-Hire/144237/.

Tandberg, David A. 2013. "The Conditioning Role of State Higher Education Governance Structures." *Journal of Higher Education* 84, no. 4: 506–43.

Tappero, Jordan W., and Robert V. Tauxe. 2011. "Lessons Learned during Public Health Response to Cholera Epidemic in Haiti and the Dominican Republic." *Emerging Infectious Diseases* 17, no. 11: 2087–93.

Taylor, Frederick, W. 1911. *The Principles of Scientific Management*. New York: Harper Brothers.

Taylor-Robinson, Michelle M. 2006. "The Difficult Road from Caudillismo to Democracy, or Can Clientelism Compliment Democratic Electoral Institutions?

Exploration of the Honduran Case." In *Informal Institutions and Democracy in Latin America,* edited by Gretchen Helmke and Steven Levitsky. Baltimore: Johns Hopkins University Press.

———. 2009. "Candidate Selection for the Honduran National Congress by the Traditional Parties." In *Candidate Selection, Party Politics, and Democratic Capacity* (in Spanish), edited by Flavia Freidenberg and Manuel Alcántara Sáez. Mexico City: Tribunal Electoral del Distrito Federal de Mexico, with the Universidad Nacional Autónoma de Mexico and the Institute de Iberoamérico de la Universidad de Salamanca.

Teodoro, Manuel P. 2014. "When Professionals Lead: Executive Management, Normative Isomorphism, and Policy Implementation." *Journal of Public Administration Research and Theory* 24, no. 4: 983–1004.

Thayer, Paul B. 2000. *Retention of Students from First Generation and Low-Income Backgrounds.* Washington, DC: US Department of Education.

Thompson, James D. 1967. *Organizations in Action: Social Science Bases of Administrative Theory.* New York: McGraw-Hill.

Thurmaier, Kurt. 1992. "Budgetary Decision-Making in Central Budget Bureaus: An Experiment." *Journal of Public Administration Research and Theory* 2, no. 4: 463–87.

Torenvlied, René. 2000. *Political Decisions and Agency Performances.* London: Kluwer Academic.

Torenvlied, René, and Agnes Akkerman. 2012. "Effects of Managers' Work Motivation and Networking Activity on Their Reported Levels of External Red Tape." *Journal of Public Administration Research and Theory* 22, no. 3: 445–71.

Torenvlied, René, Agnes Akkerman, Laurence J. O'Toole Jr., and Kenneth J. Meier. 2012. "A Test of the Public Management Model in Dutch Primary Education: The Importance of Organizational and Environmental Context." Paper prepared for Annual Meeting of Public Management Research Conference, Shanghai.

Trawick, Michelle W., and Roy M. Howsen. 2006. "Crime and Community Heterogeneity: Race, Ethnicity, and Religion." *Applied Economics Letters* 13: 341–45.

TSE (Tribunal Supremo Electoral–Honduras). 2014. "Tribunal Supremo Electoral." www.tse.hn/web/index.html.

Tsebelis, George. 1999. "Veto Players and Law Production in Parliamentary Democracies: An Empirical Analysis." *American Political Science Review* 93, no. 3: 591–608.

———. 2002. *Veto Players: How Political Institutions Work.* Princeton, NJ: Princeton University Press.

Tung, Rosalie L. 1979. "Dimensions of Organizational Environments: An Exploratory Study of Their Impact on Organizational Structure." *Academy of Management Journal* 22, no. 4: 672–93.

Turkenburg, Monique. 2008. *De School Bestuurd: Schoolbesturen over Goed Bestuur en de Maatschappelijke Opdracht van de School.* The Hague: Netherlands Institute for Social Research.

Tversky, Amos, and Daniel Kahneman. 1981. "The Framing of Decisions and the Psychology of Choice." *Science* 211, no. 4481: 453–58.

United Nations. 2013. *Levels and Trends in Child Mortality*. New York: United Nations Children's Fund.

Vallely, Andrew, Lisa Vallely, John Changalucha, Brian Greenwood, and Daniel Chandramohan. 2007. "Intermittent Preventive Treatment for Malaria in Pregnancy in Africa: What's New, What's Needed?" *Malaria Journal* 6, no. 16: 1–13.

Vandenabeele, Wouter. 2008. "Development of a Public Service Motivation Measurement Scale: Corroborating and Extending Perry's Measurement Instrument." *International Public Management Journal* 11, no. 1: 143–67.

Van Maanen, John. 1978. "People Processing: Strategies of Organizational Socialization." *Organizational Dynamics* 7, no. 1: 19–36.

Wagner, Martha. 1983. "Public Management and Private Management: A Diminishing Gap?" *Journal of Policy Analysis and Management* 3, no. 1: 107–15.

Walker, Neff, Bernhard Schwartlander, and Jennifer Bryce. 2002. "Meeting International Goals in Child Survival and HIV/AIDS." *The Lancet* 360, no. 9329: 284–89.

Walker, Richard M., George A. Boyne, and Gene A. Brewer, eds. 2010. *Public Management and Performance: Research Directions*. Cambridge: Cambridge University Press.

Walt, Gill, and Julie Cliff. 1986. "The Dynamics of Health Policies in Mozambique 1975–85." *Health Policy and Planning* 1, no. 2: 148–57.

Wamsley, Gary L., and Mayer N. Zald. 1973. "The Political Economy of Public Organizations." *Public Administration Review* 33, no. 1: 62–73.

Watkins-Hayes, Celeste. 2011. "Race, Respect, and Red Tape: Inside the Black Box of Racially Representative Bureaucracies." *Journal of Public Administration Research and Theory* 21, supp. 2: i233–51.

Wegge, Jürgen, Hans Jeppe Jeppesen, Wolfgang G. Weber, Craig Pearce, Silvia A. Silva, Alexander Pundt, Thomas Jonsson, Sandra Wolf, Christina L. Wassenar, Christine Unterrainer, and Annika Piecha. 2010. "Promoting Work Motivation in Organizations: Should Employee Involvement in Organizational Leadership Become a New Tool in the Organizational Psychologist's Armoury?" *Journal of Personnel Psychology* 9, no. 4: 154–71.

Weinzimmer, Laurence G. 1997. "Top Management Team Correlates of Organizational Growth in a Small Business Context: A Comparative Study."*Journal of Small Business Management* 35, no. 3: 1–9.

Weyland, Kurt. 2007. *Bounded Rationality and Policy Diffusion: Social Sector Reform in Latin America.* Princeton, NJ: Princeton University Press.

Whittlesey, Derwent. 1937. "British and French Colonial Technique in West Africa." *Foreign Affairs* 15, no. 2: 367–69.

Wiersema, Margarethe F., and Karen A. Bantel. 1992. "Top Management Team Demography and Corporate Strategic Change."*Academy of Management Journal* 35, no. 1: 91–121.

Wilkins, Vicky M., and Lael R. Keiser. 2004. "Linking Passive and Active Representation by Gender: The Case of Child Support Agencies." *Journal of Public Administration Research and Theory* 16, no. 1: 87–102.

Wilson, James Q. 1989. *Bureaucracy: What Government Agencies Do and Why They Do It.* New York: Basic Books.

Wittmer, Dennis. 1992. "Ethical Sensitivity and Managerial Decision-Making: An Experiment." Dissertation. http://jpart.oxfordjournals.org/.

Wood, B. Dan, and Richard W. Waterman. 1994. *Bureaucratic Dynamics: The Role of Bureaucracy in a Democracy*. Boulder, CO: Westview Press.

Wright, Bradley E., Robert K. Christensen, and Kimberly Roussin Isett. 2013. "Motivated to Adapt? The Role of Public Service Motivation as Employees Face Organizational Change." *Public Administration Review* 73, no. 5: 738–47.

Wright, Bradley E., and Sanjay K. Pandey. 2008. "Public Service Motivation and the Assumption of Person–Organization Fit Testing the Mediating Effect of Value Congruence." *Administration & Society* 40, no. 5: 502–21.

———. 2009. "Transformational Leadership in the Public Sector: Does Structure Matter?" *Journal of Public Administration Research and Theory* 20, no. 1: 75–89.

Yang, Kaifeng, and Anthony Kassekert. 2010. "Linking Management Reform with Employee Job Satisfaction: Evidence from Federal Agencies." *Journal of Public Administration Research and Theory* 20, no. 2: 413–36.

Zhu, Ling, Scott E. Robinson, and Rene Torenvlied. 2015. "A Bayesian Approach to Measurement Bias in Networking Studies." *American Review of Public Administration* 45, no. 5: 542-564.

Zweifel, Thomas D., and Patricio Navia. 2000. "Democracy, Dictatorship, and Infant Mortality." *Journal of Democracy* 11, no. 2: 99–114.

# Contributors

**Agnes Akkerman** is a professor of labor market institutions and labor relations at Radboud University Nijmegen, and is the James S. Coleman Professor of Sustainable Cooperation in Labor and Employment Relations at the University of Groningen.

**Rhys Andrews** is a professor of public management at Cardiff University. His research interests focus on strategic management, social capital, and public service performance. He has published widely in refereed journals, including *Human Relations*, the *Journal of Public Administration Research and Theory*, and *Public Administration Review*. He is a coeditor of both the *International Public Management Journal* and the *Journal of Public Administration Research and Theory*.

**Claudia N. Avellaneda** is an associate professor in the School of Public and Environmental Affairs at Indiana University. She has published considerable research on public management and policymaking in Latin America. She serves on the editorial board for the *Journal of Public Administration Research and Theory* and is a board member of the Public Management Evidence Lab in the Department of Public Policy at the City University of Hong Kong.

**Ricardo Gomes** is an associate professor of public management at the University of Brasília and director of educational research for the Instituto Nacional de Estudos e Pesquisas Educacionais Anísio Teixeira in Brasília. He is the president of the Brazilian Academy of Management. His interests include public management, and he serves on various editorial boards and is an at-large representative of the International Research Society for Public Management.

**Marlette Jackson** is a PhD student in the Department of Political Science at Stanford University. Her research interests include comparative politics and international relations.

**Mads Leth Jakobsen** is an associate professor in the Department of Political Science and Government at Aarhus University. His research centers on questions of administration and bureaucracy as well as innovation in the public sector.

**Anne Mette Kjeldsen** is an assistant professor in the Department of Political Science and Government at Aarhus University. Much of her recent research had focused on questions of public service motivation.

**Kenneth J. Meier** is the Charles H. Gregory Chair in Liberal Arts and a distinguished professor of political science at Texas A&M University. He is also a professor of public management at the Cardiff University School of Business in Wales. He is a widely published scholar on questions of public management. He has served as president of the Midwest Political Science Association, the Public Management Research Association, and the Southwest Political Science Association. He served as the editor-in-chief of the *Journal of Public Administration Research and Theory* and was formerly the editor of *the American Journal of Political Science*.

**Laurence J. O'Toole Jr.** is the Margaret Hughes and Robert T. Golembiewski Professor of Public Administration and also a distinguished research professor in the Department of Public Administration and Policy at the University of Georgia. He is past chair of the Section on Public Administration of the American Political Science Association and past president of the Public Management Research Association. He has been elected a fellow of the National Academy of Public Administration and is a senior member of the Netherlands Institute of Governance.

**Thomas Pallesen** serves as head of the Department of Political Science and Government at Aarhus University. His research centers on the interaction between politicians and bureaucrats, with a special focus on the discretion of street-level bureaucrats.

**Amanda Rutherford** is an assistant professor in the School of Public and Environmental Affairs at Indiana University. Her research interests include managerial values and decision making, performance management, organization theory, representative bureaucracy, higher education policy, and research methodology. She is the book review editor for the *Journal of Public Administration Research and Theory* and is a member of the Rising Professionals Editorial Board for the *Journal of Student Financial Aid.*

**Claire Stieg** received an MS in political science from Texas A&M University. Her research interests include public–private comparisons and performance management in the context of higher education.

**René Torenvlied** is professor of public management at the University of Twente. His main research interests are management, collaboration, and performance in the public sector, and collective decision making and policy implementation. His research integrates model-guided theoretical analysis with large-scale, empirical data analysis. He led the evaluation of the Dutch crisis management organization MH17, commissioned by the Dutch minister of security and justice. He is a coeditor of the *Journal of Public Administration Research and Theory*.

**Cameron Wimpy** is a senior researcher at Fors Marsh Group in Arlington, Virginia, where he leads social science research projects. His political science research examines questions involving comparative politics, ethnic politics, and quantitative methods. His recent research has focused on voting behavior in Sub-Saharan Africa and beyond, the diffusion of social conflict, and spatial econometrics. His fieldwork has taken him to Ethiopia, Malawi, Mozambique, South Sudan, Sudan, and Yemen.

# Index

*Figures, notes, and tables are indicated by* f, n, *and* t *following the page number.*

www.ingramcontent.com/pod-product-compliance
Lightning Source LLC
LaVergne TN
LVHW050150080826
844660LV00002B/153

* 9 7 8 1 6 2 6 1 6 4 0 0 0 *